Peter Arenyo-Davis

(174)

Queen Victoria
in Switzerland

Queen Victoria in Switzerland

PETER ARENGO-JONES

ROBERT HALE · LONDON

ISBN 0 7090 5365 7

Robert Hale Limited
Clerkenwell House
Clerkenwell Green
London EC1R 0HT

2 4 6 8 10 9 7 5 3 1

Photoset in North Wales by
Derek Doyle & Associates, Mold, Clwyd.
Printed in Hong Kong by
Bookbuilders Ltd.

Contents

Acknowledgements

Material from the Royal Library and Archives at Windsor (Queen Victoria's Journal and correspondence, watercolours and sketches by her and Princess Louise, photographs) is published by gracious permission of Her Majesty the Queen.

The author is grateful for generous help and guidance given by: Mr Oliver Everett, Librarian and Assistant Keeper of the Archives at Windsor and his predecessor Sir Robin Mackworth-Young; The Hon. Mrs Roberts, Curator of the Print Room; Lady de Bellaigue, Registrar of the Royal Archives; Miss G. Campling, Head of Photographic Services; Miss F. Dimond, Curator of the Royal Photograph Collection and Lt.-Col. Seymour Gilbart-Denham, Crown Equerry, the Royal Mews and their staffs.

Further, the author wishes to thank Moritz, Landgraf von Hessen and the Hessische Hausstiftung at the Fasanerie, Fulda (where Frau Nicolette Luthmer was particularly helpful) for permission to quote from Queen Victoria's letters to her daughter Victoria, Princess Royal of Prussia.

Grateful acknowledgement is also made to the Earl of Derby for permission to use material from the Papers of the 15th Earl of Derby, as well as to the Liverpool Record Office, Liverpool Libraries and Information Services where they are housed.

The author would like to thank Dr J.M. Fewster, Senior Assistant Keeper of Archives and Special Collections at the University of Durham Library for his help with the papers of General Charles Grey.

Crown copyright material held in the Public Record Office is reproduced with the permission of the Controller of Her Majesty's Stationery Office.

For use of material from the Hughenden Papers acknowledgement is made to the Bodleian Library, Oxford which holds the Disraeli manuscripts from Hughenden Manor on permanent deposit from the National Trust.

Illustrations from the graphical collection at the Zentralbibliothek Luzern are reproduced here by permission of the Director, Dr A. Schacher. The author is grateful to him and his staff for their generosity and patient help.

Finally, the author is greatly indebted to the many people without whose help, support and encouragement all along this book would not have been possible.

Glossary of Familiar Names

Affie	Prince Alfred, Duke of Edinburgh, Queen Victoria's 2nd son
Baby	Princess Beatrice, Queen Victoria's youngest daughter
Bids	Sir Thomas Biddulph, Keeper of Her Majesty's Privy Purse
Janie	Jane, Marchioness of Ely, Lady of the Bedchamber

For Evelyn

Author's Note

Throughout this text there are curious spellings as well as variations in the spelling of the same word, place or name. The originator's spelling has usually been retained, with a footnote in some instances to avoid confusion (e.g. Queen Victoria's 'Alten' instead of 'Olten'). The originator's abbreviations have also been retained, e.g. 'wd' for 'would', 'shd' for 'should', 'Ly' for 'Lady', 'Ld' for 'Lord'.

Queen Victoria's Journal as we have it is a transcript made by her youngest daughter, Princess Beatrice. Queen Victoria had instructed that the Journal should be burned after her death. Before doing so, the Princess copied a good proportion of the text. But we have no means of knowing how much is omitted.

In this book quotations and extracts from the Journal are in italics.

PART
One

1   Settled Desolation

On 31 August 1868 Queen Victoria, thinly disguised as 'The Countess of Kent', sat on the grass of a Swiss Alpine meadow on her way down from a 7,000 ft mountain, enjoying her afternoon tea[1] – her attendants having made light work of obstacles such as the non-availability of a kettle and the near-impossibility of finding water nearby.

This is the stuff of which British travellers in the nineteenth century were made. This is the spirit behind the peaceful conquest of Switzerland by the British. All over the country the Queen's subjects were doing similar things, some more strenuously and adventurously, some more sedately. But very few will have had to go to such lengths as their Queen to get away to Switzerland. For her, this holiday was the culmination of years of planning, hoping and plotting.

For six years Queen Victoria had been shrouding herself in seclusion. In 1868 she was in the seventh year of mourning for Prince Albert, the Prince

'He protected me, He comforted and encouraged me.'
Queen Victoria with Prince Albert at Buckingham Palace, 1854

Consort, whose death in 1861 had robbed her life of its light. She was forty-nine, diminutive in height and of late rotund, the mother of nine children and the sovereign of a quarter of the world's population. It was said that she had not smiled since the bereavement that had so shattered her. Albert had more than shared the burden of her responsibilities. Deprived of his counsel and protection she felt lost and insecure, convinced that she was not up to the task of being Queen by herself. She dreaded appearing in public. Although she gritted her teeth and performed her royal duties whenever absolutely necessary, each time the effort was agonising. She appeared stiff and aloof, whereas by nature she was the opposite.

> ... her simple and formidable character was compounded of a few basic and universal elements. By nature she was almost all the things that the typical woman is alleged to be by those who have the temerity to generalize on the subject; instinctive, personal, unintellectual, partizan, interested in detail, viewing things in the concrete rather than the abstract, and with a profound natural reverence for the secure and the respectable. With these common qualities of her sex, the Queen possessed also those of her age ... though regal, she was not aristocratic as the English understand the term. The healthy, homely German blood which coursed through her veins had imparted a commonplace, even a bourgeois tinge to her taste. But if her nature was normal, her character was not. It was too abnormally high-powered for one thing. Her enjoyments were more rapturous than the average girl's, her sentimentality more unbridled, her interest in detail more inexhaustible, her partizanship more violent, her innocence more dewy. Some strain in her – once again it may have come from Germany – had endowed her with an extravagant force of temperament; so that the ordinary in her was magnified to a degree where it became extraordinary ... To this startling fervour of feeling she added a startling simplicity of vision.[2]

This character sketch by David Cecil is in marked contrast to the traditional but woefully over-simplified perception of Queen Victoria as the epitome of the Victorian: unamused, straitlaced, prudish. Published in 1954, it was foreshadowed by others, even Lytton Strachey's more than a quarter of a century earlier, and has been followed by many a biography presenting a more differentiated picture of her personality. But the image of the severe Queen, withdrawn and in solemn black, is so deeply embedded as to have survived to this day, even now overlaying our appreciation of the sunnier and spontaneous side of the Queen's personality that struggled through as she emerged from the depths of mourning and acquired self-confidence as a monarch in her own right.

Queen Victoria's Swiss holiday in 1868 helped her along this road, but she had a long way to come. The death of Prince Albert had been such a devastating blow that she took years to come out of shock, and the rest of her life – spent more or less in mourning – trying to come to terms with her loss, although by the 1870s she had achieved a resigned balance. But during the 1860s her insistence on seclusion became a serious national problem, even raising the question of her abdication.

Her family and her courtiers did what they could, notably her then still unofficial Private Secretary, General Grey, to whom she wrote in 1863 (in the customary third person):

> ... she cannot deny that <u>he</u> is her <u>main</u> support & when <u>he</u> is away, she always

General Grey playing a
salmon in the Dee

feels <u>additionally anxious</u>. She is <u>not</u> worrying herself just now, & is calmer; but her constant & ever increasing grief – added to a terribly nervous temperament by nature (which her precious Husband knew but too well & often had to suffer from she fears, but wh <u>he naturally</u> cld <u>calm</u> as she cld at any moment of the day & night pour out <u>all</u> to him) – prevents her taking <u>anything calmly</u>.[3]

So, with her ever-present need for a father-figure and male shoulder to lean on, it was not surprising that she turned to General Grey to confide in and discuss travel plans. For example, she told him of her intention of spending three weeks in 1863 at Coburg, Prince Albert's family seat in Germany (in what used to be the province of Saxe-Coburg-Gotha) and thus a place with special associations for the Queen. She wrote to General Grey that she felt the need to go there:

… as she feels it <u>almost a duty</u> to do something for her <u>wretched health</u> & nerves, to prevent further increase of depression & exhaustion.

God knows her <u>own</u> inclination would be to do <u>nothing</u> for her health, as <u>her</u> only wish is to see her <u>life end soon</u>, but she feels that <u>if</u> she is to go on, <u>she must</u> change the <u>scene</u> completely sometimes – (if it does not affect, & she hopes it does <u>not</u>, her duties) – consequently – going to Balmoral for a fortnight or 3 weeks in the <u>Spring</u> & to <u>Coburg</u> (<u>Coburg only</u>) in the <u>Summer</u> for <u>3 weeks</u> – (besides visiting her dear Uncle at Brussels; which is a duty) & quite necessary.

Her Beloved Angel wld <u>not</u> – if He were asked & saw <u>how</u> weak & bowed to the earth with anguish & desolation she is – ever, ever <u>encreasing</u> – object to her making these <u>additional moves</u>.[4]

Those around the Queen knew perfectly well where the real problem lay. That summer Grey wrote from Coburg to a trusted Court official, Sir Charles Phipps, Keeper of the Privy Purse:

I have since had a long conversation with Princess Alice,* who says the Queen <u>is</u> very well. She got through her luncheon of 18 to the Emperor of Austria perfectly, talked a great deal – & was interested – running to the window & to see him drive away. Princess Alice also says that the Queen owned to her she was afraid of getting too well – as if it was a crime & that she <u>feared</u> to begin to like riding on her Scotch poney &c&c. She is so nice & touching in her manner that it is difficult to find the heart to urge her to anything she does not like – but after the next anniversary, we must all try, <u>gently</u>, to get her to resume her old habits.[5]

' ... *this feeling of settled desolation.*'
Queen Victoria to Crown Princess Victoria, 3 September 1867

* Queen Victoria's second daughter, the future Grand Duchess of Hesse-Darmstadt.

This was easier said than done. It was to take a long time.

She did travel. But for some years she never ventured beyond the familiar and comforting round of her own residences and those of her close family abroad. One of these was the summer house Rosenau near Coburg, in which Prince Albert had been born. Yet the Rosenau, peaceful though it was, had a drawback. There were always too many people around.

It was when staying there in August 1865, in search of peace and quiet, that a new idea started to crystallize, took hold of her and did not let go until she had put it into practice three years later.

She immediately put the idea to General Grey in a memo.

August 28 1865

The Queen does feel that she <u>must</u> try some day to spend <u>4</u> weeks in some <u>completely quiet</u> spot in Switzerland where she can refuse <u>all</u> visitors and have <u>complete</u> quiet. The first week here she <u>felt</u> the benefit of the quiet; but since last Tuesday she has not had one day's repose and since Monday has been quite overwhelmed by the number of visitors and relations so that she regrets she did not decide to stay here 3 or 4 days longer to recruit herself before starting on the journey. Seriously, she thinks that if she is alive (and alas! she must live on) <u>next year</u> she must try and do something to get a little <u>complete</u> rest for she feels that <u>her nerves</u> and her <u>strength</u> are getting <u>more</u> and <u>more exhausted</u> and <u>worn</u>. She has been talking to Kanné* and also to Major Elphinstone† but she wished the General would also speak to them, for what the Queen <u>wants</u> is to choose some <u>very retired spot</u> in a fine part of Switzerland which she could get at without too long a journey; she does <u>not</u> wish to <u>travel about</u> in <u>Switzerland</u> or to go and <u>see</u> anything very fatiguing for her strength and nerves would not stand that. She would go with a reduced party, take no horses but perhaps <u>2</u> ponies for herself to ride and <u>live as simply</u> and in as retired a way as possible. General Grey understands this from his knowledge of her Highland expeditions and she fears Kanné hardly does. Then he says that the Queen would have to sleep at Darmstadt and then go still <u>two nights</u> resting one day between! ... The Queen has a real <u>longing</u> to try it.[6]

The longing took root fast. Warming to the idea, the Queen now bombarded General Grey with quick-fire memos about it. In the first of two that she dashed off the following day, she said she had spoken to the outrider Trapp while on a drive and he had told her about a house called 'the Riss' in Tyrol in Austria which might be suitable: 'There is the <u>grandest</u> Alpine

---

* Her director of Continental Journeys.
† Governor to her son, Prince Arthur.

scenery in every direction and <u>complete</u> solitude. The Queen would prefer Switzerland as the Prince knew it and she would rather see nothing he had <u>not</u> seen, but on the other hand as <u>complete tranquility</u> and <u>solitude</u> is the chief object, that would be best obtained in the 'Riss'. Part of the suite would be left at the nearest Town.'[7]

Later that day she had an afterthought and wrote to Grey that she

> … would wish General Grey not to be deterred by hearing of the smallness of accommodation, the distance from a town and the difficulty of provisions at the Riss. The Queen <u>can</u> and <u>would</u> put up with the homeliest food and provisions. She would take her meals (excepting perhaps breakfast and luncheon) with her very small suite; she would take only 1 gentleman and 1 lady & a Dr. besides her children – & <u>very few</u> servants. In <u>short</u> to live quite on a <u>reduced scale</u> and taking only those servants who would be <u>really useful</u>. The Queen has been calculating & if we can go in <u>one</u> night & a day from <u>here</u> … the Queen thinks we might easily manage to come from Antwerp here without stopping; – we came purposely <u>slow</u> from Antwerp and Darmstadt & left very late. By leaving 3 or 4 hours earlier – & arriving here 2 hours later & going a little faster we might easily do it.[8]

So it was to be Austria.

Or perhaps Switzerland after all? But: 'It is the length of the journey,' she wrote to Grey the next day, 'wh. would make it necessary, if the Queen went to Switzerland, to spend 4 weeks there, or she could not undertake the journey.'[9]

Two days passed and it looked like Austria again, she told Grey, but staying at another house: '… a charming place … . for the Queen to go to, wh. possesses <u>all</u> the advantages & none of the disadvantages of the Riss.'[10]

And so it went on. In the event, Queen Victoria did not go abroad at all in 1866, when Prussia and Austria were at war, nor in the following year. But by the summer of 1867 she was chafing at the bit again, determinedly laying plans for a few weeks in Switzerland in 1868, in deep seclusion. Prince Albert had toured there in 1837, before their marriage, and had sent her glowing accounts and mementos[11] that she treasured. In 1864 her third son, Prince Arthur, had followed in his father's footsteps around Switzerland.

A holiday in Switzerland, if well prepared, would bring her the much longed-for repose and seclusion she needed and at the same time she would be vicariously reunited with her beloved. But this powerful urge to get away from it all and steep herself in solitude, breathing the pure Alpine air that Albert had breathed, was in head-on conflict with an equally powerful pull in the opposite direction exerted by her subjects at home. They wanted more of her, not less.

Prince Arthur on his Swiss tour in 1864. The guide A. Hofmann is on right, with rope

Her courtiers had seen trouble brewing on this score for years. As far back as 1863 Viscount Torrington, one of her Lords-in-Waiting, had said as much in a letter to General Grey:

> … there is strong pressure from without from almost the highest in the land down to the smallest boy in the streets of London to get the Queen once more to come to London. Loyalty, however inconvenient, is at the bottom of this movement. The public accept <u>no one</u> as a substitute and the danger is considerable if once that public cease to care or take an interest in seeing the Queen moving amongst them. It will not do for people to be accustomed to Her Majesty's absence. Do away with the outward and visible sign and the <u>ignorant mass</u> believe Royalty is of no value. There is not a tradesman in London who does not believe he is damaged by the Queen not coming to London.[12]

Yet here was Queen Victoria fighting tooth and nail to deprive her subjects of just these outward and visible signs of royalty – and feeling aggrieved that she was not given due credit for bearing up in spite of her widowed state and for conscientiously attending to the less public but onerous paperwork and discourse with ministers that her constitutional position thrust upon her. Even guardedly worded, constructively meant criticism of her reluctance to appear in public – even gentle persuasion that after some years of mourning she might now come more out of her shell again – all this aroused the Queen's grievous displeasure. She was especially allergic to such sentiments if they came from the press. 'She <u>is</u> shocked,' she wrote to General Grey in a memorandum, 'at the people treating her as an unfeeling <u>machine</u>, and how can they compare <u>her</u> to the Prince! He was a man, and had a happy home. She is a poor weak woman shattered by grief and anxiety and by nature terribly nervous! But she won't "heed" (as the Scotch say) those newspaper vulgarities and steadily do whatever she can and she feels and thinks is fit. She would be thankful if the General would tell her when such articles are in the papers, as then she won't read them.'[13]

But she did read them. The very next day she sent Grey another memorandum: 'Though the Queen promised General Grey not to read or take notice of those stupid unfeeling articles in the papers she can't resist sending him this one in the John Bull as she is rather amused at Queen Emma of Honolulu being held up as an example to her! They seem rather to forget (and this is always most astonishing) that the Queen has a few other duties to perform than Queen Emma!! Please return the paper.'[14]

The Queen particularly dreaded having to open Parliament. Her letter on the subject to the then Prime Minister, Lord Russell, in early 1866 is something of a masterpiece in the way it combines commitment to her role as monarch with a passionate plea for mercy:

> To enable the Queen to go through what she can only compare to an execution, it is of importance to keep the thought of it as much from her mind as possible, and therefore the going to Windsor to wait two whole days for this dreadful ordeal would do her positive harm.
>
> The Queen has never till now mentioned this painful subject to Lord Russell, but she wishes once for all to just express her own feelings. She must, however, premise her observations by saying that she entirely absolves Lord Russell and his colleagues from any attempt ever to press upon her what is so very painful an effort. The Queen must say that she does feel very bitterly the want of feeling of those who ask the Queen to go to open Parliament. That the public should wish to see her she fully understands, and has no wish to prevent – quite the contrary; but why this wish should be of so unreasonable and unfeeling a nature as to long to witness the spectacle of a poor, broken-hearted widow, nervous and shrinking, dragged in deep mourning, alone in State as a Show, where she used to go supported by her husband, to be gazed at, without delicacy of feeling, is a thing she cannot understand, and she never could wish her bitterest foe to be exposed to!
>
> She will do it this time – as she promised it, but she owns she resents the unfeelingness of those who have clamoured for it. Of the suffering which it will cause her – nervous as she now is – she can give no idea, but she owns she hardly knows how she will go through it.[15]

She did manage – just.

> *Great crowds out, & so I had (for the first time since my great misfortune) an escort. Dressing after luncheon, which I could hardly touch. Wore my ordinary evening dress, only trimmed with miniver, and my cap with a long flowing tulle veil, a small diamond & sapphire coronet rather at the back, and diamonds outlining the front of my cap.*
>
> *It was a fearful moment for me when I entered the carriage alone, and*

the band played; also when all the crowds cheered, and I had great difficulty in repressing my tears. But our two dear affectionate girls [Princesses Helena and Louise who faced the Queen in the carriage] were a true help & support to me, and they so thoroughly realised all I was going through. The crowds were most enthusiastic, & the people seemed to look at me with sympathy. We had both windows open, in spite of a very high wind.

When I entered the House which was very full, I felt as if I should faint. All was silent and all eyes fixed upon me, and there I sat alone. I was greatly relieved when all was over, & I stepped down from the throne ...

'*So thankful that the great ordeal of today was well over, & that I was enabled to get through it.*[16]

Queen Victoria opening
Parliament, 1866

The press did not miss the opportunity to echo the growing public discontent with the Queen's seclusion – in fact, it fuelled the discontent. By 1867 feeling had exacerbated to such a degree that General Grey, in answer to the Queen's request that he should 'hint as to the harm' articles such as a recent one in *The Times* was doing,[17] felt impelled to tell her as gently as possible that, however much one understood her position, she was only making matters worse for herself:

… his distress on this occasion is much increased by feeling how little he can do to prevent its repetition. But where a feeling is very general, & very strong, it is difficult, if not impossible to prevent its finding expression; & General Grey would only be deceiving Your Majesty & concealing a truth of which Your Majesty ought to be aware, if he did not add that however unreasonable the feeling may be, & whatever may be thought of the time or manner in which it is expressed, or of the time chosen for expressing it, it is the fact that *The Times*, in this article has only followed the impulse given by, what General Grey cannot conceal from himself, is a very general & a very strong feeling…. People feel, very generally, that the tone of society is much deteriorated, & that unless some check is put upon its onward tendency, it will get worse & that very serious consequences may be the result. They believe that Your Majesty is the only person who has the power to interpose any effectual check upon this state of things, & that only by Your Majesty's resuming the place which none but Your Majesty can fill.[18]

This then is the background against which the Queen in great secrecy hatched her plot of escaping to Switzerland. During the summer and autumn of 1867 she conducted a lively correspondence with Howard Elphinstone, the Governor of Prince Arthur, about where to go the following summer. At first she still toyed with the idea of going to the Tyrol in Austria,[19] but she gave this up on learning how very remote the house in question was, what a long journey would be needed to reach it and how very hot it might be in that valley. An entry in her Journal in early August suggests that she still felt almost guilty about going away like this, in her widowed state, but could justify her urge for seclusion by invoking doctor's orders and expiate her feeling of guilt by going where Prince Albert had been in 1837:

> *Had a long talk with Maj. Elphinstone about a projected visit to Switzerland D.V. next year, which Dr. Jenner is most anxious I should undertake for my health, though it is terrible to do or see anything without my beloved Albert. Still I do long to see fine scenery, & Maj. Elphinstone is kindly going to try & find a nice place for me to go to.'[20]

Elphinstone then suggested some possible places in Switzerland, to which the Queen replied in late August with a fairly clear specification.

The temperature of the places which Major Elphinstone mentions wld be totally unfit for the Queen, indeed – unless she can find bracing air – she wld <u>not</u> think of going to Switzerland <u>at all</u> – of course a <u>hot</u> sun and <u>hot</u> days she is prepared to put up with, but there must nevertheless <u>be</u> <u>fresh</u> & <u>cold</u> <u>air</u> besides.

She wld put up with a <u>few small</u> houses supposing <u>only</u> she & her children, – maids & 2 or 3 menservants lived in <u>one</u>, the ladies & gentlemen in another, & so on; that wld do <u>perfectly</u> well – indeed she wld <u>like</u> <u>that</u> <u>best</u> – & any <u>little</u> alterations necessary she wld pay the expences for having made. <u>Only</u> let us find a <u>quiet</u> spot in true mountain scenery – with fine, <u>bracing</u>! air.[21]

The Queen ended this letter by saying she hoped the secret would be kept. A few days later she added to her specification.

The Queen thanks Major Elphinstone for <u>all</u> his letters & <u>all</u> the gt. & kind trouble he has taken to further her wishes. … She will be most curious to hear all from him as to the possibilities afforded for her going to Switzerland. But later than the beginning of Aug. She c.ld not go there – nor w.ld she wish to remain longer than the 10th or 12th of Sept. It w.ld else prevent her getting <u>enough</u> of the bracing Highland air. 6 weeks of the <u>latter</u> she w.ld <u>wish</u> to have.[22]

Elphinstone went to Switzerland on a reconnaissance journey and duly reported back in October with a memorandum containing descriptions of two houses on the Lake of Lucerne that might be suitable. 'He regrets however that he cannot give further details. – It was impossible … to procure these, because, both the houses being private residences admittance could not be obtained without disclosing the object of the visit.'[23]

The private house idea was dropped, but not the location. Although Elphinstone, a careful courtier, does not presume further than that 'Your Majesty has to some extent made up Your mind whereabouts You would wish to remain',[24] the Queen's sights were in fact now firmly set on central Switzerland and she pursued this aim with ruthless determination until August 1868, in the face of all the obstacles the first half of that year was to put in her way.

These obstacles were formidable. There were dramatic political developments that demanded the presence of the monarch at the seat of government and the press was turning nasty. The Conservative government was in a minority in the House of Commons, the ailing Prime Minister Lord Derby resigned in February (to die the following year) and the prospect of a General Election loomed throughout the year. This deprived the Queen of any certainty that she would long enjoy the one stroke of good fortune that fate had vouchsafed her for years: a congenial Prime Minister in the person of Benjamin Disraeli who stepped up from being Chancellor of the Exchequer to replace Lord Derby. Disraeli knew the value of General Grey as a frank and fearless counsellor and wrote imploring him to stay on when Grey had begun to despair of ever persuading the Queen that she needed to make more public appearances.

… After we lost the Prince, which seemed to me, at first an irrecoverable blow in the conduct of public affairs, I have always looked to you as the principal means by which public business might be carried on with satisfaction to Ministers individually, and advantage to the State. It seems to me almost an act of Providence, that the Queen's private confidence should have devolved upon a real gentleman; a man of honor, intelligence, and acquirements; and of no mean experience of life, and especially of political life. I should myself deplore, as a great misfortune, your secession from Her Majesty's service.[25]

Grey's answer dwelt on the need to feel that he was being treated with confidence:

The mere suspicion that such is not the case, necessarily impairs, if it does not destroy one's usefulness, and renders such a situation as mine altogether intolerable. I cannot conceal from myself that since, on more occasions than one, I have given unpalatable opinions to the Queen, she is become reserved with me, and, in certain questions now shuts herself up with me entirely. I believe, however, that this proceeds less from any diminution of confidence, than the fears of having things pressed upon her which jar with her inclinations; and it is this belief chiefly, which induces me still to hold on in a position which, as I told you when you were here, is become very disagreeable to me.'

The letter continues with gloomy foreboding:

I wish I could think matters would mend but if, as I am determined to do, I do my duty to the Queen, honestly, I foresee that they will only become worse. However, you may be sure that I shall do nothing hastily, and I am much cheered and encouraged in holding on, by the kind and flattering manner in which you have expressed yourself towards me.

The end of this letter, however, holds out a glimmer of hope: 'Since I wrote this letter I have received from the Queen (for the first time for some weeks!) instructions which certainly go to show no want of confidence, however certain subjects may be tabooed, and though she may prefer not to hold personal communication with me!'[26]

Grey stayed on, but neither he nor Disraeli nor anyone or anything else (including the sniping of the press) could dissuade her from making things worse by resolving to go in May for some weeks to Balmoral, her residence in Scotland. Disraeli tried – yet, as he said to Grey, 'she ought not to go to Scotland, but she will'.[27] And she did. Grey had all the more reason to be anxious for the Queen because he was one of the very few people who knew that not very long after returning from Balmoral she would be heading for the Continent.

In fairness to the Queen, she had real cause for grief and anxiety on top of her self-imposed burden of honouring the memory of her dear departed with

Benjamin Disraeli

her own brand of perpetual mourning. It was taking her years to recover her balance after being deprived of her Consort, her pillar of strength. In March 1868 her second son Prince Alfred was shot and wounded in Australia by a member of the Irish Republican movement called the Fenian Brotherhood. In April she was praying for the success of a British expeditionary force against Theodore, King of Abyssinia, who had taken hostage all the British subjects he could lay his hands on in the country. Her prayers were heard: the force advanced through an almost impassable region to Theodore's fortress of Magdala and released the prisoners.

At the beginning of May a violent political upheaval was triggered by Gladstone's Liberal Opposition carrying a Resolution in the House of Commons that the Irish branch of the United Church of England and Ireland should be disestablished, since it ministered to only a very small minority. The Liberals knew that the Government could not act on a constitutional issue such as this without going to the country. Sure enough, Disraeli advised the Queen to dissolve Parliament and told her that, if she should think it best, Ministers were ready to resign at once. The Queen (understandably) refused the offer of resignation, but agreed that there should in due course be a dissolution and General Election. This finally happened in November and she spent the summer and autumn anxiously hoping that her new ally and supporter Disraeli would not be swept from office, to be replaced by the much less sympathetic Gladstone.

It is ironic that in May Disraeli of all people should have – no doubt unthinkingly – given her a cruel reminder of this possibility, in the course of a letter full of flowery thanks. The Queen had (decorously via an intermediary to Mrs Disraeli) sent him spring flowers 'as they will make his room look so bright'. Writing from the House of Commons, Disraeli immediately thanked the Queen 'for your Majesty's bright and gracious recollection of him this morn. None of the decorations, on which he sometimes has to take your Majesty's pleasure, were half as fair; and he trusts, that in their sweetness and their beauty, they may ever be typical of your Majesty's life and thoughts.' But Disraeli rather marred the effect by saying in the same letter ' … The House very serene, and about to die'.[28] Reminding the Queen of a distasteful prospect was no doubt the last thing he had in mind; but he will have been anxious to shield her from the unpleasant truth, which was that serenity was in fact in very short supply in Parliament. The place was in turmoil – as vividly portrayed by *The Globe and Traveller* on 19 May:

Will there be a Dissolution?

The temper of the Opposition becomes more splenetic and venomous every day. Whatever the PRIME MINISTER proposes, MR GLADSTONE and his allies are resolved, if possible, to thwart. Never before have the annals of the House of Commons been disgraced by party warfare so thoroughly sordid and unscrupulous. Never before has a politician – for MR GLADSTONE has forfeited every claim to be called a statesman – exhibited in a form so despicable the mingled results of personal dislike and disappointed ambition. The spirit of envy has taken mortal shape, and represents South Lancashire.

A VISION.
V——"WHY DO YOU FROWN—WHAT HAVE I DONE?"   E——"LET GRIEF PREVAIL O'ER DUTY!"

South Lancashire was Gladstone's parliamentary seat. *The Globe* supported the Conservative Party.

To add to the Queen's worries, the press had now become even more outspoken than before in its strictures on her absences from the centre of affairs. She was particularly aggrieved when one such article appeared in *The Globe* in mid-May, just after she had made a great effort by not only entertaining at Buckingham Palace but also laying the foundation stone of the new St Thomas's Hospital in London. The article acknowledged these public activities as the dawn of a new spring in relations between the Sovereign and her loyal subjects, but deplored her intention of nipping it in the bud by betaking herself away again almost at once.

The Queen with her Subjects

It is with no feigned satisfaction or perfunctory sense of duty that we chronicle the graceful discharge of one of the most important functions of Royalty by HER MAJESTY yesterday. The deep shade of sorrow which the death of the illustrious and much-loved PRINCE CONSORT cast on the SOVEREIGN and Court of England has for some time obscured the lustre of the Crown. ... The people ... ever and anon ... have looked hopefully and anxiously to see the Monarch ... rise from the sombre shade and once more appear before her people with bright, if chastened mien; resuming the responsibilities of her exalted station, and again performing the duties of her peerless state....

The monarch is not only the ruler but also the head of the nation. In the wearer of the Crown centre the force and vitality of the national body corporate. From the occupant of the Throne, as from a fountain, flows all honour. From the dynast depends all dignity. What the sun is in the planetary system the SOVEREIGN is to the social system.... If the head is clouded in grief, the whole body suffers. If the fountain flows feebly, honour is at a low ebb. If the dynast is hidden from view, dignity comes to be disregarded. If the sun is eclipsed, vigour, growth, and harmony are endangered in the social system.

... With profound respect ... we venture to give expression to the desire that an impression to the effect that HER MAJESTY meditates an early departure for her far-off home in the Highlands may even now prove unfounded. ... A Royal birthday spent in the Highlands ... withdrawn from us would doubtless be enjoyable to the Royal Family, but in some sort a misfortune to the nation.

The Queen reacted violently. On the day this article appeared she wrote a defensive letter to Disraeli, saying she was prepared to return earlier than contemplated from Scotland 'if anything ... very serious should render it necessary – but she is completely done up by the fatigue of these few days ... [She has had so] much anxiety & worry during the last 2 or 3 years of every kind & sort that it is beginning to tell very seriously on her health & nerves – wh. are both very much shaken – ... The Queen would not have written all this to Mr. Disraeli now, had she not been much annoyed & pained at an article in this Govt's *Globe*, (wh. she understands is a Govt. paper) wh. she considers a most ungrateful return for the very gt. exertions she has made this season ...[29]

On this day the Queen also appealed to Theodore Martin, a man of influence with the press:

Mr Martin has been so kind and feeling, and knowing so well how the Queen's health and nerves are shaken – therefore will understand how very <u>great</u> the efforts made this year have been – a week in London, <u>three</u> Drawing-rooms, and the great ceremony yesterday, from which she is suffering <u>much</u> to-day; he will accordingly not be surprised at the indignation and pain with which she read the Article in *The Globe* to-night, and her great anxiety therefore that he or Mr Helps should try and prevent similar Articles appearing in *The Times* and *Daily Telegraph*. Every increased effort is rewarded by such shameless Articles; and the discouragement and pain they cause are <u>very great</u>. ... Were she not to get away for three to four weeks (and <u>no</u> public service <u>can</u> suffer, for communication is very rapid) she believes she would <u>completely</u> break down. They even <u>grudge</u> the Prince of Wales going down for <u>three</u> days to spend his poor widowed mother's birthday <u>with her</u> (for the first time since '61!). It is very cruel! The Queen hears it is not <u>at all</u> the general feeling, and that people are really anxious about her; but she really <u>is</u> feeling <u>utterly</u> worn out; and <u>does wish some</u> newspaper would point out <u>how</u> much she <u>has</u> <u>done</u>, and how necessary it is to keep her well enough to go on, for else she may be unable to do so.[30]

Her appeal failed. Six days later *The Times* thundered forth. In stinging phrases the article lambasted the Prime Minister for not impressing on the Queen the necessity for her, as constitutional Head of State, to be at hand at this time of political crisis:

On Monday night the Queen's Ministers were twice defeated in the House of Commons. ... There is a Ministerial crisis, which may dissolve either the Ministry or the Parliament. This being the state of things, the public has been astonished by another contemporary incident. In the same paper of yesterday which contained the news of MR DISRAELI's defeat and his motion to report progress on the Scotch Reform Bill it was announced that the QUEEN, with her family, had left Windsor Castle the evening before, at half-past 6 o'clock, for Balmoral. Thus, at the very hour when a most important debate was proceeding – a debate on which the question of life and death to Government or to Parliament might turn – the first person in the State, to whom recourse must be had in every momentous juncture, was hurrying at full speed from the neighbourhood of the capital to a remote Highland district, six hundred miles from her Ministry and Parliament. In the month of May, at a time when the business of the Nation is at its height, and interests of every kind cause people to congregate in London – at a time when it is especially necessary that the SOVEREIGN should be accessible to her Ministers and to the Legislature, we have the whole Court withdrawn to a distance which renders any personal communication impossible.... MR DISRAELI is 63 years of age, and, though mentally energetic, it would be too much to ask him to rush to the Highlands at

Balmoral Castle from the
opposite side of the Dee

Limited Mail speed and return within 48 hours. So HER MAJESTY must be communicated with by messenger, if at all; and, however the communication is made there must be an inconvenient lapse of time before the answer is received....

We must think, therefore, that it was an act of culpable neglect on the part of the Minister not to inform the QUEEN that the political prospects of her government were so doubtful as to demand her presence at or near the seat of the Legislature....

There was worse to come. The next day a report was telegraphed to Balmoral of an extraordinary incident in Parliament. An MP had in the House of Commons formally raised the question of her abdication, by asking 'whether it be true that HM the Queen has been compelled through delicate health to retire from England during the remainder of this session; and if so, whether it is the intention of Her Majesty's Government, out of consideration to Her Majesty's health, comfort and tranquility, and in the interest of the Royal Family and of HM's subjects throughout the Empire, and especially of this Metropolis, to advise Her Majesty to abdicate.'[31]

This Question, in the words of the *Pall Mall Gazette*, 'was received with a condemnatory shout of "order" from all quarters of the House, was rebuked by the Speaker for the disrespectful terms of the question and [the MP] apologized for his offence against the good taste and the etiquette of Parliament'.

The Queen felt goaded beyond endurance. She followed up her letter to

Disraeli with another – a letter that contained the ultimate threat:

> She <u>thinks</u> it vy important that the question of her <u>state</u> of health <u>once</u> for <u>all</u>
> shld. be <u>understood</u>. – It is simply this: The Queen's health – & nerves –
> <u>require</u> in the spring time a <u>short interval</u> of bracing mountain air &
> comparative quiet – or she <u>must</u> break down completely & <u>if</u> the public will <u>not</u>
> take her – as she is – she must <u>give all up</u> – & give it up to the Pr. of Wales. – No
> doubt they wld. wish her to be always in London for <u>their</u> convenience … but
> the Queen <u>can't</u>…. The Queen's looks belie her & <u>nobody</u> believes <u>how</u> she
> suffers.[32]

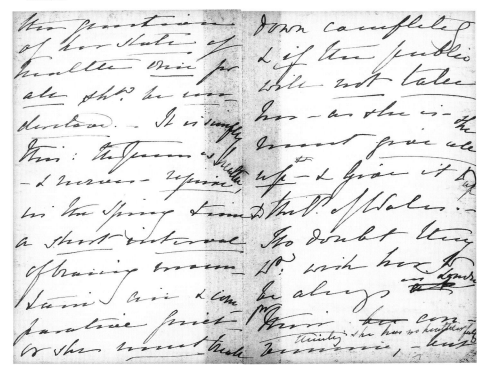

Facsimile of pages from Queen Victoria's letter of 22 May 1868 to Disraeli, in which she threatens to abdicate

The Queen asked Disraeli to have the matter authoritatively raised in consultation with her physician, Sir William Jenner, adding in a dig at General Grey that it ought to have been done long ago and that her own people had 'never been wise or judicious in this'.[33]

Queen Victoria was certainly right in thinking that her looks belied her real condition. General Grey, writing to his wife about the gilly* dance on the occasion of the Queen's birthday in the last week of May, rather unchivalrously bore out her point: 'Princess Louise looked really lovely at the dance, and tho' H.M. did <u>not,</u> no one who saw her could <u>for a moment</u> have surmised that her <u>health</u> required care!'[34]

---

* Grey's spelling.

But of course the Queen's state of mind was a different matter.

As the turbulent month of May drew to a close the tide of public censure had turned and was beginning to ebb. The Sovereign's Birthday on 24 May saw the press handsomely – but still guardedly – making amends for their earlier strictures, in an outburst of loyalty and understanding for her parlous condition; the Queen was also much comforted by a letter from her eldest daughter, the Crown Princess of Prussia. 'Your dear, loving, warm-hearted letter of the 20th,' she wrote back, 'reached me on the morning of my poor, sad ... birthday – so full of recollections – so far off. The <u>present</u> has now become a reality & is like a different life. You speak so dearly & affectionately & I do so long to fold you to my heart – <u>my</u> <u>own</u> <u>own</u> <u>own</u> loved <u>1st born</u>! – but you <u>must</u> <u>bear</u> with your poor old Mama, for her head gets so tired & she is so fagged & wasted that I fear you will find her a dull, tiresome companion....

Victoria, Crown Princess of Prussia, the Queen's eldest daughter

'But I do gratefully accept what God <u>has</u> sent to cheer ... & comfort me.'[35]

During the rest of her month at Balmoral the Queen did not fail to study and react to the long accounts of the Parliamentary Debates prepared for her by Grey and the hurried appraisals sent by Disraeli. As usual she also conscientiously dealt with all the voluminous paperwork that came her way. While all this was going on she must have been wondering how she was going to break the news of yet another absence – and half way across Europe at that – relatively soon after returning to England. Throughout these troubled months she had clung tenaciously, as if to a lifeline, to her project of escaping to Switzerland for a complete rest and change. But she had shared the secret with only two or three people, those concerned with the arrangements that were being made for the journey and accommodation.

Even these few were too many. Writing to her mother from Potsdam in early June, the Crown Princess, Victoria, said she had heard from her father-in-law, the King of Prussia, that 'you are coming to Switzerland in August. Is that true?'[36] The Queen wrote a damage-limitation letter explaining her need for secrecy,[37] but she must have spent the month having nightmares about the cat being let out of the bag in London and turning into a fierce British lion that roared its disapproval of her abandoning her realm for foreign climes.

Scotland did her good: she felt stronger and better for it and had to tear herself away, as she wrote to the Crown Princess on her last night, adding: 'It is now near 11 – & still vy light – there is such charm in that soft, clear light.'[38]

Back in Windsor, the Queen found life even more unbearable than she had feared. Not only did she have to take part publicly in the dreaded English Season, but she had come straight from the invigorating air of her beloved Scottish glens and forests into a fierce heatwave. Her body was built for cool weather, not high temperatures, and she suffered accordingly. Hardly an entry in her Journal or a letter of hers at this time is without some reference to the heat and what it was doing to her.

But she soldiered on. June 20 found her taking a one-and-a-half hour march-past of 24,000 troops. *Very tired but greatly pleased and gratified* says her Journal. Yet on the same day she wrote to the Crown Princess that 'the heat is so fearful today that I can hardly hold my pen … so unwell with violent headaches and sickness since I came back that I am quite shaky.'[39]

Two days later she faced the music again and went to Buckingham Palace for a monster Garden Party.

At 5 the alarming moment arrived & I went down into the garden…. Quantities of people on the lawn whom I had to recognize as I went along & after nearly 8 years seclusion, it was vy. puzzling & bewildering.[40]

There were Tyrolean singers and a band. The Queen talked and had tea with the Royal party in a tent. *This over, I slowly walked back to the Palace, talking to people on the way. Felt quite exhausted & faint & I had seemed to be in a dream, so totally unsuited to the scene.*[41]

Twenty-four hours were enough for her at Buckingham Palace. She was back at Windsor by the following afternoon and sweltered there ('overpowered by the heat') until she could decently get away to her island retreat of Osborne, on the Isle of Wight, where it was no less oppressive but at least she was away from Windsor, 'that dungeon'.[42]

There should have been one more ordeal before she could be released to go to Switzerland: the Speech from the Throne proroguing the Parliamentary Session until the autumn. But fate was kind to her and the speech was delivered on her behalf by the Lords Commissioners. The speech, drafted as usual by the Government, had of course been submitted to her. In her Journal of 30 July she wrote of holding a Privy Council *before which I saw Mr. Disraeli, who spoke kindly about the speech, saying that he felt so grateful to me for suggesting a slight alteration in the last paragraph, which I thought as it 1st stood might have fettered the Govt. in any future liberal policy. All the Cabinet agreed about the alteration, but none had thought about it.*

So that was satisfactorily dealt with. Furthermore, the Season was drawing to a close, and those who could were intent upon getting away for country pursuits. As *The Gentleman's Magazine* put it: 'The London Season begins with the reprieve of the partridges and the pheasants, and ends with the death warrant of the grouse.'

One major problem remained. The solution proposed for it was about to be put to the test.

2   Incognita

The big question-mark still hanging over Queen Victoria's Swiss holiday as she prepared for departure in early August 1868 concerned her urgent need for privacy. Was she going to travel half way across Europe, braving a record heat-wave in order to recruit her health and strength in glorious surroundings, only to be plagued by the very public attention she was trying to escape from? Was she going to find the total seclusion she so desperately sought? Time would soon tell, but meanwhile she at least had the satisfaction of knowing that she had all along taken every possible precaution.

Total secrecy was out of the question. If she had ever thought that she could make such a journey secretly and go undetected for a month in a country crawling with her own subjects as well as holidaymakers from far and wide, she would soon have abandoned the thought. Of course the Swiss hotel-keepers and staff already then knew what was good for them: travellers high and low could rely implicitly on their absolute discretion. But the public at large, although by that time used to the spectacle of foreign grandees lording it in their resorts, might have taken more than a passing interest in a personality as well known as the Queen of England. And she could hardly have gone about in disguise.

So the Queen did the obvious thing. She changed her name. In doing so she took advantage of a convention as practical then as it is paradoxical to us today, a device breathing the spirit of an age that observed a well-defined – and in many ways genial – code of conduct: the incognito. By announcing that she was going abroad as 'The Countess of Kent', the Queen was letting it be known that she was not expecting to be treated as Queen, but as an (almost) ordinary traveller.

To our modern ears the very word incognito has the distant echo of a long-vanished age of manners. For Queen Victoria the device was a readily available possibility, and it promised relief from torment. It was marvellously effective: all she had to do was to announce she was going incognita and governments would take no official notice of her, the press would stay at a safe distance and the public would not pry. Everyone would know who she was, but nobody would bother her, since she would be going about as an unknown countess. The authorities were thereby elegantly absolved from the need of paying their respects to a Head of State, and the press and public were implicitly requested to leave her in peace.

Queen Victoria had used the device before, and it had worked reasonably well. She was now fervently hoping that it would serve her even better at this agonizing time for her escape to Switzerland – an escape which had taken three long years to become a reality. Although at the outset in 1865 she had considered both Switzerland and Austria, Switzerland was the obvious choice. Apart from its growing fame as 'the Garden of England', it was where Prince Albert had toured in 1837 – a sojourn from which he had sent the young Queen he was soon to marry several mementos.[43] She kept these, which included a pressed Alpine rose from the Rigi, in an album which she said she took with her wherever she went. Then, in 1864, her son Prince Arthur with his Governor Major Elphinstone had gone on what amounted to a sentimental journey, following the same route and very much encouraged by his mother.

High in the Queen's esteem for his discretion and loyalty, Howard Elphinstone put his knowledge of other countries and their languages to work in order to find suitable accommodation for her in Switzerland

Clearly the Queen had to go to Switzerland. In 1867 when she started planning in earnest, Elphinstone was the obvious person to recruit as a fellow-plotter. She was uneasily aware that it was going to be difficult to sell the idea to her subjects, who were already discontented at her withdrawal from public life and all-too-frequent absences from her capital. But she also felt, at heart, that she was not yet ready to be fully back in the swim. Thus, come what may, she was determined to do what she needed – to get away whenever she could. However, she was anxious to postpone for as long as possible the difficult moment of issuing an announcement.

The first thing was to decide where to go. Elphinstone threw himself into the task with enthusiasm, suggesting a host of possible destinations. The Queen rejected them all for being too hot. So he set off to reconnoitre in Switzerland and recommended two private houses he had 'cased' near the Lake of Lucerne. These too were rejected and the search was resumed early in the following year, 1868.

The Queen knew what she wanted when she wrote to Elphinstone:

> The simplest fare, 2 of my cooks enough. Probably the Queen would take 2 <u>Ponies</u> and a carriage, but <u>no</u> horses. Inquire as to what the carriages of the country are. Perhaps some new cushions might make them comfortable enough not to necessitate the Queen taking her own carriage which would probably not be so useful for that country – Are the horses always driven from the box or not? It would be more convenient if there were room for 2 on the box – as the Queen would not feel <u>safe</u> if she had <u>not</u> Brown <u>with</u> her, and he would not be able to communicate with the people nor would he know the country. Inquiries must be made as to the water etc....[44]

Towards the end of March the Queen, still moving only within the tiny circle of those in the know, sent a memorandum to General Grey in which she, almost hesitantly for her, broached a subject that she knew very well was going to spell trouble: two long summer absences.

> With regard to what she stated yesterday she would <u>just</u> repeat in writing what she said. Sir William Jenner wishes the Queen to have 4 weeks or a months <u>complete</u> change of scene and as <u>much</u> <u>mental</u> rest as possible, and for that (not to break in upon some weeks of the bracing Highland air which is equally necessary to her health) it is essential she should not be detained in England beyond the 7th or 8th August: and she is therefore anxious to know whether something could <u>not</u> be done (<u>as it is a case of health</u>) to permit this, should Parliament be prolonged beyond that period.
>
> The Queen's whole system her nerves, stomach etc are all very much shaken by the 6 years and more of unassisted labour and responsibility, added to the terrible grief which for the first 3 or 4 years quite overpowered her strength; then came years of much anxiety both public, and domestic and last year especially she was <u>very sorely</u> tried in <u>many</u> ways.
>
> She feels it a duty to her family and people to do all to prevent her getting worse and becoming incapable of continuing her duties at all'.[45]

What the Queen was after in this letter was to anticipate and get round a potential show-stopper: could she go abroad with Parliament still in session? And there were other considerations. Queen Victoria, although not Head of Government, at that time still exercised more direct influence on decisions than in her later years. Apart from that, the Royal Assent was (and is) needed for every piece of legislature. When the Lord Chancellor, Lord Cairns, was consulted on the subject, he produced a splendid Opinion:

Absence of the Sovereign from Her Dominions
Confidential Memorandum
It was formerly the custom, when the Sovereign was about to leave the Kingdom, to appoint Lords Justices, by Letters Patent under the Great Seal, to exercise during the absence of the Sovereign certain portions of the Royal Prerogative.

The last occasion when this was done was in 1821, when His late Majesty King George the 4th was about to proceed on a visit to the Continent.

Since that time, no appointment of Lords Justices has been made.

When Her Majesty was about to visit Germany in 1845, the late Lord Campbell, in the House of Lords, enquired whether Lords Justices would be appointed, and suggested that it would be unconstitutional not to do so. The Lord Chancellor (Lord Lyndhurst) said the question had been carefully considered both on that occasion, and also when Her Majesty had visited France; and that the Government, acting on the advice of the Law Officers, were of opinion that there was no Law or rule requiring the appointment of Lords Justices; that a Secretary of State would attend Her Majesty; and that the increased facilities of communications made the former precedents no longer applicable.

The latter reason is, at the present time, still more forcible.

Beyond, therefore, the regular communications between Her Majesty and Her Majesty's Ministers for the purpose of taking Her Majesty's Pleasure, and obtaining the Royal Sign Manual – which can be conducted with more or less dispatch according to the exigency of the case – the only matter which requires to be considered is the Royal Assent to Bills in Parliament.

There can be no General Commission to give Assent to Bills: nor can there be a Commission to assent to a Bill until the Bill has passed all its stages in both Houses – There will probably be ample time to transmit and return Commissions in regular course for all Bills other than the Appropriation Bill.

As to the Appropriation Bill, it is generally the last which passes through the Houses of Parliament; and, when it has passed, both Houses must wait until the Commission with the Royal Sign Manual is returned.

Any delay as to this, would be best avoided by sending beforehand to the Secretary of State, or Minister in attendance on Her Majesty, a Commission, with the date in blank, for giving Assent to the Appropriation Bill. On the Bill passing the last stage, a telegraphic message could be sent to the Secretary of State, who would insert the date in the Commission; submit it for Her Majesty's Signature; and at once transmit it by Special Messenger to the Lord

Chancellor. Probably all this could be done in 24 or 36 hours.[46]

Most satisfactory, if wordy. It meant that the Queen was let off the hook even if Parliament were still in session when she went to Switzerland – an increasingly likely eventuality in view of the uncertain political situation.

Her immediate problem was to get through the spring with all its anxieties and do whatever possible to win understanding for her month in Balmoral from May to June.

By early June she had weathered the Balmoral storm and was feeling calmer. So it must have been a real blow to her when a letter arrived at the beginning of June from her eldest daughter Crown Princess Victoria in Germany asking whether it was true that she was going to Switzerland in August.[47] Realizing that her cover had been blown, the Queen wrote back:

> I am very much surprised at what the King told you about my plans. Of course for very long I was very uncertain as to what I cld. do – but Sir Wm Jenner was very anxious I shld. go to Switzerland quite incognita, & as quietly as possible – for a complete change of Scene – thinking it might do my nerves good. But I told no one, except those 2 or 3 on whose secrecy I can implicitly rely. I can receive no one, neither children, relations or acquaintances, for else it becomes what the Rosenau was each time – a gt. fatigue and excitement. You will at once, dear Child, see the necessity for this line being drawn. I wld. have told you before – but having to keep it quiet as long as possible here …[48]

The Crown Princess then replied that 'I quite understand your journey to Switzerland, indeed I did so before you told me about it, it was Ct. Bernstorff*[49] who wrote it in an official despatch a week or 2 ago. I hope it may do you good and what an enjoyment is in store for you.'

No doubt; but first there were troubled waters to sail through. It was now clear that the moment of truth was upon her: an announcement would have to be made fairly soon – especially since she had finally decided upon her accommodation in Lucerne and arrangements for the journey itself had to be got under way. Perhaps the trip could be kept under wraps a little longer, at least until she had made her eagerly awaited public appearances in London. But she could at least share her thoughts about it with the Crown Princess. ' … You shall hear all about my Journey – but I am going to see no sights. All Picture Galleries & Exhibitions as a rule I have been obliged to give up – as I am quite unequal to them. I am able for very little & I don't think I shall be

---

* Sure enough, Count Bernstorff, the long-time Prussian Ambassador to London, had somehow winkled out the secret and reported on 30 May (in French, as protocol demanded) that arrangements had been made for the Queen to spend August in Switzerland. Of Lord Stanley, though, he only said that he would spend the Parliamentary recess 'in the country'.[49]

able to make any long excursions – for I get tired very easily & <u>sun</u> heat I positively <u>cannot</u> bear. Your 2 sisters & Leopold – my <u>inseparables</u> go with me. It is to <u>Lucerne</u> that I am going (please don't betray this) & I have taken the Pension <u>Wallis</u> <u>there</u> …'[50]

Staying in a pension on the Continent was a radical departure for the Queen. On her previous trips abroad she had always stayed in residences belonging to members of her family. The Pension Wallis belonged to Robert Wallis, an English lithographer who had moved to Lucerne from his birthplace in Germany and had married a local Swiss woman. Although originally something of a hot-head and radical when first in Switzerland during the momentous 1840s, he had settled down and established a successful lithography business. This enabled him to branch out and build a select, intimate 'pension', which opened for business in 1866. The whole of it was rented for the Queen's stay. Commanding glorious views over the lake, the house occupied a prime site on a hill called the Gütsch, just outside the town.

With an admirably secluded Swiss base thus secured, the next step was to

Lucerne, seen from the
Gütsch

ensure privacy while travelling. Wheels were set in motion to this end on 1 July, when General Grey wrote a private letter to Disraeli:

As the time is now approaching, within 5 or 6 weeks, when the Queen intends to go abroad in search of that peace & repose which the state of her health renders so essential, I write to you, by Her Majesty's desire, to say that Her Majesty has fixed upon a residence about 1/2 an hour, or 3/4 of an hour distant from Lucerne, & will proceed there in the first days of August.

In order to derive the full benefit from this excursion, it is absolutely necessary that Her Majesty's privacy should not be unnecessarily disturbed. She therefore proposes to travel under a real, not a half & half, incognita, as when she went to Coburg, & I will let you know, as soon as it has been decided on, the name under which it will be her pleasure to travel.

It is Her Majesty's wish to be treated entirely as a Private Individual, going abroad for her health, & it is therefore her intention resolutely to decline every offer of anything like Royal Honours, & all visits that may be offered by Relations, or Members of Foreign Royal families. I write in the same sense to Ld. Stanley,* to beg that he will clearly explain his wishes in this respect to Mr Lumley,† & to request that he will not only use his own best endeavours, but try to obtain the cooperation of the local authorities, whenever it may be necessary, to prevent her being intruded upon by the world.

It is from her desire to secure this quiet that H. M. has hitherto been silent on the subject of her intention to go to Switzerland, & she trusts with entire confidence in you to do whatever may be in your powers to further Her wishes.

Nothing will probably be going on during H.M.'s absence. Parlt. will be up, & you will be all preparing for the coming Elections, while all seems peaceable on the Continent. She does not know, therefore, that the presence of a Minister will be necessary. But should you think it unadvisable that H.M. shd. remain for four weeks abroad, without being in reach of one of her responsible Advisers, one of the Ministers might easily come out to Lucerne, as for his private convenience; & there he is, as I have already said, at only 1/2 an hour, or 3/4 of an hour's distance from Her Majesty. – I will write again, about the mode of communicating with the Queen while abroad. I will only say now that, in order to preserve her incognita inviolate, H.M. does not wish anything to be addressed to her as <u>Queen</u>.

Yrs very truly

C. Grey

* The Foreign Secretary.
† The British Minister to Switzerland in Berne.

Since writing the above the Queen has expressed a wish that the Ld. Chancellor shd. be asked whether there would be any objection to Her Majesty assuming the title, when abroad, of Countess of Chester. The P. of Wales is Earl of Chester. – H.M. does not wish to take the title of Dss. of Lancaster under which she has before travelled, & which is not favourable to the strict incognita she desires to maintain.[51]

There was an objection: the Princess of Wales was Countess of Chester and the Queen could hardly hijack one of her daughter-in-law's titles (although, as Sovereign, she theoretically was entitled to do so). The upshot of the ensuing consultation was that the Lord Chancellor, Lord Cairns, wrote to Disraeli that 'The Duke of Edinburgh is Earl of Kent: so that if Her Majesty thought fit to use the Style of Countess of Kent, the difficulty as to the title of Countess of Chester, arising from that being one of the dignities of the Princess of Wales, would be avoided.'[52]

On 7 July the Queen's Journal records a discussion with Disraeli: ... *Talked of my journey abroad & my taking the title of Css. of Kent, a fine old title & now one of Affie's.*[53] Affie, her second son, was Prince Alfred, Duke of Edinburgh and of Saxe-Coburg-Gotha.

Later that month it was finally judged opportune to issue a public announcement about her forthcoming journey, the wording having been decided upon after correspondence between General Grey (its drafter), Disraeli and a hesitant Queen.

The Queen will leave England early next month for a short residence in Switzerland.

As Her Majesty goes abroad entirely on the recommendation of her Physicians, in search of the change of air and repose which they consider so essential to her health – she will maintain the strictest incognita during her absence – refusing even the visits, as well as the attentions usually paid to Sovereigns when travelling on the Continent and in such circumstances.[54]

This news was, of course, immediately seized upon by the press, but by this time the sting had (for the time being) been drawn from the long-standing feud about her absences. For one thing, the ground had been well prepared this time (after the Queen's sternly expressed annoyance that the public relations aspect of her earlier stay in Scotland had been bungled by Court and Government). For another, the London Season was coming to an end. The gentry were heading for their country places – and, indeed, many of them for Switzerland (as were increasing numbers of less privileged people). So there were no reproaches.

The Globe, 1 August 1868

THIS MONTH'S INTELLIGENCE

The Queen will leave Osborne on Wednesday for a short residence in Switzerland, under the advice of Sir William Jenner, who will accompany Her Majesty. Lord Stanley will leave London a few days afterwards, and will be at Her Majesty's commands. Her Majesty will maintain a strict incognita during her residence so that Her Majesty may be able to command a few weeks of complete repose which, with change of air, is deemed highly necessary for Her Majesty's health.

The day before this article appeared Disraeli had written to the Foreign Secretary, Lord Stanley: 'Remember to exercise your large influence with the Press, to say as little about our friend as possible.'[55]

Lord Stanley, Foreign Secretary

Stanley did so to good effect. He was the Cabinet Minister appointed to be at hand in Switzerland in order to transact any public business requiring the Queen, but also to keep unwanted visitors (that is, everybody) from her doorstep. Stanley was an odd choice. The heir to the Earldom of Derby, he was a living example of the gulf between the old British landed aristocracy and a Royal Family not yet pukka in their eyes. He inclined to defeatism and was something of a pessimist. On hearing of the Queen's intention to get away from it all in Switzerland, his first reaction (noted in his diary) was characteristic: 'A strange report that the Queen is going to pass a month in Switzerland. If true, she will give offence to the Irish, who expect a visit: and to the Emperor, as she will not pass thro' Paris: while she will be mobbed by tourists of all nations, and half killed with heat, which always, as she says, makes her ill.'[56] Hardly balm to the ear of a Queen already jittery over this aspect of her forthcoming tour.

When Stanley went to Windsor to present the Brazilian Minister, he observed: 'The Queen well, but growing enormously fat: complains much of her health: talks of her Swiss tour &c. I warn her against heat and tourists, by whom she will be mobbed to any amount.'[57]

Stanley was, to say the least, an indifferent performer in Parliament. *The Times* wrote of one of his speeches during this disastrous 1868 session ' ... His amendment was smothered in his own confusion.' *The Gentleman's Magazine*, although admitting that with him 'you may always reckon upon sound manly sense', called his articulation 'terribly disconcerting. It is zigzag and blurred.'

Draft of Lord Stanley's letter to the British Minister in Berne, as amended by the Queen

Yet he was, after all, Foreign Secretary and the logical choice to be Minister in Attendance. However, the Queen could do without his kind of encouragement. She was prepared to tolerate him – but at arm's length. When she saw the letter he had drafted to the British Legation in Berne, the Swiss Federal capital, announcing that he would be 'in attendance on the Queen',[58] she firmly crossed out this phrase and inserted her own amendment – as a result of which the letter that actually went to Berne had her revised wording: 'In obedience to the Queen's commands I shall be at Lucerne though not in actual attendance on Her Majesty during Her stay in Switzerland.'[59]

The earlier part of this letter to Berne spells out the ground rules laid down for the way the Queen's visit was to be treated by officials in Switzerland.

I have already informed you that the Queen proposes to pass a portion of the present summer at Lucerne; but as it is Her Majesty's intention to maintain during Her stay in Switzerland, as well as on Her journey there and back, the most complete incognita, travelling under the name of Countess of Kent and declining all Royal Honours, it will be proper that you should make a communication to that effect to the Federal Authorities, and request them to make a similar communication to the Cantonal Authorities at Lucerne. It may be right to add, however, that Her Majesty's government rely on the good will of the Federal and Cantonal Authorities to provide in other respects for the comfort and freedom from molestation of the Queen during Her stay at Lucerne.

Her Majesty will not require the attendance of yourself or any member of your mission at Lucerne during the whole time of Her residence at that place, but you should be at Lucerne (in plain clothes) with any members of your mission on Her Majesty's arrival on the 7th of August, so that you may receive Her Majesty at the Railway Station and take any commands which She may see occasion to give to you.[60]

One who had high hopes of the visit was the British Consul in Geneva, who in a flowery hand wrote a despatch to Stanley:

My Lord,

I am informed that Her Majesty the Queen intends coming to reside at Lucerne next month, that place being in my Consular district and also that Her Majesty will probably visit Geneva, on her outward, or homeward journey. I write to your Lordship, to solicit the grant of a sum of money sufficient to provide me with a Dress Uniform, in case I may require one, on any occasion during Her Majesty's stay in Switzerland.

I may mention that I have never received anything for any outfit since my appointment, and I certainly cannot afford the expense from my private purse, already sufficiently taxed in the service of the Public since I have had the honour of holding my Consular appointment at Geneva, & for now more than 8 years.

I hope your Lordship will consider I am making a right application on the present occasion. If I am expected, not to have anything to do with Her Majesty's visit either at Lucerne, or perhaps through this city, then I can continue to do without the Uniform – but in any case I really cannot afford myself, the expense of what, I believe amounts to some £50.0.0.[61]

This request was in vain. His Lordship not only refused point blank, but instructed the Consul to stay well away. All he got for his efforts was extra consular office work.

As the day of departure drew near, preparations went into top gear. Moving Queen Victoria's Court to Switzerland for a month occasioned a flurry of letters and telegrams between various members of the Royal Household, the Royal Mews, the Admiralty, the French authorities via the British Embassy in Paris and the Swiss authorities via the British Legation in Berne. It was a smoothly co-ordinated exercise conducted with military precision without benefit of typewriter or telephone, but with liberal use of the telegraph.

To appreciate just how modest the Queen was in her Swiss domestic requirements compared to what she was used to (and had to put up with) at home, it is enough to glance at the 1868 Royal Household List.

Part of Queen Victoria's Household in 1868. There were also numbers of housemaids, wardrobe maids and dressers (to say nothing of Table Deckers, a Wax Fitter, Coal Porters and a host of others)

88   HER MAJESTY'S HOUSEHOLD.

LORD CHAMBERLAIN'S DEPARTMENT, S.W.

Lord Chamberlain, The Rt. Hon. the Earl of Bradford.
Vice ditto, Rt. Hon. Lord Claud Hamilton, MP.
Comptroller, Hon. Spencer C. B. Ponsonby.
Chief Clerk, Thos. C. March, Esq.
Inspector of Accounts, Daniel Tupper, Esq.
First Clerk, G. T. Hertslet, Esq.   *Second ditto*, F. W. Jennings, Esq.
Office Keeper, Geo. Brinkworth.
Office Messengers, C. Hitch, Richd. A. Tilley, and Wm. Dawson.
Private Secretary to Her Majesty, Lt.-Gen. Hon. Charles Grey.
Keeper of Her Majesty's Privy Purse, Maj.-Gen. Sir T. M. Biddulph, KCB.
Secretaries to ditto, Henry T. Harrison, Esq., and Doyne C. Bell, Esq.
German Librarian, Hermann Sahl, Esq.
Personal Servants, Mr. Rudolph Löhlein, and Mr. John Brown.
Jäger, Mr. Spencer S. D. Cowley.
Paymaster of the Bedchamber, W. Hampshire, Esq.
Ladies of the Bedchamber, Dowager Duchess of Athole, Marchioness of Ely, Countess of Gainsborough, Countess of Caledon, Viscountess Clifden, Lady Churchill, Dowager Lady Waterpark, and Duchess of Roxburghe.
Extra Ladies of the Bedchamber, Dowager Duchess of Norfolk, Dowager Countess of Mount Edgcumbe, and Viscountess Jocelyn.
Maids of Honour, Hon. Lucy Maria Kerr, Hon. Flora C. I. Macdonald, Hon. Caroline F. Cavendish, Hon. Emily Cathcart, Hon. Horatia Charlotte Stopford, Hon. Harriet Lepel Phipps, Hon. Florence Catherine Seymour, and Hon. Mary Louisa Lascelles.
Extra Maid of Honour, Hon. Eleanor Stanley.
Bedchamber Women, Lady Caroline Barrington, Viscountess Forbes, Hon. Mrs. G. Campbell, Viscountess Chewton, Hon. Mrs. A. Gordon, Lady Codrington, Lady Sarah Elizabeth Lindsay, Hon. Mrs. Robt. Bruce.
Extra Bedchamber Women, Mrs. Pratt, Lady Augusta Frederica Elizabeth Stanley, and Lady Charlotte Copley.
Honorary Bedchamber Woman, Hon. Lady Biddulph.
Lords in Waiting, Earl of Haddington, Viscounts Torrington, Strathallan, and Hawarden, and Lords Bagot, Crofton, Skelmersdale, and Raglan.
Extra Lord in Waiting, Admiral Lord Byron.
Grooms in Waiting, Hon. M. Sackville West, Lt.-Col. W. H. F. Cavendish, Col. Hon. Aug. Frederick Liddell, Lieut.-Col. Hon. Charles Hugh Lindsay, MP., Rear-Adm. Sir Wm. L. G. Hoste, Bt., Col. Lord Jas. Chas. Plantagenet Murray, Sir Henry Seton, Bt., and Maj.-Gen. Francis Seymour, CB.
Extra Grooms, Hon. Sir Chas. Aug. Murray, KCB., and Lieut. Walter George Stirling, RH. Art.
Master of the Ceremonies, Gen. Hon. Sir Edward Cust, KCH.
Assistant-Master, Col. Charles Bagot.
Marshal of the Ceremonies, Hon. Spencer Lyttelton.
Gentlemen Ushers of the Privy Chamber, W. C. Master, Esq., the Hon. Fred. Byng, Chas. Heneage, Esq., and Gen. Sir J. M. F. Smith.
Gentlemen Ushers, daily Waiters, Sir W. Martins, Hon. Spencer C. B. Ponsonby, Edwd. Hamilton Anson, Esq., and Adm. Sir Aug. Clifford, Bart., CB.   (*Black Rod*).
Assistant Gentleman Usher, Sir Alex. Duff Gordon, Bart.
Grooms of the Privy Chamber, A. Blackwood, Esq., J. F. Campbell, Esq. (of Islay), Col. E. S. Claremont, CB. and Hon. Roden Berkeley Wriothesley Noel.

LORD CHAMBERLAIN'S DEPARTMENT.   89

Gentlemen Ushers and Quarterly Waiters in Ordinary, Henry Greville, Alfred Montgomery, Wilbraham Taylor, Esqrs., Major-Gen. H. S. Stephens, Capt. R. T. Bedford, RN., Col. Howard Vyse, Capt. W. Ross, and Commander C. G. Nelson, RN.
Extra Gentleman Usher and Quarterly Waiter, John Geo. Green, Esq.
Grooms of the Great Chamber, Messrs. Thos. Gibbs, F. A. André, John Wood, John E. Parry, James Burbidge, Edward Thomas, D. Collins, Wm. Bagley, and A. G. Butcher.
Librarian, Jas. M. Berry, Esq.
Librarian in Ordinary at Windsor Castle, B. B. Woodward, Esq.
Poet Laureate, Alfred Tennyson, Esq.
Examiner of Plays, Wm. Bodham Donne, Esq.
Bargemaster, Mr. J. A. Messenger.   *Keeper of the Swans*, Mr. J. Hamilton.
Governor and Constable of Windsor Castle, Capt. Count Gleichen, RN.
Keeper of the Jewel House, Tower, Colonel Charles Wyndham.
Exhibitor of the Crown Jewels, Tower, Mrs. Ann Cram.
Pages of the Back Stairs, Geo. Fleming, Gilbert Sprague, G. J. Searle, W. Shackle, and S. Maslin, Esqrs.
State Pages, Samuel Shepperd and Joseph Hill, Esqrs.
Page of the Chambers, Frederic Wagenrieder, Esq.
Pages of the Presence, First class, R. K. Taylor, C. Doll, and W. Tuppen, Esqrs.   *Second class*, J. Carver, C. Robertson, and G. Waite, Esqrs.
Pages, Mess, Messrs. John Kennedy, Geo. Phillips, and Wm. Wiltshire.

HOUSEKEEPERS.

Buckingham Palace, Miss Thornton.
Windsor Castle, Mrs. Thurston.   *St. James's*, Mrs. Elizabeth Nash.
Osborne, Mrs. Elizabeth Smith.   *Frogmore*, Mrs. Harriet Hoath.
State Apartments, Kensington, Mrs. Fred. Sayer.
Private Apartments, Kensington, Mrs. Roberts.
State Apartments, St. James's, Lady Smith.
Hampton Court, Mrs Heaton.   *Kew*, Hon. Mrs. Hodgson.
Clarence House, Mrs. S. Pritchard.   *Claremont*, Mrs. Henderson.

Inspector of Buckingham Palace, Richard Cripps, Esq.
Inspector of Windsor Castle, William Seabrook, Esq.

QUEEN'S BAND OF MUSIC.

Master, George Anderson, Esq.   *Conductor*, J. C. E. Nickel, Esq.
Musicians, Messrs. Wm. Best, H. G. Blagrove, G. Hardy, Jno. G. Waetzig, Wm. Henry Card, John Buels, John Day, James W. Gunniss, Geo. Horton, Edward Remenyi, Wm. Egerton, Orluff Svendsen, John Rendle, A. W. Chisholm, Victor Buzian, Thos. Edgar, Wm. Handley, Fredk. B. Jewson, W. H. Hawkes.
Serjeant Trumpeter, Joseph Williams, Esq.
Eight Trumpeters, Chas. Schröeder, A. F. Germann, C. Betts, Edw. Card, Henry Malsch, W. G. Cusins, P. J. Paque, Wm. Egerton, jun.

SERJEANTS AT ARMS.

E. Gordon, J. A. Peacock, Chas. Sisson, Esqrs.; Maj.-Gen. H. S. Stephens, Sir Alexander Campbell, Bart., Norman Macleod, Esq., Capt. John Woodriff, RN., and Thos. Chas. March, Esq.
Attending the Lord Chancellor, Lieut. Col. Hon. W. P. M. C. Talbot.
Ditto, the House of Commons, Lord Charles J. F. Russell.
Queen's Messengers, Messrs. T. Hill, W. Peel, H. Gibbs, and C. Hull. (*In attendance on the Lord Chamberlain*), Mr. John Macpherson.

Simplicity with comfort was the Queen's watchword for Lucerne, so her establishment there consisted of what, by royal standards, was a skeleton staff. Three carriages were sent out to Lucerne; one of them, on her insistence, was a particular favourite of hers, the Balmoral Sociable, specially modified for picnics, which was conveyed by ship from Aberdeen. It, together with ponies, the Queen's bed (which she mentions some years later in her Journal as having been with her in Switzerland[62]) and other paraphernalia arrived in Lucerne a few days before the Queen – an event that was duly reported not only in the local press but beyond: in Berne, readers learned from their newspaper *Der Bund* that numerous servants had brought utensils for the kitchen from England and that 'for weeks purveyors of victuals have been learning to prepare these after the manner of the English Court, for example making sandwiches in perfect cube form with butter and ham, to be enjoyed for breakfast and which are really very tasty'. The Queen also engaged one or two local maids, one of whom she took back with her to England. Then there was her trusted Highland servant John Brown, his brother Archie and three other Highlanders, as well as grooms and helpers.

During the month before leaving for Switzerland the Queen stayed at Osborne but found that the sea air brought no relief from the overpowering heatwave that was brooding over the whole country. She was counting the

Osborne House, Isle of Wight

days until her departure, but with growing trepidation. A spate of letters to the Crown Princess gives insight into the Queen's state of mind and body during these trying weeks. ' … tho' my present life has taken a fixed form & shape & I have accepted help & comforts gratefully & feel comparative Behaglichkeit, I dislike going abroad exceedingly & wld. rather stay at home'.[63] And a week later: 'Osborne is really like Africa, quite intolerable. I wish I cld flee to some iceberg to breathe.… I fear I shall not find much cooler air in Switzerland & in that case I wish I was not going there, for it is misery to move & be active and one cld enjoy nothing. People talk of its being so hot. But it can't be worse surely than here – & at any rate the nights are cool, & that makes up for the day.'[64]

The Queen had been dreading 'the large family party at Osborne more than I can say, for I am pining for rest & quiet.'[65] Her forebodings about this month at Osborne were well-founded. The Crown Princess was told about the Queen's daughter-in-law, the Princess of Wales, and her four-day-old baby: 'Alix continues to go on quite well, but I thought she looked pale and exhausted. The baby – a mere little red lump was all I saw; & I fear the seventh grand-daughter & fourteenth grand-child becomes a very uninteresting thing – for it seems to me to go on like the rabbits in Windsor Park! The present large family party is very far from enjoyable or good for me.'[66]

The Queen then referred to what the Crown Princess had written to her (' … nothing is better for the nerves than rising very early and having a walk before breakfast, and going early to rest – but this I think you do not like, and it does not suit you'[67]). The Queen's reaction is illuminating:

Going to bed early & getting up early would be a total impossibility for me. The night is the only quiet time for me – & I feel able for work then & not in the morning early. Darling Papa was very different & so are some people – but I find the greater part in this country do what I do. Walking before breakfast does not suit all – & never did me. However I shall try when I am abroad to <u>modify</u> it a little. I generally <u>now</u> breakfast at a <u>1/4 to 10</u> or <u>1/2 p. 9</u> (the <u>last</u> is what I <u>wish</u> to do – but I often can't get up early enough for that) & I generally <u>am</u> in bed by 1/2 p. 12. That is the time I <u>wish to keep to</u> – but it constantly is 1/4 to 1 & even 1 o'clock, especially when we come home late & dine late wh. is unavoidable in <u>this heat</u>.[68]

In another letter the Queen wrote that she was suffering from an extremely obstinate 'dérangement', as she called it. 'I dare say, I shall be all the better for it tho'! – For I don't perspire & am always in a dreadful dry, burning heat & that I suppose has found its vent in this way. It is fortunate to have a few days to recover before I start on my long journey. The scenery will no doubt repay me, but I dread the whole thing a good deal.'[69] So much so that her body protested even more, as she told the Crown Princess a few days later: 'I have been very unwell this week. The Diarrhea never stopped till yesterday & then I had <u>one</u> of my most violent sick headaches with violent <u>retching</u>. I hope however I am better now, but the unusually gt. heat near the sea affects the bile & I think I shall be better for the change.'[70]

No wonder that ' … As the time for my journey approaches, I feel nervous and anxious. Travelling <u>alone</u> without dearest Papa is a gt. trial, but Kanné arranges everything <u>so</u> well & <u>so</u> <u>quietly</u>, that he really makes it as easy as <u>possible</u>.'[71]

Her Director of Continental Journeys, J.J. Kanné, had been pressed into service alongside the indefatigable Elphinstone.

'The Queen begs Col. Elphinstone to be sure to write or to speak – to Kanné about Brienz & the Rosenlaui, for that <u>is</u> the <u>one</u> thing she <u>does</u> long to see. – The carrying up and down is not the slightest objection to her. –

She much rather <u>a</u>void the Grindelwald.'[72]

As always, Elphinstone acted immediately. In the event, though, neither Brienz nor Rosenlaui were in fact visited during her Swiss stay – nor did the Queen explain why she preferred to avoid Grindelwald, one of Switzerland's finest and already then most popular resorts. 'The Queen thanks Col. Elphinstone very much for all his very satisfactory letters & for the explanations to Kanné. She will let Pcess Louise reconnoitre the St Gotthard & hopes it <u>may</u> be <u>effected</u>.'[73]

Arrangements had been made for a daily Messenger to ply between London and the pension in Lucerne. The Queen had told her daughter to ' … write always either to Madame la Comtesse de Kent, Pension Wallis, Lucerne or to Gräfin v. Kent, Pension Wallis, Luzern. I travel under that name and nothing is to be directed to me – from here or elsewhere – otherwise.'[74]

Wednesday, 5 August, was *the* day. The Queen's laconic Journal entry is in surprising contrast with what must have been her state of mind, for it was on that day that she left Osborne for Switzerland.

> *August 5*
> *A very fine morning. – Breakfast out as usual & sitting a little while with Alice. Then took leave of her, Louis, & the 4 dear little Children, with regret. – At 1/4 p. 12 left our dear peaceful Osborne with our 3 Children, feeling sad at the parting with dear Alice. May God protect & preserve her, but I do feel a little anxious about her health. – Janie E., the Biddulphs, Col. Ponsonby, Sir William Jenner, Fräulein Bauer & Mr. Duckworth are with us.** We rowed out to the 'Victoria and Albert' & were off by 1.*

The Equerry Colonel Ponsonby portrayed what it was like on board in one of his lively and outspoken letters to his wife:

We left Osborne about half past 12. The Yacht as usual with all the Officers looking like Lord High Admirals. Molyneux and one or two others I knew but there were several new ones. Among others Lord Charles Beresford who has been appointed for his gallant conduct in saving a man's life at sea. And a Mr. Acland and a Mr. Fanshawe who had both been appointed by mistake. Fancy what idiots the Admirals must be. However they are smart looking young men tho they are not the sons of Dr. Acland or Admiral Fanshawe. I am writing in my cabin in mid channel, there is scarcely any motion – but there was just a swell about luncheon time which made Bauer turn green – but she was quickly restored by champagne. Poor Mary Bids is suffering from toothache. I persuaded her to drink wine at luncheon which got rid of it – but it has come on again. I have been in long converse with Kanné who has explained most of the arrangements at Lucerne. He thinks we return on the 5th of Sept. There is so much in the Yacht that reminds me of a passage I had in her some years ago to Antwerp, and also back again. We arrived at about 6 o'clock – A French officer came on board – and then an American from the American man of war – but that was all. The Consul, an old man with an enormous beard came also – He knew Bids and has pointed out the improvements which have taken place since you were here, which seem to be the construction of a long range of baths and nothing else. For books Jenner bagged Letters of Pliny, which he says are interesting from Osborne and I took 'Belisaire' which he says is renowned for

---

dulness. Jane Ely offered me some books and told me that the Correspondence of Marshal Saxe was improper. So lent me the Danvers papers which sent me to sleep. We are to land at 10 and then go on to Paris so as to arrive tomorrow morning. I believe the Q is going to be photographed and then see the Empress and thats all.[75]

The Queen's own account of the crossing is short and to the (nostalgic) point:

> *… August 5*
> *As soon as we had passed the Needles, there was a ground swell & I had to go below, remaining there till we reached Cherbourg at 1/4p. 6. How it reminded me of the past, all seemed unaltered, & yet all is so changed for me! What used formerly to be such a delight makes me low & sad now. Dined in the deck saloon with Louise, the 2 Ladies & Ernest L. We left the yacht at 1/2p. 10, & trans-shipping on to the 'Alberta', entered the inner basin, from which we stepped on shore in the arsenal. Everything was kept quite private & a few steps took us to the train.*

This was the saloon train that the French Emperor Napoleon III had placed at the Queen's disposal for her journey to Lucerne via Paris.

LE SALON D'HONNEUR.

LA CHAMBRE A COUCHER.

The Emperor Napoleon III's saloon train

We had the Emperor's compartments, all communicating with one another & our servants near us.

IN FRANCE – EN ROUTE

Luxuriously appointed though the Emperor's train was, it rattled. The night journey from Cherbourg to Paris for a stop-over at the British Embassy with her Ambassador Lord Lyons did the Queen's jangled nerves no good at all.

Nor did things improve when she alighted in the capital, hoping perhaps for some early morning fresh air. Her Journal takes up the story.

> *August 6, Paris*
> *Could get no sleep, the carriage rocking so dreadfully. At 7 we reached Paris in a blazing heat. Ld. Lyons met us at the station, & I drove with the Children in his carriage straight to the Embassy, where I had been for a few minutes 13 years ago. Strange did it seem to me to find myself again in this great & famous capital, which I entered in such pomp & never visited but with state 13 years ago with my precious Husband & now <u>alone</u> & in such a different quiet way! Ld. Lyons took us at once upstairs, where there are fine large rooms. Had some breakfast & then washed & dressed. Afterwards sat in the garden, which is very pretty, reading & writing, till near 12, but the heat & fatigue fairly drove me in, & I remained lying quietly.*

In the afternoon the Queen put aside her newly assumed incognito for a short while in order to receive a courtesy call. It was to cost her dear.

> *... August 6*
> *at 1/2p. 3 received the Empress Eugénie, who had kindly come from Fontainebleau on purpose to see me. The Emperor is at Plombières. She remained about 10 minutes & brought 3 Ladies & 4 Gentlemen.*

Then the Queen did a terrible thing. She refused to return the Empress's call. Unroyal behaviour, a blot on Anglo-French relations that shocked France. For a Head of State a courtesy call is a solemn act symbolizing the state of relations between countries, not an empty show of social grace. In the nineteenth century, tightly governed as it was by etiquette, refusal to return a call was an even more grievous snub than it would be today. Queen Victoria had committed a gaffe of the first order and its echo was to pursue her throughout her stay in Switzerland. It was all taken very seriously, except by the Queen herself. Pleading extreme tiredness, she rested, '*overpowered by the heat*', and had some light dinner at 6, but then rather marred the effect by going on a long sightseeing drive through Paris as if nothing had happened, noting how

> *the absence of smoke makes all look bright & clean, but I regret the endless new formal building destroying all the picturesque old streets. We started at 1/2p. 7 & it was very hot in the train.*

Not many people had turned out to see the Queen go by in Paris, although there was a minor Fenian incident. However, her brief stay was in the full glare of press publicity on both sides of the Channel and expectations were high. It was obvious that the French wanted no truck with this Countess of Kent nonsense. They wanted the Queen of England. The Paris correspondent of the (London) *Court Journal* had read too much into the visit, but he reflected the mood in Paris:

> The arrival of her Majesty Queen Victoria is regarded as the great event of the season at Court, and already are gossiping speculations at work as to the purport of the visit, for no one in these days can be brought to believe that so mighty a resolve could be taken by her Britannic Majesty without some more important motive than the mere passage through Paris and the few hours' personal interview with the Empress Eugénie.'

Little did this correspondent know the Queen's condition. He went on to report rumours of a projected European summit meeting, for which this visit in Paris might have been a preparation.

> The Emperor is supposed to press urgently for a general rendezvous of the Capital Sovereigns of Europe at Darmstadt, where the prospects of the ensuing winter might be discussed. But Prussia objects to meet Bavaria, and declines *in toto* to shake hands with France. Austria would rather not sit opposite Prussia either, and Russia refuses point-blank to stand within gunshot of Austria.... The Emperor of Austria consoles himself with the reflection that he is not the only one left out of the Imperial circle. Napoleon III stands likewise looking wistfully at the merry game being played by his brother Sovereigns in which he is not invited to share, and as he walks up and down the vulgar little pasteboard promenade at Plombières, ruminates on the best and most effectual trick which he can play to disturb the enjoyment of the revellers.

In this atmosphere of political unease, with states, especially France and Prussia, eyeing one another suspiciously for signs of aggressive intent, it was only to be expected that the Queen's every move would be keenly watched for any hints as to whether Albion was favouring France or Prussia. The cynicism of the *Pall Mall Gazette*'s Paris correspondent was not wide of the mark: 'Everyone is getting tired of an armed peace which is exhausting the country, and more than one Liberal journal calls lustily for hostilities in order that tranquility may be restored.' By receiving but not returning the Empress's call, Queen Victoria kept France guessing and left the Emperor without a much-needed show of British support.

So much for the Queen's incognito on her first day abroad. Things could only improve – but in the matter of the unreturned call they did not. The Foreign Secretary, Lord Stanley, arrived in Paris in the evening en route for Lucerne 'by the common train'[76] as he put it, and was briefed by the Embassy after Lord Lyons had seen the Queen off in Napoleon III's saloon train.'They said the Queen's visit had gone off well,' he noted in his diary, 'but were evidently vexed at her refusing to call on the Empress.... It is no doubt a mere form, and there was the excuse of want of time, but it is just on these points that the Imperial Court, as being <u>parvenu</u>, is touchy.'[77] Stanley wrote in similar vein to Disraeli: ' ... the only contre-temps was the great Lady's absolute refusal to return the Empress's call, which as a matter of ceremony she ought.'[78]

But it soon became clear that the French were taking it as more than a trivial slight. Stanley called on the French Foreign Minister Moustier and General Fleury of the Imperial Court, whom he found 'deeply mortified at the Queen's incivility to the Empress (it is nothing less): he could not help alluding to it more than once, though very civilly.'[79]

This is more than could be said of the French press, ever on the lookout for knocking copy about the British. Stanley sent Disraeli the mildest of the articles, in *Figaro*, which he thought would amuse him.

The Queen of England in Paris

Hardly had her Majesty Queen Victoria arrived at the Embassy yesterday than she dismissed her suite and remained alone. She retired to her simply decorated, austere room and rested until lunch. Lunch was taken en famille, not even Lord Lyons being invited to the Royal table ...

After lunch Her Majesty walked in the garden, seated herself there and spent at least one and a half hours reading the philosophical and religious works of the Prince Consort.

The Queen was fatigued. Prey to extremely painful attacks of neuralgia since the death of Prince Albert, travelling causes her great discomfort and she cannot undertake journeys of any length with impunity.

Her accompanying physician Dr Jenner, who has prescribed complete rest and the sojourn in Switzerland, yesterday interposed with the Royal traveller to abstain from excitement and observe absolute calm.

So she spent the entire afternoon in complete isolation without the slightest distraction, in the Embassy garden. The Queen was still in her travelling clothes and in place of a day bonnet wore a cap recalling those of Mary Stuart.

In the meantime, the Empress had arrived at the Tuileries from Fontainebleau.... After lunch, in other words about half past two, her Majesty the Empress, wearing a mauve tulle dress with a matching hat topped by a spray of trembling osprey feathers, set out with her retinue in two-horse ceremonial carriages to the Elysée from whence she would visit the Queen at half past three.

Queen Victoria hurried through the drawing-rooms, arriving below the vestibule and descended the staircase to meet the Empress whom she embraced with a show of great friendship and effusion. The Empress, having presented her retinue in one of the first morning-rooms, left them with the persons accompanying the Queen and with Lord Lyons. Their Majesties, separated from all these people by a morning-room, retired to an official drawing-room next to the magnificent Throne Room and spent twenty minutes in conversation. The Queen, while escorting the Empress back, expressed her sincere regrets that owing to her fatigue and indisposition she was unable to receive the Empress in the manner she would have wished.

The Queen greeted the members of the Empress's suite, accompanied the Empress to the foot of the peristyle and embraced her once again. The Empress then took her leave and departed to the Elysée.

For an hour and ten minutes the Empress and a crowd of onlookers waited in vain, exposed to the elements, for the Queen's return visit. The crowd murmured its dissatisfaction and manifested its sympathy in favour of the Empress. Finally, no longer able to count on the return visit of her sister-in-royalty, the Empress requested Mesdames Paulet and Jacquot to disrobe her, the ceremonial carriages were dismissed and at five minutes past five the Empress and her suite left the Elysée in open carriages for the Gare de Lyon and Fontainebleau.

This incident of considerable importance preoccupied the crowd which, in interpreting the apparent refusal to return the visit, evidently misjudged the reasons which had prevented Her Majesty Queen Victoria from returning the call. But public sentiment neither reasons nor comprehends: the crowd was dissatisfied and on her departure the Empress was the recipient of the acclaim which was a consequence of the public frame of mind.

Let us say that at the Embassy there was surprise at the Queen's eschewing a return visit and she was earnestly requested to do so. But as loyal chronicler we should add that the Queen was so exhausted and prostrated by fatigue and suffering that her indisputable goodwill was vanquished by the circumstances.

This was not the end of the story.

THE QUEEN IN SWITZERLAND

On the morning the Queen arrived in Switzerland, *The Times* in its main leading article came out with a veritable hymn of praise on the glories of Switzerland and on how fortunate the Sovereign was to be allowed at last to revel in them. The last paragraph contains a plea that would no doubt strike a chord with many a plagued twentieth-century Royal.

LONDON. FRIDAY, AUGUST 7, 1868

In a rapid journey HER MAJESTY has crossed the Channel to Cherbourg, gone by train to Paris, and thence proceeds by way of Troyes and Bâle to the Lake of Lucerne, where the Royal party are expected to arrive this morning. Every one will be disposed to congratulate HER MAJESTY on having chosen so noble a region as Switzerland for her autumn tour and on making so beautiful a spot as Lucerne her first residence. To a large proportion of the QUEEN's subjects the Swiss mountains are not new, though they can never grow old. Every year hundreds of English people of all ages pass over certain well-known tracks, and delight their eyes with the sight of the most magnificent natural objects which Europe can boast. The most frequented spots, the most hackneyed routes, present the most glorious forms of mountain, lake, or waterfall; for the places are visited and, it may be, vulgarized in direct proportion to their beauty and their fame. Thus, the least adventurous of the travelling public – the 'procession of cockneys' – are acquainted with regions whose names are household words wherever there is any feeling for grandeur and sublimity. But it is the ill fortune of Royalty to be less free in its movements than the meanest of its subjects. The middle-class family which can spare a very moderate sum has its way made every year smoother for its Swiss tour. The railways south of the Thames once passed, it finds comfortable travelling at reasonable rates, and hotels where the food is made palatable and where it is possible to drink the wine. No wonder that the attractions of fine scenery, new and more lively modes of life, with the comforts of good accommodation offered by people who thoroughly understand the business of entertainment, should attract the QUEEN's subjects, and it seems almost a pity that exalted dignity or public duties should forbid the highest personages in the world to share these pleasures. But certain it is that even now Monarchs are very much restricted, or, in obedience to custom, have very much restricted themselves from visiting foreign parts. The younger branches of the reigning Houses do, indeed, see the world, though even they must go with a certain kind of State, and must be worried almost to death by the pertinacious curiosity of the crowd, particularly of genteel English. The Crowned Head must as a general rule be content to bear its weight of dignity in its own land. The tradition is against the locomotion of Sovereigns, and it will take many years before it dies out. The political relations of States, and the significance which rumour attaches to many Royal movements, tend to keep Sovereigns at home, since, though they may avoid ceremonial receptions by the use of an *incognito*, they cannot throw off their identity nor attain perfect privacy and irresponsibility. However visionary may be some of the drawbacks to the happiness of Monarchs which moralists profess to discover, there can be no doubt that they are deprived to a certain extent of free intercourse with the world, the free gratification of curiosity, and pursuit of adventure.

It must be remembered, then, that the QUEEN now, for the first time, goes among the Alps. For the first time she will see the transcendent beauties of the Lake of the Four Cantons, the Righi and Pilatus, with the distant mountain ranges which shut in the view; for the first time she will explore those shores where every turn discloses something grand and rare, unparalleled, at least, in these regions of the globe. How much the QUEEN feels the charm of mountain scenery those who have read her Journals in the Highlands need not be told. Her surprise and delight at the objects which she met in those northern tours are expressed with the utmost simplicity and sincerity. If, then, the brown hills of Scotland affected her with such emotion, what must be her pleasure in looking for the first time on the mighty masses of the Alps, with their clothing of snow and glacier, their waterfalls, their pine forests, and all those natural features which once seen are never forgotten! We sincerely hope that the QUEEN will have strength and spirits to see a good deal of Switzerland. Such a foreign excursion is likely more than anything else to give strength to the body and elasticity to the mind, to remove the depression caused by long-continued sorrow, and to make the sufferer take a new and brighter view of life. There can be no doubt that one of the best remedies even for bodily ailments is change of scene, and the meeting with entirely new objects, both living and inanimate. The benefit which doctors often attribute to what is called 'change of air' is more often caused by a break up of the monotony of ideas, and is a moral rather than a physical influence. In Switzerland it is difficult to say which is the more new and strange, the aspect of nature or the human life which accompanies and has grown out of it, and to one who has not been much abroad we can well imagine that a month in this most beautiful of European regions would produce a more beneficial effect than any number of changes of place between one point of Great Britain and another.

As the 'Countess of KENT' travels for the benefit of her health, and for that reason dispenses with the courtesies which foreign authorities would offer, we hope that English tourists will respect the privacy of the Royal party. Loyalty is no doubt a very excellent sentiment, but it can be cherished without invading its exalted object at every turn of her daily walks; nor has it, indeed, any real connexion with that vulgar curiosity which makes a well-dressed English mob rush after a Prince as if he were some extraordinary animal, exhibited for the first time. It is not unnecessary to make these remarks, since the fact that the QUEEN is at Lucerne, and that only well-to-do English people are likely to be found there, may be no protection to her; for, unhappily, respectable people are the greatest offenders in this respect. The QUEEN has gone on a tour which we all hope will be a pleasant one; let all assist in making it so, by abstaining from importunate loyalty. Sovereigns seldom have the opportunity

The Queen's Suite at Lucerne

Princess Louise, Queen Victoria's fourth daughter, aged 20

Prince Leopold (*left*) and Prince Arthur (*right*), Queen Victoria's fourth and third sons, aged 15 and 18

Princess Beatrice, Queen Victoria's fifth daughter and youngest child, aged 11

The Hon. Lady Biddulph, Hon. Bedchamber Woman (wife of Sir Thomas)

Revd J.R. Duckworth, Prince Leopold's Governor

The Queen's Suite at Lucerne

Colonel Henry Ponsonby, Equerry to Queen Victoria

Jane, Marchioness of Ely, Lady of the Bedchamber

Sir Thomas Biddulph, Keeper of the Privy Purse

Sir William Jenner, Bart., MD., Physician-in-Ordinary to Queen Victoria

Fräulein Ottilie Bauer, Princess Beatrice's Governess

of laying aside their majesty with their Crown and Robes; on these rare occasions, then, let them have the agreeable freedom of a lower station.

The Queen was accompanied in Switzerland by a few particularly congenial members of her Household.

The party also numbered five Highlanders, including the stalwart Highland Servant John Brown and his brother Archie, resplendent in their kilts but, surprisingly, attracting little attention. Hovering in the background were her Continental courier J.J. Kanné and the Swiss guide A. Hofmann, who had earned his spurs for his guiding of Prince Arthur and Elphinstone's 1864 Swiss tour.

Queen Victoria, 1868.
'Of late years, especially since the sad loss of her husband, Queen Victoria has undergone a great change, both in mind and body. The charm of her presence always rose more from the natural expression of an amiable disposition than from any regularity of feature or grace of manner. Her eyes are blue and bright, her hair dark, and her complexion is now somewhat sallow. It is marked by deep lines of affliction, and yet those do not make her expression less attractive. In the approaches of age she has gained that which may be called the beauty of goodness.'
From *Sketches and Anecdotes of Her Majesty the Queen, the late Prince Consort, and other members of the Royal Family*, selected and arranged by J.G. Hodgins (Sampson Low, 1868)

PART

Two

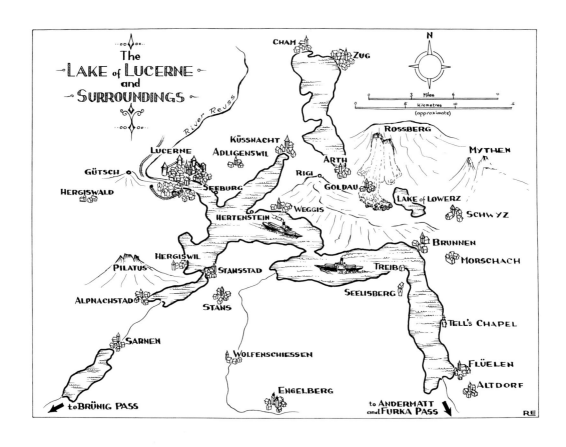

The
LAKE of LUCERNE
and
SURROUNDINGS

CHAM
ZUG
River Reuss
N
Miles
Kilometres
(approximate)
ROSSBERG
MYTHEN
KÜSSNACHT
ADLIGENSWIL
LUCERNE
ARTH
GÜTSCH
RIGI
SEEBURG
GOLDAU
LAKE of LOWERZ
HERGISWALD
SCHWYZ
WEGGIS
HERTENSTEIN
BRUNNEN
MORSCHACH
HERGISWIL
PILATUS
STANSSTAD
TREIB
SEELISBERG
ALPNACHSTAD
STANS
TELL'S CHAPEL
SARNEN
FLÜELEN
WOLFENSCHIESSEN
ALTDORF
ENGELBERG
to BRÜNIG PASS
to ANDERMATT
and FURKA PASS
RE

3 Haven

After a second night on the train, this time not quite so sleepless, Queen Victoria steamed across the north-west frontier of Switzerland and into Basle at seven o'clock. Breakfast was brought into the saloon and they were soon off again on the way to their destination, Lucerne.

The Queen's Journal entry for this first Swiss day is long and detailed, her pen stimulated by new surroundings and by the triumph of having at last reached the haven she had dreamed of all these years. She begins with an account of the journey from Basle to Lucerne:

August 7
From here the scenery is lovely, though unfortunately one does not see any of the highest hills. All looked so fresh & green. We passed the valley of the Birs, celebrated for a gallant defence of the Swiss in the 15th century. Our next stop was at Sissach, after which comes a longish tunnel & an immense one 5 minutes long, after Laufelfingen. During the making of it 50 men were buried alive.

The Emperor Napoleon III's saloon train

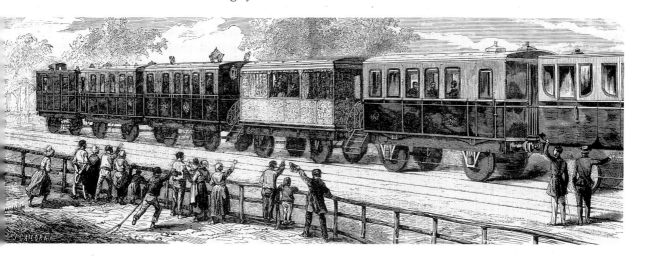

Tunnelling technique was in its infancy when this, Switzerland's longest tunnel at the time, was built in the 1850s. Hence the accident.

The upper Hauenstein tunnel, then Switzerland's longest, at its opening in 1858

What the Queen does not mention in her Journal is that the tunnel, and indeed the whole line, was designed and built by British engineers. This omission says much about the predominant British image of Switzerland, which had undergone a sea-change during the nineteenth century. Whereas before that time attention had been focused on the cities, on politics, religion, trade and industry and intellectual life, the focus shifted with the awakening of enthusiasm for the beauties and excitement of the Alps in the eighteenth century. The magnetic attraction of the mountains became so strong that by the time of Queen Victoria's visit Switzerland meant lakeside and mountain resorts to holiday in, with perhaps only a night or two spent in a city to see the sights and with villages as a picturesque contrast.

Yet relations between the two countries had for centuries been many-sided, close and as time went on increasingly cordial. The Swiss played no small part in British public life, and Switzerland underwent an industrial revolution that paralleled or followed British lines, often adapting British technology and methods. Much British investment and know-how went into the development of the country's rail network. There were even wild flights of fancy such as a project for a direct line between the Suez Canal and Denmark. If Queen Victoria had known that the line she was travelling on was British-owned, and that the tunnel was an early engineering marvel brought about by her subject Thomas Brassey (without benefit of powerful machinery), she would surely have at least mentioned this, and Princess Beatrice – a dutiful daughter to the last – would have copied it.

More likely she was never told. It would have been an unromantic irrelevance, as remote from her present purpose as was any thought about, say, the Anglo-Swiss trade treaty of twelve years earlier. Or indeed her own urgent intercession on behalf of Switzerland in 1857, when Prussia had mobilized and was marching on the Swiss in order to reinforce their claim to Neuchâtel, a Prussian Principality which had recently declared for membership of the Swiss Confederation. Later, as she sailed on the Lake of Lucerne in her chartered ship, she never knew – or if she did, she did not think it worth mentioning – that another steamer plying the lake had been built in England and brought overland from Basle to Lucerne.

She was coming to Switzerland to get away from it all, and one can almost sense Queen Victoria's impatience to put the world behind her from the way she continues her account of that first day in Switzerland.

> *… August 7*
> *We stopped for the last time at Alten,* * *the central station for all the Swiss railways. Passed the Lake of Sempach, extremely lovely & blue, with wooded banks, & then began the most glorious scenery, mountain peaks, towering one above the other in the most wonderful way, till we at length came close on Lucerne, passing the splendid emerald green coloured river of the Reuss. My own dear Scotch sociable was at the station, driven from the box with 4 horses by a local coachman, & I entered into it with the Children. Kanné sat on the box & Brown behind.*

'You may like to know <u>how</u> we go about. Almost always in a (Scotch) Sociable, the guide Hofmann sitting on the box with the Coachman, a safe but dreadfully slow man who drives 4 in hand, & Brown in a dickey behind wh. has purposely been added & under wh. is a box wh. I have to all my Sociables these last 2 years, in wh. goes the luncheon & tea baskets &c. Sometimes, but for short drives, I also use my Waggonette, & then no guide goes.'
(From Queen Victoria's letter to her daughter, Crown Princess Victoria, 19 August 1868)

For weeks the press on the Continent had been relaying speculation, then confirmation of the Queen's forthcoming visit to Switzerland. The arrival of her horses, carriages and baggage at Lucerne a few days ahead of her had also been duly noted in the Swiss press. Now, as she herself stepped out of the train at Lucerne and looked around anxiously, she will have been greatly relieved to find that her incognito was doing its work: the Swiss Federal authorities and local officials had taken the hint and were staying away.

* Alten/Olten.

Not so the public. The local press reported that the Lucerne police, in full strength and gala uniform, had difficulty in keeping the eager crowd at a respectable distance. The Queen was described as 'a woman of about 50, not tall, fairly corpulent, with a red face and clad in mourning for her departed husband'.

The Queen's account of the day continues with mounting enthusiasm.

> *... August 7*
> *Drove through a small part of the town, which is most picturesquely situated, up to our house, called Pension Wallis. The drive up was very hot, & took about 1/2 an hour from the station. Not many people out & no authorities. The view from the house & above all from my sitting-room window, overlooking the Lake with the town in front,*

> *skirted by the most glorious mountains, & brilliant verdure in the foreground, is something ideal. Really it was like what I had dreamt of, but could hardly believe to see in reality! How much dearest Albert wished I should see Switzerland, how he admired it, & how everything beautiful makes me think of him! The small house is very snug & comfortable & felt very cool, & there is room for all of us, excepting the*

Pension Wallis. On the left, the '*Châlet quite adjoining*' mentioned in the Journal

Biddulphs & Col. Ponsonby, who live in a Châlet quite adjoining. Had some breakfast directly after we arrived, & then washed, dressed & rested. Luncheon was at 2 in a good sized Diningroom.

View of Lucerne and surroundings from the Gütsch. (Oil painting by J.J. Zelger, 1868, commissioned by Queen Victoria)

… August 7

Again resting. – At 1/4 to 6 took a drive with the 2 Ladies, the Guide Hofmann, sitting on the box with the coachman & Brown behind on the rumble. We went through a fine wood of all kinds of trees, on emerging from which one suddenly came upon Pilatus 7,300 ft. high, on the highest peaks & summits of which are very pointed rocks. The whole was glowing in the setting sun, what is called here 'Alpenglühen'. It was glorious & the evening pleasantly cool. We passed most picturesque châlets, with galleries, many overhung with vines. It looks so pretty to see them dotted about the hills. The Rigi, 5,910 ft., one has constantly before one. The vegetation nearly goes to the top of it & one can plainly see the Hotel at the top. Home through the town, a little before 8, quite delighted with our 1st drive. – The 2 Ladies, Sir Thomas, Col. Ponsonby & Sir Wm. Jenner dined with us. Afterwards we sat out, looking at the town below.

Later Lady Ely will have slipped away quietly to write the first of the private letters that the Prime Minister had requested of her. In order to keep an eye on the Queen at long range, Disraeli had an impressive intelligence-gathering network: the Queen herself, not at her prodigious best as a correspondent while in Switzerland, but still keeping up a steady flow of black-rimmed memos and letters, with her opinions on affairs of state such as the appointment of Church dignitaries and with accounts of her activities; then the Foreign Secretary Lord Stanley, Ponsonby, Biddulph, the press, and, as on this first day, Jane Ely. After giving a detailed account of the day and hoping that the Queen would like the place ('it is most private'),[80] she loyally and with monumental understatement took the Queen's side on the great Issue of the Unreturned Call in Paris: 'The Queen felt too tired to return Her Imperial Majesty's visit, which was rather a disappointment, I believe.' The letter ends on an emollient note: 'The Queen told me, the other evening, you suited her so well & understood Her Majesty, which was a great comfort to her & you were so sensible & kind, the Queen said.'[81]

The following morning the Queen awoke refreshed.

August 8
Very hot, but I slept without moving, & the beauty of the morning was very great & a feast for the eye. We 4 breakfasted together, in a charming spot, in the shade, near the house, & I sat & wrote in a little summer house close to the stables, till near 1. The air was very pleasant, though the sun scorching.

One of the letters the Queen wrote that morning was to her eldest daughter Victoria, Crown Princess of Prussia:

What am I to say of the glorious scenery in Switzerland; the view from this Hse

wh. is <u>vy high</u> is most wonderfully beautiful with the Lake – Pilatus, the Righi &c – & I can <u>hardly</u> believe my eyes – when I look at it! It seems like a painting or decoration – a <u>dream!</u> –

We took a charming drive last night round below Pilatus by Krienz – & the evng. lights – the beautiful woods & <u>all</u> so green & fresh (whereas with us all is parched & burnt) was <u>quite</u> too delightful. It was cool & pleasant. The heat of the sun is fearful but the air is so pure & light it refreshes one. I am sitting writing in a vy pretty little Summer House – near the House – wh. is shady & fr. wh. you have lovely <u>peeps</u>....

I hope to take a fine drive this afternoon to get a <u>sight</u> of the Glaciers & Jungfrau. Now goodbye & God bless you.[82]

Watercolour of the same view, by Princess Louise, 8 August 1868

Later that afternoon the Queen and her two daughters went on their first drive through Lucerne and along the lake, taking their tea with them, *'lost in admiration of all we saw, & which is so difficult to describe'*.[83] They returned at eight, the Queen remarking that it was still very hot.

The weather was also the first thing she noticed the next morning, a Sunday:

'After luncheon sketching the heavenly view from my window. All the highest hills could be seen, reaching up to the very clouds!' (Journal, 8 August 1868) Watercolour by Queen Victoria, 8 August 1868

> *9 August*
> *Most dreadfully hot. – Breakfast out at 9 & sat out writing, until we had service at 12, performed by Mr Duckworth in the Diningroom.*

Such services were being held all over Switzerland, which – as a German tourist remarked – was a free country occupied by the British. With colonizing zeal and religious fervour they were building their own churches all over the place, even in the mountain hamlet Arolla at 6,500 feet altitude; where there were no English, Scottish or local churches to use, the public rooms of hotels would be pressed into Anglican service. Not everybody appreciated this, including the author Samuel Butler who, touring Switzerland in 1869, wrote: 'As much as possible I keep away from English-frequented hotels in Italy and Switzerland because I find that if I do not go to service on Sunday I am made uncomfortable. It is this bullying that I want to do away with.'[84]

An afternoon drive took the Queen along the Emmental with fruit trees, houses and *'through such a picturesque small village, with a Church & Convent & as one wound up the hill, one could hear the bells ringing for Vespers. Got out & took our tea, which was most refreshing, under a tree.'*

The Queen had come to Switzerland for a complete change – but there were limits. Never once during all her stay did she miss out on her afternoon tea. This was no mean achievement: there tended to be an absence of tea-making infrastructure on mountains and glaciers, apart from which the Swiss have never been great tea-drinkers. But, as we shall see, Victorian ingenuity invariably prevailed; neither did the Queen complain on the very rare occasions when she had to wait until 6 o'clock.

... August 9
After passing the Emmenbrücke, the whole range of mountains, surmounted by glaciers & snow-topped ones with the Titlis, 13,000 ft. high, could be beautifully & clearly seen, all glowing with that pink hue, which lasts but a very short time. – Dined outside, & remained sitting out till 1/2p. 10.

The Queen's first week in her Lucerne hideaway settled down into a sedate routine of walks, rides, drives and long periods in the garden, resting, writing or painting. She liked her early morning rides on her pony Flora in the *'deliciously cool'* fir wood nearby, although Flora was *'frantic with the horse flies, which pursue man & beast here!'*[85]

Unfortunately there were annoyances: the press reported that the Queen had taken exception to the peace of the Sabbath being disturbed by the noise of bowling coming from a nearby public garden ('the perpetual thunder of these Royal Salutes', as the *Court Journal* put it) and that she had offered the princely sum of 2,000 francs (£80 at the exchange rate of that time, 25 francs to the £) to stop the sport on Sundays – but to no avail.

There were a few excursions on the lake. The first one stimulated the Queen into making four sketches from the steamer *Winkelried*, kept at her

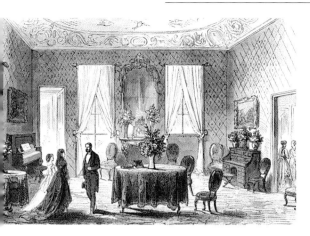

Pension Wallis: the Queen's drawing room (*left*) and the Queen's bedchamber (*right*)

disposal during her whole stay. Carriages would be taken on board so that part of an excursion could be made by road, picking up the steamer again at another point.

August 11
The air seemed fresher, when we were out at breakfast, but whilst I was sitting out, it got much hotter again.... At 12 started with Louise, Janie E. & Sir T. Biddulph, driving down to where a steamer was waiting for us. Embarked taking our carriage on board with us & steamed off at once. Pleasant air & most splendid views as we went along. Hofmann explained every place we passed. We came to Tell's Chapel, under which

The steamer *Winkelried*, used by the Queen during her stay

William Tell's Chapel on the shores of Lake Lucerne, near Flüelen

we stopped for a while. The height of the mountains & rocks here is stupendous & we were told chamois were to be found.... Truly glorious was the view, as we approached Fluellen, the Urirothstock, with snow, rising splendidly above it, & lower down richly wooded mountains, made a most beautiful picture. We lay quite close enough to Tell's Chapel, which is open in front, to see the curious old fresco paintings on the wall, representing incidents in his life. Here it was that he jumped out of the boat & was saved in the midst of a storm. Had our luncheon on board the steamer. The Lake a most marvellous sapphire blue and emerald green colour, changing from one to the other. Luncheon over, we went on to Fluellen, where we disembarked, our carriage being easily unshipped & at once drove off through the very picturesque town built up against the mountain. Drove some time along the Lake, on the celebrated Axenstrasse, hewn through the rock with many tunnels. The heat was unfortunately so great, that I could hardly enjoy it. Stopped in a shady place to take our tea, & went on to Brunnen, where we again got on board the steamer. Only a few people had assembled at the pier. The great composer Wagner's Villa, not far from Lucerne, was pointed out to us. Got home at 1/2 p. 7. Heavy clouds had gathered & a thunderstorm broke forth, continuing with violent rain for 2 hours. The echo in the mountains makes the thunder seem very loud.

Tunnel on Axenstrasse

The Queen wrote to her eldest daughter Princess Victoria about this first excursion:

> … It was most splendid & nothing can exceed the beauty of the Lake in any direction. The view up to Weggis – to Brunnen & Fluelen – with those splendid peaked mountains all wooded & the Urirothstock in the midst is really quite overwhelming. Then on to Stanzstadt … with the splendid Pilatus overhanging the Lake to the right – & the Lake itself, that wonderful colour – varying from saphire blue to emerald green – is too glorious![86]

The Equerry Colonel Ponsonby gave a lively account of the previous evening at the pension in a letter home to his wife. Some of the Queen's suite had taken an exploratory trip on the steamer that afternoon:

> At 4 Louise Leopold Duckworth Bauer Bids & J. Ely & I went to Lucerne to our steamer which was in waiting. Most luxurious with chairs etc., and we have tea on board. We went up to the other end of the lake and visited Tells Chapel & then back only just in time for dinner. The Queen with Mary Bids had been driven in by a thunder storm. Discourse at dinner about William Tell. I'm sure says the Queen if there is any doubt about his existence Colonel Ponsonby don't believe in him. 'Well Mum it is curious there is a similar tale told of one

Dining room of the Pension Wallis and Princess Louise's sketch of Sir Thomas Biddulph ('Bids' or 'Father Jim')

Toko of Denmark.' Whereupon Bids split into instant clatter of laughter. I got this from 'Myths of the Middle Ages'. Toko was 300 years before Tell. Jenner horrified 'But you don't believe in Toko?' Of course I hadn't expressed such opinion but being then pressed I denied all belief in Tell and Toko and said the story was a very old Indian one. Jenner indignant. Murray says Tells chapel was built by 114 people who personally knew Tell. Louise says that Froude says these 114 people are myths as much as Tell…. Kanné tells me that Mr Brown and Dr. Jenner will drive him mad. J.B.* of course asks for everything for the Queen as if he were in Windsor Castle, and if anything cannot be got he says it must – and it is. Jenner who has never seen foreign <u>L.</u>† before runs about to each in a state of high disgust and says they must be entirely altered – Jenner is right of course – but he rather over estimates the idea of bad smells, because perched up here there are not except in one or two places.[87]

Although the Pension Wallis was almost new, an entry in the Lord Chamberlain's 'Statement of Her Majesty's expenses on Tour in Switzerland' shows that to fit it for Royal occupation a goodly sum was spent on the local purchase of furniture, carpets, baths and sundries, glass, china, looking-glasses, a telegraphic apparatus and, to put Jenner's mind at rest, a prodigious amount of cleanser for the patent WC. The total came to £407.0.1 – a lot of

* John Brown.
† i.e. lavatories.

money in those days, but not extravagant; by comparison, as much as half that amount had been spent for entertainment during one evening a month earlier, on the occasion of one of the rare State Balls at Buckingham Palace, for the hire of marquees and tents and the attendance of Mr. Dan Godfrey's Quadrille Band (Mr. D. Godfrey and 36 Performers).[88]

Jenner's fears on the score of Swiss sanitation were unfounded. Neither the Queen nor any of her entourage caught anything untoward. On the contrary, the Queen was on the mend and venturing further afield. A drive around Lucerne elicited a Journal entry about the Lion Monument:

Lion monument, Lucerne

August 12
Drove up to see the Lion Monument put up to the memory of Louis XVI's poor Swiss Guard, who were all killed in the Revolution of the 10th of Aug. 1793. ⃰ *Got out & went close up to look at it. It is most*

⃰ In fact it was in 1792 that the Swiss Guard were killed, defending Marie Antoinette during the storming of the Tuileries.

striking, grand & touching. The lion is hewn in bas relief, out of the rock, represented lying pierced & dying, grasping with his paws a shield on which are the Fleurs de Lis of the Bourbons.

... August 12
Stopped to take our tea in the carriage ... Our very slow but safe coachman drove beautifully through the very narrow streets & round the sharp corners.

The Queen was obviously relishing her new-found freedom. But she was, after all, the Head of State and was not let off the hook completely. The umbilical cord with London was never broken, although Disraeli knew what was good for him and made sure his sovereign was bothered as little as possible. In any case, with Parliament in recess and the summer holiday season in full swing, there was no great political activity. Messengers arrived, but especially at first the Queen was in no way overworked. During this first week, for example, Sir Thomas Biddulph wrote on her behalf to Disraeli, conveying her approval of some Ministerial appointments, and adding for good measure: 'There is no inconvenience from Tourists or Inhabitants, who behave very well.'[89]

The Foreign Secretary Lord Stanley was also under-employed at the time. He was on hand to take care of any foreign or other affairs that might blow up. Kept at arm's length by the Queen and staying in a Lucerne hotel, he was having a hugely enjoyable – and very energetic – holiday, with very few calls on his time to distract him from his marathon 'rambles',[90] as he called them. These kept him happily occupied for many hours every day, whereas it took him only a few minutes to deal with the correspondence brought by the messengers. During his first week his royal duties consisted of nothing more onerous than fending off some people who wanted to call on the Queen. Among these was a Dutch aide-de-camp, sent by the King of Holland to pay his respects to the Queen, and even the Papal Nuncio in Berne, who had hoped that he could personally convey the Pope's good wishes.

The British diplomatic staff in Berne called on Stanley but did not get near the Queen. In his diary Stanley records a thumb-nail sketch of the Swiss, given to him by the Minister, John Savile Lumley, the head of the Legation:

Lumley talks about the people, praises them highly, says their politics are very pure, their offices miserably paid, but they continue to get capable men to fill them: there is really, and not only in name, an open career: one of their leading politicians in his youth helped his father who kept a small cabaret: and such cases are not rare. There are no very rich people, fortunes in general are moderate: but pauperism is unknown. They work hard, and in addition to their farms, follow some trade or other occupation which keeps them from idleness in the winter. They have moreover the exceptional advantage of having perhaps a million sterling brought yearly into the country by foreigners.[91]

Very likely the Queen kept well away from such unholiday-like conversation, in line with her policy of having a complete change and keeping her involvement in affairs of state to an irreducible minimum. By now, the end of her first week in Lucerne, she was well ensconced in her quarters on the hill, she had got her bearings and was chafing at the bit to go further afield.

It was not to be.

4 Frustration

As the days wore on Queen Victoria became more and more aware that there was something seriously wrong – and getting worse by the day.

Nature had set the Queen's thermostat at a sub-Arctic comfort level: she felt well at Balmoral, for example, while others shivered, but found 'normal' temperatures unpleasantly hot, and real heat unbearable. One of her aims in choosing Switzerland for this holiday had always been to find 'bracing air',[92] and this expectation grew during the summer of 1868 as England baked in the fiercest heatwave for decades.

The journey to Switzerland had not been easy, with Paris *'in a blazing heat'*[93] already at 7 a.m. after a sleepless night in a rocking train, followed by another night in the *'very hot'*[94] train to Basle. But the first day in Switzerland had made up for it all, and she found the evening pleasantly cool.

The rest of her first week was hot by any standards. In fact, the Queen had got away from the English heatwave only to walk straight into an almighty one in Switzerland. It was Queen's weather with a vengeance. The Swiss had been having a cool summer; promptly upon her arrival the greatest and longest heatwave in living memory set in – and broke just after she left. Not quite what the doctor ordered …

The Queen felt the heat, of course, but at first there was much to distract her from it: exhilaration over her new surroundings, the glory of the scenery and relief at having successfully managed her great escape. But by mid-August, the beginning of her second week, when the novelty had worn off and the mountains beckoned, the heat was really getting to her. And not only the heat, but a phenomenon called Föhn, an ill wind brought about by the meeting of cold and warm air over the Alps, with associated abrupt changes in air pressure.

People react very differently to Föhn: some do not even notice it, some have minor symptoms such as light-headedness which they shrug off, others get leaden feet and violent headaches. Queen Victoria was clearly susceptible. It says much for her determination of spirit that she battled against the symptoms and got on with her holiday, even though the weather was putting paid to the Alpine expeditions she yearned for. Central Switzerland during that second week of the Queen's stay was plagued not only by Föhn but by recurring thunderstorms and showers that made the air oppressively damp and shrouded the mountains in mist. Not very amusing.

Her Journal entries for these days are mostly laconic about her feelings, referring only to headaches and heavy air. But she was more outspoken in her letters to her eldest daughter Victoria. At the beginning of this trying week she was still putting a brave face on it:

I believe it is quite exceptional here to have such dreadful heat <u>all</u> day with <u>hot</u> nights. Yesterday was better after another dreadful thunderstorm on Thursday Evng. & pouring rain. But today it is again very hot tho there is a pleasant air. It prevents my undertaking <u>any</u> lengthened expeditions for the day – or riding or walking wh. is <u>vy provoking</u>. – I have had some very pleasant & beautiful afternoon drives – quietly & peaceably from 5 to 8 – or a little before. – We breakfast out about 9 & then I sit out writing – in the shade, but more I cannot do in the heat. This will show you how <u>far</u>, how <u>very far</u> from well, poor, old Mama is – & it depresses & discourages me. <u>Home</u>, at least Scotland, is the <u>best</u> place for <u>me</u> for my health, <u>that I feel</u>. Perhaps (if I live) in some years I may be better. It is God's Will & whatever He sends – sorrow, or joy, or suffering, or comfort must <u>all</u> be borne with meek submission and gratitude! – Still, for all that, I am very glad I am here & can see God's most <u>glorious</u> Creation – as I am sure it can <u>no where</u> be surpassed.[95]

Below the Schwarzenberg. Watercolour by Queen Victoria, 16 August 1868

The Foreign Secretary, Lord Stanley, was invited up to the Pension Wallis and noted in his diary that he saw the Queen afterwards: '... she in good spirits, and pleased with the place, but complains of heat, and Jenner says it is too much for her, and almost makes her ill ... I thought her in good humour, which is by no means always the case.'[96] To the Prime Minister Stanley wrote: 'The great lady keeps herself very close: I saw her last Sunday in excellent looks and high good humour: she said little of public affairs, but what she did say was to blame the opposition, and express decided sympathy with her ministers. She hoped the elections would go well. She seems to pass her time chiefly sitting in her garden, and driving out in the evening at a tremendous pace ... We have had great heat for some days, which she suffered from (and indeed it was such as I have never felt in Europe) ...'[97]

The Queen, never one to suffer silently for long, soon gave full vent to her frustration, and on 19 August she wrote to Princess Victoria:

This climate is dreadful ... so damp & clammy when it is not boiling – & I get dreadfully tired & have constant headaches & little appetite. <u>Beautiful</u>, beyond belief – but oh! for our dear Highland air & solitude! How different that is. And everyone of us feels it. – We have had a gt deal of rain, since that frightful heat on Saturday or Sunday when there was a stifling chirocco – der <u>Föhn Wind</u> – On Monday when we had settled to go to Engelberg – it poured, so we gave it up – & then cleared, – & we had a fine drive – but nothing long, in the afternoon. The drives about here however are <u>quite</u> beautiful & I am totally unmolested.

Yesterday we again settled to go to Engelberg & <u>again</u> had to give it up. We started at 10 & went as far as Stanzstadt by steamer but it rained & the mist hung so low that we gave it up – & went to Brunnen. Here we disembarked (we

'Turning up by a small village we came upon Lake Lowertz, along the banks of which we drove. In the centre is a small island & there are the ruins of an old Castle Schwanau.' (Journal, 18 August 1868)

Landslide of 1806,
Goldau.
*'As one passes along the
Lake, one comes upon
great scenes of
devastation, which
continue for at least a
mile. Rocks & stones are
hurled about in every
direction, many to a
distance of 100 yards, &
some are of gigantic size.
1400 people are said to
have perished.'* (Journal,
18 August 1868)

always take our Carriages with us on board) & drove thro' Schwytz – by the lovely lake of Lowertz to Goldau where there was that most extraordinary & wonderful landslip of the Rossberg – on wh. occasion the stones were hurled to an <u>immense distance,</u> – the whole having the appearance of a mighty ruin. Here in a quiet spot overlooking the lake we lunched (Louise, Leopd., Ly. Ely, Col. Ponsonby & Mr Duckworth were with us) – a guide, Brown & Archie (who go about unmolested or noticed in their <u>Kilts</u>) attending us. Unfortunately it rained a little the whole time. We then drove thro' <u>Goldau – Arth</u> charmingly situated on the Lake of Zug at the foot of the Rigi, – (by this time it cleared & became <u>vy</u> fine & vy hot again) – we drove along the lake under trees – such beautiful Wallnut* trees, beeches etc. & vegetation I never saw – on to <u>Zug,</u> a most picturesque old Town – beautifully situated – to Cham – a sort of 1/2 way Hse., – near a Station, where we had to wait 3/4 of an hour, for our horses to rest. And we were obliged to take our tea (brought with us) in a stuffy Tea-garden, near a Skittle ground!! No one was there & not a soul knew us, but it was very <u>unpoetic.</u> Then I <u>sketched</u> & we drove home – at the rate of 3 miles an hour – by 8.[98]

* The Queen's spelling.

Woman in local costume. Sketch by Princess Louise

Reporting on the Queen's condition to Disraeli, the gentle Lady Jane Ely came out with another masterpiece of understatement: 'I think The Queen has suffered a good deal from the heat & Her Majesty finds the air a little too relaxing for her here. ... I know you will not betray me about it, but The Queen looks languid & tired I think.'[99]

In other words, she was under the weather and something had to be done about it. At this stage many a twentieth-century holidaymaker would have given up and gone home. But not Victoria Regina. She had come for bracing air and bracing air was what she was going to get. A planned expedition to the lakes of Brienz and Thun, taking in Interlaken, was abandoned and the courier Kanné despatched to reconnoitre one of the highest Alpine passes, the Furka which, as the Queen put it in her Journal, '*he thinks may be a good place for me to get some pure, fresh mountain air*'.[100]

Jane Ely promised Disraeli to write and tell him 'how the change answers. ... You must not be anxious about The Queen, for I am sure it is only the heat of the weather that affects her, for Her Majesty eats and sleeps well.'[101]

Meanwhile, even during this week of frustration, there were consolations in the form of short spells of bearable, even good weather.

August 17
A bright fine afternoon. Drove with Baby & Mary B., at the back of the town, up a high hill by Adligenschwyl, a small village, through a beautiful wood where we stopped for tea. Everywhere quantities of blackberries (of which we have excellent tarts) & heather, which made it feel quite like dear Scotland. Walked a short way & then drove by rather a steep hill, home by Seeburg & the town. The mountains glowed again in the setting sun & looked too beautiful. The town is very gay, so many people of every kind & sort out on the Parade & some very curious figures! It was pleasant, but very damp. – Janie E. read to me after dinner.

Another source of comfort to the Queen must have been the realization that her incognita was being respected everywhere. She was not being mobbed by her own subjects or by other tourists, as Stanley had feared. The

Swiss were showing exemplary reticence and courtesy and, snug in her little pension up on the hill, she was away from prying eyes and safe from intruders – except one.

An unknown man had been stopped in the grounds of the pension trying to gain entrance and saying he needed to see the Queen. First suspicions that he was a terrorist (it would not have been the first attempt on the Queen's life) were dispelled, and when it turned out that the intruder was English he was taken under police custody to the British Legation in Berne. The rest of the story was told by the British Minister Lumley, writing to Lord Stanley:

On the 19th inst. I received from Sir Thomas Biddulph a telegram from Lucerne to the following effect: 'There is a man named Wood who seems mad and who wants to see the Queen. The police have sent him today at half past one to the British Consul, Berne. Can you get him sent to England or away.'

Yesterday evening the man was brought to the Legation by a gendarme and, as I was not in Town, he was sent to my house in the country in a hired conveyance …

The man, who was shabbily dressed, said he was an architect in search of employment. He appeared to be a harmless monomaniac, his fixed idea being that he had a secret mission to the Queen, which necessitated his immediate return to Lucerne. He complained that his effects, consisting of a small hand bag, had been searched by British detectives at Lucerne & that some important papers had been taken from him, that he had not been allowed to remain at Lucerne long enough to receive money which he expected in a day or two, and that he had been sent in charge of the police from Lucerne to Berne where he found himself without the means of paying for a night's lodging.

I told him he had committed a misdemeanour in endeavouring to force his way into the Queen's residence; that as long as he was in Switzerland he would doubtless be under the surveillance of the police & that if he chose to remain in this country I could do nothing for him, but that if he made up his mind to return to England I would pay his expenses.

He said that as his mission had failed he would prefer going to England; I accordingly paid his lodging for the night, had a second class place taken for him by the early train this morning for London & gave him a small sum for his food on the way.

The enclosed account contains a statement of the expenses I have incurred in this business, which I shall be obliged if your Lordship will direct to be repaid to me through my Agent at the Foreign Office.[102]

The statement included SFr. 1 for a room in a pension, SFr. 1.50 for breakfast and SFr. 2.50 for dinner with wine. The incident was widely reported, with first suppositions that the man was a Fenian giving way to later rectification along the lines of Lumley's letter.

There is no mention of the incident in the Queen's Journal as we have it. Either she did not deem it worthy of mention, or Princess Beatrice omitted to copy what the Queen had written. Perhaps she was not even told of the incident on the day it happened. In any case, Kanné soon returned from his reconnaissance trip, having seen the inn on the Furka and found it good, and preparations got under way for a few days' stay there.

Yet there were still affairs of state that engaged the Queen's sense of duty and disturbed her conscience. For example, she had grave reservations about a candidate for a Church appointment whom Disraeli was urging upon her. In Switzerland the Queen could shed many of her royal burdens, but not her preoccupation with steering the Church of England down a middle course – a concern given urgency by the predominant role played by the Church in the life of her subjects. It left her only once for a few days. To ensure that her forthcoming stay in the mountains would be a real holiday within her holiday, the Queen gave instructions that no official papers were to be sent up after her. This was to be the climax of three years of hoping, scheming and planning.

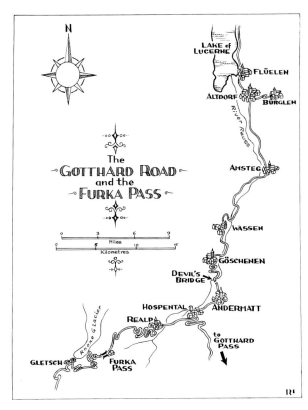

The route of Queen Victoria's most adventurous excursion in Switzerland, 22 to 25 August 1868

5 'Purer, Lighter Mountain Air'

When the Queen left Lucerne early in the morning of 22 August she had spent two weeks in or fairly near the sheltered environment of the Pension Wallis. What she was now embarking on in her quest for 'fresher, purer, lighter air' (as she put it in a letter to her daughter Victoria[103]) was a far cry indeed from her usual afternoon drives. It was nothing less than a journey into the high Alps, first up the valley leading to the St Gotthard Pass, one of Europe's great north-south routes, then (turning off before the pass itself) up to the Furka Pass, well above the tree-line, and far higher than the Queen had ever been before. She proudly noted the height in her Journal.

August 22
Hotel Furca
8,000 ft. high
Got up early, & at a 1/4 p. 8 left Lucerne with Louise & Janie E., driving quickly down to the steamer, where we embarked & found Sir T. Biddulph & Sir Wm. Jenner. The mist still hung heavily on the mountain tops but gradually lifted & the Lake looked lovely as we steamed to Fluellen, which we reached in an hour. Got at once into our carriages, there being 3 besides our own, in which I went with Louise & Janie E.,

(*below*) Flüelen, starting point of the road leading to the St Gotthard and the Furka (*below right*) Tell's chapel at Bürglen

Hoffmann on the box, & Brown behind. We went with the usual Poste very well driven with 4 small horses with bells on their harness. Sir T. Biddulph & Sir Wm. Jenner followed directly behind, & then the maids & men servants, the luggage behind, all with 4 horses & bells. Went straight up into the splendid mountains. Three miles beyond Fluellen, we came to Altorf, the capital of the canton Uri, also extremely picturesque. Passed over a bridge over the rapid stream of Schächen & saw the village of Burgh, where Tell was born & a small Chapel commemorates where his house is supposed to have stood. We soon came to where one looks up Surenen Pass, behind which Engelberg lies, immensely high mountains rise on either side. Several poor women came up to the carriage with baskets of fruit, one of which we took, gladly eating its contents, as we were very hot & thirsty. We next reached Amsteg, quite in the mountains. From there the road ascends & one goes along the rapid, foaming, dashing Reuss which forms constant waterfalls, the valley narrows, & one has the most grand mountains before one. Almost up to

Wassen

the very tops one can see those picturesque little châlets dotted about with the brightest greenest grass. I wish I could describe properly the beauty of all. Though the sun was scorching, the air was pleasant & cool in the shade. At about 1, came to Wasen, very finely situated, where we stopped outside to take our luncheon & give the horses a rest. Went on again, winding along & crossing bridges over the Reuss. Half an hour brought us to the Göschenen Thal, where the scenery became very wild, & assumed very much the character of our Highlands, only much higher and grander. A few fir trees grow amongst the rocks & even a little hay was being made and collected, where one could not imagine a goat could go.

Normal practice in a small country where, especially in Alpine valleys, every inch of arable soil is precious. Apart from the near-inaccessibility of the mountainside terrain, there was the ever-present danger of avalanches, falling rocks and landslides to contend with.

> *… August 22*
> *Got out & walked a little & again when we came to the celebrated Devil's Bridge. The road is very steep, but broad & there is plenty of room for carriages to pass one another. In spite of very sharp corners & the tremendous height at which one finds oneself overlooking yawning & frightful precipices beneath, I did not feel frightened, for the horses were extremely quiet & the driver very good.*

For centuries, travellers crossing the Alps had felt very frightened indeed. In 1188 the monk John de Bremble on his way to Rome summed up the general feeling: 'Pardon me for not writing, I have been on the Mount of Jove, on the one hand looking up to the heavens of the mountains, on the other shuddering at the hell of the valleys. Feeling myself so much nearer heaven that I was more sure that my prayer would be heard, Lord, I said, restore me to my brethren that I may tell them that they come not to this place of torment.' And a century later Adam of Usk had to be blindfolded on his way over the St. Gotthard Pass.

New and old Devil's Bridges

… August 22
At the Devil's Bridge the waterfall is so immense, that one feels the spray in one's face. It is magnificent, & we were all enchanted. How wonderful to think of the French Army having marched over this fearful pass & before the splendid new bridge was built. The old ruined one is still to be seen. The whole is called the St. Gothard road, but this is the Göschenen Pass. Passed through two tunnels which were built to prevent the avalanches regularly sweeping the road away. We met many tourists in carriages & on foot with 'Alpenstöcke'. In a short time we emerged from this tremendous Pass, & came upon a large flat where Andermatt lies. Further on we came to Hospenthal where the character of the houses changed, the wooden châlets there being stone ones instead. Here we changed horses, as well as our excellent driver, who had driven us with the same horses from Fluellen, about 24 miles! Instead of going up the St. Gothard we went straight on, passing Realp, another little village, where the Inn is kept by a monk whom we saw standing at the door. Very shortly after Realp, we began the tremendous ascent of the Furca, over the Sidli Alp, which took us 3 hours till we reached the desolate little Inn. As we rose we saw the Spitzenhoerner, rising up in the strangest points. The whole of this road which goes up in zig-zags has only been made since 2 years. Unfortunately the mist began to come down, & as we got higher & higher it became very cold & damp. Kanné was in a great state of fidget to hurry us on. At length, just as we came in sight of the desolate little house, the mist cleared off enough for us to see what was close to us & by 7 we reached our destination. It is in fact a miserable little 'Schenke', very small rooms poorly & badly furnished, but clean, & not uncomfortable, if there were only fireplaces as one would find in every small Highland Inn. I have a small room opening into the dining room, which I can use as a sitting room, & up a small staircase are our bedrooms. Got our dinner at 1/2p. 8. It blew dreadfully & rained, & was very cheerless.

Not as cheerless, though, as the welcome that had awaited a weary Swiss traveller the night before. He poured out his indignation in a letter to the Berne newspaper *Der Bund*, which (with an upsurge of republican spirit for once getting the better of its otherwise friendly attitude towards the Queen) published it under a prominent headline:

The Countess of Kent on the Furka

The following has been sent to us by a reader: It was last Friday evening towards half past seven, when, hungry and sore from a strenuous walk, I arrived at the local inn at the Furka pass, where I intended to take accommodation for the night. The dusk had already set in, thick clouds of mist were hanging in the air and it was getting uncomfortably cold. I had come from

(*previous pages*)
Furka, road and inn where the Queen stayed for three nights. Watercolour by Princess Louise, 23 to 24 August 1868

Hasli im Hof via Grimsel and Rhonegletscher; no wonder my eyes were glowing in anticipation as I hurried towards the cosy inn. It lies about 50 paces off the side of the road, where a waiter, dressed in a black tail-coat, and a female colleague had already taken their position to welcome arriving guests (as I assumed).

Determined to evade a lengthy welcoming ceremony, I proceeded towards the house across the grass. Suddenly I heard the voice of the waiter calling from behind. 'You wish to stay at the hotel? I am sorry, but it is not open to receive guests today. The whole hotel is reserved for the Queen of England for the next three days.'

I was thunderstruck, unable to believe my own ears.

'Impossible,' I cried. 'It would be utterly foolish of the Queen to monopolize the only house on the pass for herself.'

'But it is so,' the waiter replied, 'you will have to look for other accommodation, I am afraid.'

'Well, since the Queen has taken up all the rooms, I wouldn't mind sleeping (in a rudimentary bedstead) in the hall,' I told the waiter.

'I am sorry I cannot oblige you, Sir, but I have been ordered not to let anyone into the hotel.'

'So, have the Queen and her retinue arrived yet?' I demanded to know.

'No, she is expected tomorrow or the day after tomorrow.'

'But that is preposterous,' I cried, realizing that about half a dozen irate wayfarers, among them an elderly lady, had gathered in front of the hotel, joining me in my angry protest. The grumbling and complaining which now ensued would have created quite a stir in Her Gracious Majesty's ears. Some began to circle the house in search of another entrance, but to no avail: the Queen's cook in ordinary, standing guard at the entrance, seemed quite determined to defend it with his life. – To cut a long story short, we had to leave, whether we liked it or not, if we wanted to find a place to rest our weary bones. Some of us went towards the Rhone glacier; I myself, however, decided to walk on towards Realp, where I finally arrived at 9.30 in the evening, hungry, tired out and utterly infuriated. As I was told then and several times since, many travellers were turned back in the same rude manner that day, and they all complained about the appalling impudence with which they had been treated. It seems indeed rather impudent of the Queen to book the only inn on the pass without notifying wayfarers and to have it closed to the public long before she has even arrived. The inn-keeper who lends his name to such questionable practices in my opinion deserves to be publicly denounced.

As we see it, the whole incident can be ascribed to the excessive zeal of the Queen's retinue and the avarice of the inn-keeper.

In reply to this complaint the proprietor said he had indeed turned away guests but that travellers had been notified by his colleagues earlier along the route and he had even set up a little stand in one of the outbuildings offering food for famished travellers. And anyway, he was quick to point out, the traveller in question was 'ill-natured, comported himself rudely and threatened to smash the door'.

The Queen's descent upon the hotel got around: the American J.H.B. Latrobe remarked on it in his book, *Hints for Six Months in Europe*, published in Philadelphia the following year. 'The hotel of the Furca was taken possession of by the Queen of England and her suite not long after the writer's visit in 1868, and the common wayfarers were referred to a very modest shanty – it would be called in America – across the road'.

On the day the Queen travelled to the Furca, Stanley in his Lucerne hotel had raised a lordly eyebrow and written to Disraeli about 'the lady', as he was wont to refer to the Queen: 'I have only seen her once, for about ten minutes, and now she is gone to the Furca, where having taken the whole of the only inn, she has practically closed the pass against travellers for three days.'[104]

WATERSHED

After her first night in the high Alps on the Furka Pass, the Queen may have been wondering whether she had made a ghastly mistake in letting herself be brought all this way only to freeze in bed and be blanketed in fog. She even complained about the cold – and for her, that meant something. On the other hand, she may have been restless because she was not yet acclimatized to the rarified air at that altitude.

Very likely the Queen did not lose sleep through feeling guilty, or being sorry for the travellers whom her courier Kanné had edged out of the inn she was occupying. In fact, she had probably not even been told. Such sordid details may well have been kept from her: her stay on the Furka was going to be the zenith of her whole holiday in Switzerland and she would need to be shielded from anything as unpleasant as this. There was something else to keep her awake.

August 23
Woke frequently from the cold. There were only 42 degrees in my room! There was a dense fog & occasional snow & sleet. The people were not hopeful of its improving. – After our breakfast remained writing till 11, when I said I really must go out. Suddenly at that moment, the sun came out, allowing the splendid mountain tops, rearing their heads to the very clouds to be seen. Some were tipped & some entirely covered with snow.

This was the turning point of the Queen's stay in Switzerland. As the sun broke through that morning, her holiday finally fell into place.

… August 23
Walked with Louise & Janie E., Hoffmann & Brown following on the road leading to the Rhone Glacier & on to Brinz, about a mile. We were

in the greatest admiration of the splendid panorama before us, all the mountains so softly lit up, white with snow & with the loveliest blue tints. The Weisshorn & Randenhorn, the former, one of the highest peaks in Switzerland, were pointed out to us, also the Fleschhorn & Wasserhorn, which are close to the Simplon. We could see the Todtensee, a small lake, quite high up, where a number of French were thrown in, which gave that dreadful name to the lake. Close to the Hotel are the Matterhorn* & another smaller, very dirty looking glacier. One is quite in the midst of them! The air is most beautiful & light, & enabled me to accomplish, what was quite a long walk for me. We met many carriages, all of a primitive kind & tourists on foot with their napsacks & Alpenstöcke. Heard the curious whistle of the marmottes. – When I came in read Prayers, etc. Lunched below as we dined. Both gentlemen greatly delighted by the scenery & air. – Afterwards started with Louise & Janie E. in the sociable, with only a pair of horses, for the glacier, driving along part of the road we had walked in the morning, & on a mile & 1/4 we came to the 1st corner of this most wonderful and precipitous road & in another moment came, as it were, quite close upon the glacier, the effect of which cannot be described. One can hardly believe it is real, it seems almost like something unearthly! The road descends in 7 great zig-zags & with this marvellous glacier piled up in huge boulders of solid ice, with peaks like rocks, looked so alarming & steep, that I asked to walk down. It was really more alarming to <u>look at</u> than <u>in reality</u> to drive. We went down quite slowly & then trotted along the road which overlooks the

Upper part of Rhone Glacier. Watercolour by Queen Victoria, 23 to 24 August 1868

* One of the Queen's very few topographical errors or perhaps a mistake made by Princess Beatrice in her transcription. What she saw was the Muttenhorn (sometimes spelt Muthorn), to the south of the Furka. The Matterhorn is far away and well out of view from around the Furka.

glacier, the level mass of which looks as if it had come down like soup &
hardened.

… August 23
After 1/2 a mile we stopped and got out, intending to go down on to the
glacier. They wanted to carry me in a chaise à porteur, down the steep
bank above it, but I refused & with the help of an Alpenstock & Brown's
strong arm got down all right. When we came to the roughest highest
bank of stones I would not go any further but let Louise go on with
Hoffmann & Brown, to the glacier, sitting down & watching them with
Janie E., talking to the good humoured Swiss men in their blue blouses,
who had wanted to carry me. Louise & her companions went on a good
long way, stepping across some of the crevasses. When they came back, I
was carried up & we got into the carriage again, & took our tea. A large
herd of at least 100 cattle were grazing on the hillside, with nice bells
round their necks. Went on a little after our tea & sketched as we went
up very slowly, gazing with astonishment at the marvellous glaciers.
Home by 1/4 to 7. The air, brisk & cold.

View from the Queen's
sitting room in the inn
on the Furka, by
Princess Louise, 24
August 1868

August 24

There had been a frost in the night, but the day was perfectly splendid, & the mountains so clear. After breakfast remained sketching the splendid view from one of the windows. At 11 walked out with Janie E., going first upon a very small glacier below the house, where I picked up some fine crystals & found some pretty flowers. Lovely blue gentians were brought down from the Gothenstock for me. There seem to be so many flowers that are not seen elsewhere. Then walked with both Louise & Janie, the same way as yesterday. The sun was so warm & the view so splendidly clear. Got a little way up the hillside, at the foot of the Furcahorn, & sat down & sketched. On our way out we looked at the cows, small, but so pretty, which had come much nearer & talked to the boy who was herding them. He showed us the curious stick with 2 leather thongs attached to a chain, fastened to it, which he uses to drive the cows with. – Resting & writing – out driving at 1/2p.3 on, & down the same fearful road as yesterday. Twice we had to meet carriages & were going down on the outside which terrified me, though I was astonished at not minding it more. We again gazed with wonder & astonishment at the splendid glacier. When we got down, we found 2 horses quietly waiting, which the coachman (a careful good driver) fastened on behind our carriage & thus we trotted on, quite to the foot of the glacier, where the Rhone runs out from underneath it, in a thick white stream. Went up to the Hotel du Rhone Glacier, where a good many people seemed to be stopping. Here, we had to get out, however we got on as quickly as we could, & Alpenstock in hand, walked about 1/2 a mile along a path, crossing a little stream over rough stones, till we came to the glacier itself where it was level. With the help of Brown & Hoffmann I walked a little way on it & back. It cracked a little, but the thickness of the ice is quite enormous. It looks brown & rather dirty.

The same view from the Queen's sitting room. Watercolour by Queen Victoria, 24 August 1868

From the foot of the Furkahorn. Aug. 24. 1868 —

Louise then went to a cavern with Sir T. Biddulph, which is scooped out in the ice a good long way. I walked slowly back to where Hoffmann had kindled a fire, & where we sat on the grass under a small bank, watching the water boil in a <u>casserole</u>, a <u>kettle</u> being unknown in these parts. Had some delicious tea, then hurried off to our carriage, to which 4 horses were now attached. Went off in grand style, the whip being well smacked & the good little horses encouraged by that peculiar 'hau-ip', which the men here constantly call to them. On the level we got on fast, then came that tremendous long ascent of certainly 1000 ft., which took us 5 quarters of an hour to accomplish. We met men, who go up daily into the mountains to milk the cows, & carry milk & butter, even cheese, on their backs. Often these are conveyed in small carts, drawn by poor dogs.

From the foot of Furkahorn. Watercolour by Queen Victoria, 24 August 1868

The moon shone out over the glacier, as we were driving back & it & the mountains looked too beautiful. Hoffmann & the driver yodelled as we went along. Got in at 1/2p. 7.

Next morning the time had come for Queen Victoria, now tingling with mountain air, to return to her pension in Lucerne.

August 25
The morning was rather dull & misty. – Slept extremely well & did not suffer from the cold, though there had been snow in the night. Never had a better appetite, the air reminded me so much of that in our dear Highlands. – At 1/2p. 10 we left the Furca, where … we had spent a most interesting time, & I shall ever look back with pleasure & thankfulness, to have been able to see all these wonderful works of nature. Everyone, high & low, was so amiable, cheerful & helpful & we lived so completely together like a family, that the recollection of it will be most pleasant. The luggage started before us, but the 3 other carriages kept together with ours. Came down very quickly & that very steep part seemed as nothing to us, in comparison with the 1st day. The Febia (sic) was well seen, as we left the little house standing in all its wild solitude. We walked down part of the steepest part, as I wished to warm my feet. Came down in an hour & 40 m. to Hospenthal, having taken 3 hours to go up! Here we changed horses, getting our excellent driver of the preceding day, who Hoffmann says is the best in the country! We came very shortly in sight of the Devil's Bridge, where we got out to look at the waterfall & admire the stupendous rocks, which are so grand & wild. Walked a little way & met a whole party of Pifferari, in their most picturesque, though dirty dress, who were returning to their native place Caserta. They began to play their bagpipes (3 men, with about 4 or 5 boys). There was a little imp who kept dancing about, more like a monkey than anything else, holding his

On the St Gotthard road after Wassen ('*Wasen*') Sketch by Queen Victoria, 25 August 1868

black Calabrian hat for money. The next rencontre was a string of 5 diligences, who were toiling up the very steep ascent. Got into the carriage again, driving as far as the Göschenen Bridge, where we scrambled up to some level grass, above the road & sat down to have our luncheon. Remained sketching for a while, then drove past Göschenen & looked up the splendid Pass of Süsten, which goes up to a glacier of the same name, – past the Teufel's Stein, an immense stone just above the river. Stopped shortly after Wasen, to make a sketch as the scenery from there had a totally different character, but we were pressed for time. Went on very quickly through beautiful country, passing the Pfaffensprung, where a Priest is supposed to have jumped with a young girl across the river! At Amsteg we watered our horses & took 2 leaders, then drove slowly on to Altdorff & Fluellen, which we reached at 1/2p. 5, going at once on board the steamer, where our luggage had already been for 2 hours. Off we steamed, & had one very heavy shower of rain & a great deal of wind. We were glad to get our tea on board. Got home at 1/4 to 8 & found dear Arthur & Col. Elphinstone, who are staying at Lucerne & arrived 2 days ago. We talked much at dinner of all we had seen. –*

While the Queen was away on this expedition with Princess Louise, Lady Ely, Sir Thomas Biddulph and the solicitous Sir William Jenner, those who stayed behind (the other two children, Leopold and Beatrice, Lady Biddulph, Colonel Ponsonby, the Revd. Duckworth and Miss Bauer) were left to their own devices at Lucerne. Ponsonby caught the spirit of how they spent their time in a letter to his wife:

Upon the 'Cats away the Mice will play' principle, we are going it. We went out this morning at 9 and tomorrow at 8.30 so I haven't time to write much as we are out all day. Today we went to Alpnacht & then drove to Lungern, had luncheon in a field & rambled in woods. Leopold and Beatrice quite delighted – Mary Bids low at seeing beautiful distant alps and not being at Furka – and so home. On my way I met Ld Stanley's private Secretary who with Ld S are furious with me … They got a telegram from England that all were anxious about the Q. and the Fenians and he Ld S knows nothing. Yet it turns out there has been an arrest and he Ld S was never informed of it. I tried to pacify him. There was an arrest I know but of a mere idiot. He wrote to ask to see the Q and Baker the policeman being sent to him found he was half foolish – & communicated with the Swiss police and he was sent home to his friends. It

---

* Prince Arthur, the Queen's third son was on a tour of Switzerland with his Governor, staying at a Lucerne hotel because there was no room at the pension.

may have been wrong of Bids not to tell Ld S but really it was so trifling an affair he thought nothing of it. Of course till he returns I cannot say – but I think in my own mind he ought to have told Ld S. So they have written me a little letter which I am to give Bids. However all that nonsense abt Fenians is bosh ... Much talk of the danger of the St. Gotthard road – which she had been led to expect – but didn't find. The latter part beautiful – so like the Spittal of Glenshee!! The Furka itself like Lough ... [illegible] ... (St Paul's like Crathie Church just as much) the air clear and Scotch etc. To Helena a full description of the road up 'I can scarcely believe it is Sunday' says D ... Mr Woodruffe the clergyman here has gone up the Rigi but hinted he had gone to officiate at the Furka – which is generally believed here. – D indignant at the appt of Hugh McNeile to be Dean of Ripon a regular electioneering apptmt – and is so afraid that Peterboro will also be the same. Bids writes from Furka that it is fine – but very cold – only stoves there and very small but comfortable. They had all been to see the Rhone Glacier.[105]

Sunrise, 4 a.m. as seen
from Pension Wallis,
Lucerne, 1868.
Watercolour by Princess
Louise

6   Exploration

Having tasted true Alpine air, Queen Victoria now wanted more, and Central Switzerland certainly had much more to offer – not only air but spectacular views and a variety of places to explore.

The next stage of the Queen's Swiss stay consisted of a number of active – some even ambitious – one-day excursions during which she could top up on bracing mountain air as well as experience and glory in new sights and places. Each of these expeditions alternated with a day of rest.

To begin with, she spent a quiet day in and around the pension, resting after her long return journey from the Furka. It happened to be the departed Prince Albert's birthday, which the Queen invariably commemorated:

> *August 26*
> *This dear blessed day came round again! How changed now, but I always try to keep it as a holiday, & make it bright & cheerful. I know my beloved one would wish me to be cheerful, & would rejoice in seeing me take an interest in all I see. Gave all the Children trifles. Arthur came up to breakfast, which we had out of doors. Dawdled about a little & wrote some letters in the summer house. – Drove in the afternoon with the 4 Children, as I always like to do on this beloved day, going in 2 carriages. Took our tea with us. A very fine evening. Coming back we dropped Arthur near the Schweizer Hof.*

Strengthened after this day of rest, the Queen was now looking forward to going up the Rigi – by then the best known mountain far and wide, and one she saw every time she looked across the lake from the pension. Foremost in her mind will have been the thought that it was from the Rigi that Prince Albert in 1837 had sent her the cherished alpine rose which she took with her wherever she went.

> *August 27*
> *At 10 started ... & went on board the steamer on which we took our ponies & grooms. In about 40 minutes we reached Weggis, quite a small quiet place, where the ponies were at once disembarked & 2 horses of the country were provided for Janie E. & Col. Ponsonby, Arthur insisting on*

walking. Mounted our ponies, 4 Swiss men leading the other horses & carrying the luncheon & tea baskets, cloaks, etc. There was a good deal of mist in the mountains, but the sun was very hot. Directly behind the small town, the ascent began & at once dreadfully steep. We had gone but a short way when all on foot took off their coats. We met many funny looking people coming down, mules carrying their luggage piled up on their packs, and we saw ladies being carried in chaises à porteur. Hoffman called out frequently to us to stop & rest a little. The road winds along in constant sight of the Lake, but it was very misty & we had no good view. When we came to a spring, the poor sweating horses & streaming men, had a drink. For a short while there was some very steep climbing. At length we came in sight of Rigi Kalt Bad, about 1200 ft. below the summit, which is 5,910 ft. & as everyone seemed overpowered

Inn on the way up the Rigi

with the heat, we stopped about 10 minutes in the shade afforded by another small châlet, where refreshments were sold. In a few more minutes we got to the Rigi Kalt Bad, an immense Hotel, where people stay. 2 or 300 people turned out, & as we passed under the Hotel, a Band struck up 'God save the Queen' & people fired off some little guns, at a distance ... Halted once more & then went up in another 1/2 hour to the Rigi Rothstock just below & opposite the Rigi Staffel, another Hotel in sight of the Rigi Kulm. Reached this at 1/2 p. 1, & in a shady place sat down on the grass to rest & have our well earned luncheon. It had cleared very much & the splendid Alps of the Bernese Oberland were seen to great advantage. There are quantities of beautiful blue gentians growing on the top, & all the way up & down. We remained here about 3/4 of an hour & looked down on Rigi Klosterli. Mounted our ponies again & rode in another 1/2 hour to the Rigi Kulm, where there is a very large Hotel where people stay the night, in order to see the sun rise. We

On the way from
Kaltbad to Rigi Staffel
and Rigi Kulm

did not get off, but remained at the top for about 10 minutes gazing at the splendid view. We saw, though not very clearly, an immense way all over the flat land & the Lakes of Lucerne, Zug, etc. on the one side & on the other, all the finest, highest mountains of the Bernese Alps, with their snowy peaks. There were 3 stalls with things to buy & a high sort of stand, people climbed up to see the view.... Rode a little over the other side looking down on Goldau, the Lake of Lowerz & the Muota Thal. Then we left. I got off & walked nearly as far as the Staffel, then mounted my pony again, & came down an easier way, reaching Untersee baden, (a fort at the foot of the steep part of the Rigi), at about 5. There, in a meadow, we had our tea, getting some hot water from a little inn. Remained nearly 3/4 of an hour & sketched a little, then went on, a steep descent winding through lanes overhung with endless fruit trees, getting in another 3/4 of an hour to Küsnacht, where at the end of the town we found our carriages & drove home as quickly as we could by Seeberg, dropping Arthur near the Schweizer Hof. Got back at 8, all feeling, that

it had been a most successful day. – Only 4 to dinner. –

That night the Queen slept well but noted next morning that she was very stiff. She went for a walk, wrote letters, painted, took a drive with Princess Louise, had tea in the open (recorded as usual in the Journal) and sketched *'one of the pretty Swiss houses close to Kriens'*. After dinner, Jane Ely read to her – one of the normal duties of a lady-in-waiting.

The Queen was now ready for another attempt the following day to go to Engelberg, a mountain village which was already a popular resort for British visitors. Here she was to make history by being the first female monarch –

Seeboden, on the way down from the Rigi. Watercolour by Queen Victoria, 27 August 1868 (*see previous page*)

The celebrated panorama from the summit of the Rigi

and even more remarkable, the first woman – to set foot in the inner sanctum of the celebrated Roman Catholic monastery of Engelberg.

The way there took the Queen and her party over the lake to Stansstad, where they disembarked and drove first to Stans.

It was two o'clock by the time they reached Engelberg.

August 29
Lunched on a grassy bank, about 10 minutes distance from the village. We sketched a little afterwards, though there was no distant view & then walked to the village, to see the Monastery, which is a curious one, from its great antiquity. We first stopped at a Châlet, close to the road, where a nice looking but very poor girl was weaving silk. There were hardly any people in the village, but 2 or 3 had their suspicion, as to who we were. We walked by the Gasthaus straight into the Church, hearing the sounds of the organ. Vespers were going on, & I went close up to the altar steps. Service was going on behind the rails, reminding one much of our Cathedral services. The music was very fine. We had to wait about 10 minutes until the service was over, as we wanted to go over the Monastery. At the conclusion, the Priest in his golden vestments stood with the acolytes, swinging their censors before the immense High Altar. Then all the monks, one after the other, came out & knelt in a side Chapel, where there was a most ugly image of the Madonna & Child, in a silver & gold dress. The Church is a fine large one, but white washed, & in bad taste. Directly the service was concluded Hoffmann beckoned to me to come on & we went past the altar into a passage, where we were met by 2 or 3 Priests, one of whom, a younger man, showed us very civilly everything. There are 30 monks, but their dress is more like that of ordinary Priests, merely a cowl in addition to the black soutane. We were taken into the Sacristy, where we were shown their fine Plate & very rich vestments, a curious old Pastoral Staff & Crucifix, likewise some vestments worn by the 1st Abbot in the 11th Century when the Monastery (for Benedictines) was founded. Some of the vestments were

'*Stanz is a picturesque old town, with several Churches & a fine new monument, a marble group of Arnold Winkelried being killed & lying on the ground, with the spears in his arms.*' (Journal, 29 August 1868)

'*There is also an ugly old statue of him.*'
(Journal, 29 August 1868)
Arnold von Winkelried was a Swiss hero who helped his countrymen to victory against the Habsburgs in 1386 by stepping forward and concentrating the enemy spears upon himself, thereby opening a way into their ranks

Near Engelberg.
Sketch by Queen
Victoria, 29 August 1868

marked by Agnes, wife of the Emperor Albert. A heavy smell of incense pervaded the Sacristy & lower passages. We next went up a flight of stone steps to the Library, very rich in Missals, some of which were shown us. We all wrote our names in the visitors' book, I signing myself as Countess of

Engelberg Monastery visitors'
book, 29 August 1868

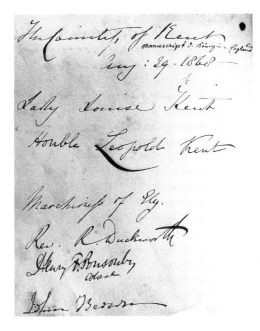

Kent & Louise & Leopold as the Lady Louise & Honble. Leopold Kent. Saw the Gallery into which open all the cells & were taken into the Principal's room, most comfortable, with a piano & violin in it, & to the large room used for ceremonies, where more embroideries were shown us. We looked into the 'Klostergarten', & then left, entering our carriages at the outer gate.

It was no mean thing for a woman to have been invited into the heart of a Roman Catholic Monastery – and the Head of the Church of England at that. The Abbot, Anselm Villiger, recorded the visit in his diary:

She came during Vespers, visited the Sacristy, the Library, the Great Hall and also desired to see a cell. She enquired about the number of monks, their way of living and daily routine etc. She was very gracious and friendly. Her retinue included a Prince, a Princess, Lord Chamberlain, Ladies-in-Waiting etc. During her excursion to Engelberg she visited only the Monastery, to the surprise of many visitors. Her bearing was very simple. It appears she had taken her midday meal in the shade of the stone on the Rüttimatt. Both she and her retinue spoke very good German. I accompanied her to the Monastery gate where a large number of visitors had gathered.

Both the Abbot and the local newspaper reported that the Queen was simply attired and not wearing a crinoline.

> *... August 29*
> *We bought some trifles & some Edelweiss, which is found near there. The horses held up badly driving down the long hill, & Benz, the coachman was nervous, having not put on properly 2 shoes, besides the break, the result being that the carriage kept twirling about, 1st one way, then the other, which frightened me very much. Instead of going to Stanzstadt we went to another picturesque village where we re-embarked & had our tea on board the steamer. It was cold & windy on the water. Got home a little before 8. –*

A quiet Sunday followed, with the Reverend Duckworth holding a service in the pension as before. The Queen turned to family matters and pondered a letter she had received from Crown Princess Victoria about her grandson, young Prince Wilhelm, the Crown Princess's son who later became Emperor of Germany from 1888 to the end of World War I. In answer the Queen wrote:

> What you told me of dear Willy interested me very much. I share your anxiety especially as regards pride and selfishness. In our days – when a Prince can only maintain his position by his character – pride is most dangerous. And then besides I do feel so strongly that we are before God all alike, and that in the twinkling of an eye, the highest may find themselves at the feet of the poorest and lowest. I have seen the noblest, most refined, high-bred feelings in the humblest and most unlearned, and this it is most necessary a Prince should feel. I am sure you, darling, who never had any pride will feel and understand this well.[106]

An afternoon drive with Louise and Arthur (with *'tea in the carriage'*[107]) gave them a fine view of Pilatus. The weather was promising well and it was decided to go up Pilatus the next day.

> *August 31*
> *A fine clear morning. – Arthur came to breakfast & at 1/2 p. 9 we drove off in 2 carriages, I with Louise & Janie E., in the sociable, Arthur & Col. Ponsonby in the next. The ponies had been sent by steamer to Alpnacht, which we drove to. The day was very pleasant & clear, but not particularly hot. The views were beautiful. Just short of the town of Alpnacht we found our ponies with 2 jaded beasts for Janie E. & Col. Ponsonby & boys to carry our luncheon & c. Started at once, Arthur walking the whole time. I rode good old 'Flora' & Louise 'Sultan'. The road, mostly dreadfully stony, loose slippery, sharp stones, very trying for both man & beast, but with the exception of the last 1/2 hour to the top,*

Queen Victoria and suite ascending Pilatus. (Oil painting by J.J. Zelger, 1868, commissioned by Queen Victoria)

not near so steep, though more tedious than the Rigi. We went steadily & slowly through beautiful woods of beech, spruce & silver fir. Châlets are sprinkled about here & there & many cows grazing with bells around their necks, which sounds so pretty. What makes the ascent less trying, is that one constantly comes to level parts, for a short distance. Stopped for a few minutes at a small 1/2 way house to get a little water. Soon after came to one of the prettiest spots possible, wild rocks tumbled about, with some grass & small 'Senn Hütten'. Many wild flowers grow there. In the woods there were quantities of cranberries & blaeberries & c. The views became more & more magnificent, as we emerged from the wooded parts. The sun having come out it was very hot, & feeling tired, besides being hungry, it was nearly 2, refused to go to the top, till we had had our luncheon. Sketched a little afterwards, & then remounted our ponies, riding up the <u>very</u> steep ascent, which was disagreeable, owing to the dreadful loose stones. In 25 minutes, however, we got to the top, where the view is most extensive & magnificent, & the air was fine & pure. We could see the following Glaciers: Blümli Alp, Ischingli, Jungfrau, Silberhorn, Moench, & Eiger, besides all the other well known nearer mountains, & the Lakes of Sarnen, Lucerne, Baldegg, Sempach &

Mauen. Our own fine Lake was beautifully seen, looking towards Fluellen. There was still one steep extreme point, called the Esel, which can only be got up to on foot, so I preferred remaining below sitting in front of the big Hotel. All, but Janie E. & Hoffmann went up & I employed my time in sketching, making some little purchases, & writing my name in the visitor's book. We had not met a soul going up, excepting 2 or 3 Senner, & the Hotel seemed quite empty. Soon after 4 we commenced our descent, I walked, not without difficulty, held by Brown's strong arm & with a good stick. Got on my pony again, where we had lunched, but the others walked on further. Passed by a spot where a cross is made on a stone & a stick placed, showing where a poor Scotch gentleman, Thomson, by name, died quite suddenly, about a week after we arrived at Lucerne, leaving a young widow at the Hotel! Rode right down to the bottom, 'Flora' going in the most perfect manner, without once making a false step. Louise walked down the greater part of the way. Stopped for about 20 minutes, to take tea, which was very welcome. We then restarted, & by this time the views became more & more glorious, the setting sun making the sky crimson & orange, while it cast that wonderful soft rosy light on the snowy peaks. Add to this the cobalt blue of the nearer wooded mountains, & the whole makes a

Queen Victoria on *Flora*
(with John Brown)

*picture of indescribable beauty. The moon rose splendidly & cast a fresh
beauty on everything, as the light faded away. It was getting rapidly
dark as we came down, which we did by 1/2p. 7. In a moment were off
in our carriages & Benz drove fast, nevertheless it was 9 before we got
back, much pleased at our successful day, which not having been so hot,
was less tiring than when we went up the Rigi. The drive home by
moonlight, reflected in the Lake was most lovely & romantic. – We had
our dinner as quickly as possible. –*

By way of contrast, Lord Stanley with his Private Secretary Sanderson had
'done' Pilatus two weeks earlier, in a manner more typical of British travellers
in those days. Here is his account:

Up at 5, light early breakfast. Started at 6, reached Hergeswyl in 40 minutes:
engaged a man and horse in case of accidents, and began the ascent. Sanderson
after walking a little way was seized with palpitations of the heart, and rode all
the rest. I walked, and was glad to find that two years of sedentary life had left
me still able to face a steep hill without discomfort. The first two hours of the
way we were among pastures and fir-woods, with fresh running streams, and
when we turned, noble views of the lakes. The last hour was passed in
mounting a steep ravine covered with loose stones, by a corkscrew path, rather
trying to wind and legs. Reached Klimserhorn hotel at 10 exactly, having been 3
hours on the way. Breakfast there, mounted the little hill behind the inn,
lounged, then on to the highest point, 40 minutes further, through a curious
cleft in the rock, where a ladder has been fixed. The height is 7300 feet, or
nearly 6000 above the lake. Noble view of Bernese Alps. Back to our hotel,
rambled slowly down, Hergeswyl at 5 P.M. and home by 6, well pleased with
our day, and very little tired. We had not above 7 hours of walking, but on
rough ground. The heat was not great on or near the top, but on coming down
again we felt it oppressive.

The ascent to the Klimserhorn is about 5400 ft. from the plain, which being
done in 3 hours gives 1800 ft. per hour, or 30 ft. per minute, or 6 inches per
second: a rather rapid rise. Taking the weight of a full-grown man at 180 lbs.,
the power used is that required to lift 90 lbs. 1 foot per second: a convenient
formula. In general I have found that 1200 ft. vertical rise per hour is fair work,
allowing for irregularities of ground.[108]

Fair work indeed, compared to twentieth-century holiday habits. Apart from being a classical scholar, Stanley also had a degree in mathematics.

The Queen, after her own day on Mt Pilatus at the end of August, was now clearly feeling the full benefit of her holiday. There was another week to go – another week of living in the close family environment which was so precious to her. The only outside pressure was coming from the Swiss guide Hofmann with his welcome suggestions of new places to discover, new views to enjoy, and she was far away from the public responsibilities that had been so intolerably burdensome. The weather was now more settled and she complained far less about the heat. There was a new culprit: dust, which the drier air sent swirling up from roads and paths, but she took this in her stride. And it was a matter of pride to her that she was getting fitter, as she noted in her Journal the day after the great Pilatus ascent.

> *September 1*
> *A very fine, very hot morning. – Breakfast out & then writing in the summer house. – Not very tired or stiff, less so than after the expedition to the Rigi. – Saw Ld. Stanley, who spoke of poor Ld. Howard de Walden's death, quite sudden, from apoplexy.*

Howard de Walden had been British Ambassador in Belgium, a country already then caught up in the power-game between France and Prussia. In addition, the King of the Belgians was Queen Victoria's cousin. So the choice of a successor to this important post would have been of immediate concern to the Queen and her Foreign Secretary. The Queen and Lord Stanley also spoke about two other matters on this occasion. Neither are mentioned in the Queen's Journal (as transcribed by Princess Beatrice before burning the original) and both were no doubt unwelcome intrusions on her holiday – especially the first, which concerned what amounted to a game of hide and seek.

This was nothing less than another chapter in the long-running drama of the Queen's Paris Gaffe. Ever since the Queen refused to return the Empress Eugénie's call on her in Paris, and particularly as the time of her return to England via Paris approached, the British Ambassador in Paris, Lord Lyons – anxious to avoid another diplomatic disaster – had been working hard to bring about a meeting between the Empress and a reluctant Queen en route back home.

All available forces were put into action. Letters passed back and forth between Paris, Lucerne and London: Lyons to Stanley, Stanley to Disraeli, Disraeli to the Queen, Biddulph to Stanley and Lyons, Stanley to Ely, Ely to Disraeli … Machiavellian skills were deployed on all sides, culminating in a pincer movement on the Queen. This was executed by Jane Ely and allies just before the Queen's ascent of Mount Pilatus. Flushed with victory, she hastened to tell Disraeli:

> I spoke to The Queen last evening, in consequence of Lord Stanley's anxiety about Paris & told her the soreness felt about the Empress's visit not having been returned & that it was much wished it should be paid on the return ... & that Ld Stanley mentions it through me, not wishing to do it officially. The Queen objected very much at first, but Princess Louise & Lady Biddulph backed me up & she was so nice about it, The Queen & said, she would go and see the Empress, but with as little state as possible ... Lord Stanley no doubt will tell you, but I thought I would send you this pleasant news, quietly. I hope nothing will prevent it now, it seems it is the German relations which have been the stumbling block & the feeling that they say, the Queen is more friendly to France, than Prussia, however all that will come right, forgive my indiscretion.[109]

It was Lord Stanley who delivered the coup de grâce during his interview with the Queen in her pension on 1 September, as recorded in his diary:

> Drove to Pension Wallis, saw the Queen (she kept me waiting nearly 2 hours), who had been up Pilatus yesterday on her pony. She was in good spirits and good temper: and consented to call on the Empress when passing through Paris: which is good as it stops the mouths of mischief-makers. Probably she feels that after passing the whole day in exercise she cannot well plead illness as an excuse for not doing the usual civilities. Ly Ely helped usefully to bring her to understand this, and Ld Lyons was anxious about it.[110]

The Queen had given in, but a small hope was left to her. Stanley immediately telegraphed to Lord Lyons, transmitting that hope: 'The Queen will call on the Empress if the Empress is in Paris when she passes through. But she hopes that neither the Emperor nor the Empress will alter on her account any arrangements they may have made.'[111] Aware that they had won the battle but perhaps not the war, Stanley also wrote to Disraeli:'Dear D., I have settled with H.M. about her return. She will visit the Empress, if the latter is in Paris when she passes through. So that is all satisfactorily arranged. Even if no meeting takes place, the offer of one is something.'[112]

So far so good, but the dénouement was yet to come.

The other subject discussed between the Queen and Lord Stanley that day was the appointment of a new Bishop – a matter of constitutional importance to the Queen as Head of the Church of England, and of political importance to Disraeli as leader of the Conservative Party marshalling its forces for the forthcoming general election.

Now, on her hill above Lucerne in Switzerland, Queen Victoria, Supreme Governor of the Church of England, looked the politician Lord Stanley in the eye and spoke like the mid-nineteenth century sovereign that she was. Stanley's diary records the scene:'She talked no politics, except that speaking of the new bishop who has to be made, she said she would have neither a ritualist, nor a strong party man of any sort, but one of moderate opinions.'[113]

Writing to Disraeli, Stanley amplified on this:

Rigi.
Watercolour by Queen Victoria, 3 September 1868

The great lady was in high spirits and good humour, and talked more freely than I had ever heard her: but not a word about politics, except about the new

bishop that will have to be appointed. On that subject she said that she did not like strong partisans, they were apt to give trouble, she would have no one who leant to the ritualistic side, but should prefer a moderate man who would not give offence. I expressed no opinion, not knowing what might have passed between you, and fearing to do more harm than good. Not a syllable about elections.[114]

Having dispatched Stanley, the Queen now reverted to holiday mode. She lunched, wrote and painted and went on a drive, *taking our tea with us. It was very dusty & hot. The moon had risen, as we drove back, reflecting itself beautifully in the Lake.*[115]

Pilatus, from the lake. Watercolour by Queen Victoria, 3 September 1868

7   Incognita – the Acid Test

It was now three and a half weeks since the Queen had arrived in Lucerne, in the full glare of international publicity and hoping against hope that she would not be mobbed, that her incognita mantle would shelter her from being importuned and that the gloomy forecasts of pessimists such as Lord Stanley would be proved wrong.

Her hopes were fulfilled. As the Queen and her retinue anxiously scanned the British press – sent out daily, with an extra set for 6 August – they were probably relieved to find that the papers were not only exercising self-discipline by not hounding her but were calling on their readers to give her a break (couched, of course, in suitably flowery nineteenth-century prose). For instance, on the Queen's first day in Switzerland *The Spectator* came out with a blistering broadside:

> The Queen … will, her subjects hope, benefit as much by her holiday as if she were the wife of any Member of Parliament. She will not benefit, however, if watched, and hunted, and criticised as her sons have lately been. The conduct of the British public, and particularly of the well-fed section of it, in this matter is utterly disgraceful to them, not only as independent citizens, but as worshippers of rank. If they must be flunkeys – and they must be, or they would cease to be British – let them show their flunkeyism by reverent regard for the Queen's wishes, and let Her Majesty enjoy Mount Pilate without a hundred opera-glasses directed on her face.

Before, during and after the journey to Switzerland, the British press followed her every move at a respectful distance, and throughout the holiday there were short factual bulletins on her comings and goings. Earlier mentions of her being fatigued gave way later to reports of improving health and spirits. Harmless enough, but the Queen would have preferred no reporting at all of her movements, except when she drafted a bulletin herself.

It was not all plain sailing during the first two weeks. A correspondent of the *Daily News* reported:

> For a day or two after her Majesty's arrival she was, I am told, too fatigued to take much exercise, and confined herself almost entirely to the grounds of the mansion, and when she was able to go beyond them she at first suffered a good

deal from the impertinent curiosity of the tourists staying here. Wherever she drove she was followed by crowds of people; and so intolerable did the nuisance become, that I am told it was on one occasion found necessary to engage beforehand, as for the Royal party, all the vehicles in Lucerne in order that the public might be deprived of any means of transport. Whether in consequence of this hint, or as the result of greater familiarity with the presence of royalty, I know not; but her Majesty is now allowed to drive about the neighbourhood without being exposed to this kind of unpleasant intrusion.

Another correspondent noted that '... we have here a number of our own country people and Americans, who may be very 'distinguished', but do not look so.' Back in July Sir Thomas Biddulph had said 'what I fear most is tourists – mostly Americans.'[116] Events seemed to bear him out, as reported in *The Court Journal* at the end of August:

The Americans are, it seems, particularly desirous of seeing the Queen, and they pester Britishers with all manner of inquiries about her Majesty, the best means of approaching her, &c. One Briton, bored with questions from a Yankee lady, put it to her how he could be expected to satisfy her curiosity when all his personal knowledge of his august Sovereign was confined to seeing her drive in the park occasionally (he spoke of the days in which the Queen went into the park), and that he knew no more of her Majesty's household arrangements than he had been able to collect from contemplating the outside of Buckingham Palace. At this the Yankee lady evidently felt that she had been talking to a fellow who was nobody; and really she had reason to regret her loss of time,seeing that in any half dozen or other Englishmen she might have found two or three at least, who, judging from the manner in which they talked, were her Majesty's most intimate friends, and were going to Lucerne on her express invitation. But, overcoming her annoyance at conversing with so humble an individual, the fair Yankee cried, 'Well! I never saw a Queen, and of all Queens I am most anxious to see Queen Victoria! Tell me, at least, how I can recognise her Majesty if I should happen to meet her out of doors.' 'If you see a lady clad simply in black, driving in an open carriage, with two young ladies with her, and another carriage following, you will probably have the Queen and the Princesses, her daughters, before you!' 'A Queen like an ordinary lady! Well, I can't realise that anyhow!'

Sir Thomas need not have worried. As it turned out, that was as far as people got. *The Lady's Own Paper* wrote reassuringly that 'the great people are not mobbed'. And even that notorious sceptic Lord Stanley had to admit that there was 'an absence of population' around the Queen.[117] This also applied to any notables who might have hoped to call on the Queen. No 'incognita-crashing' for them, although there would have been quite a parade: amongst those holidaying in Lucerne at the time were the Count of Flanders, brother of the King of the Belgians, Charlotte, the widowed Empress of Mexico (herself prudently incognita), Archduke Henry of

Austria, to say nothing of French, Austrian and Bavarian ministers and no less than three Rothschilds. Queen Victoria's incognita kept them all at bay.

As for the Swiss, the Queen made an almost universally favourable impression on them. There was the initial unpleasantness over the noise from the bowling-alley near the pension and the republican rumblings occasioned by her monopolizing all the available accommodation on the Furka. But apart from that, what particularly struck the Swiss wherever she and her suite went was the Royal visitors' 'simple apparel' and 'modest comportment'. If anything they regretted the speed at which she was in and out of the places she went to. One who brilliantly met this problem head-on and overcame it (rather too spectacularly) as the Queen passed through Basle on her way to Lucerne achieved notoriety in a local newspaper:

> ... the keeper of the buffet at the railway station charged Queen Victoria and a suite of 30 persons 700 francs for a breakfast of coffee, eggs, and cold meat, being at the rate of 23 francs a head. The Bâle people are very indignant at this extortion, but the *restaurateur* would probably justify himself as the English innkeeper did who presented George III with a bill of one guinea for a slice of bread and one egg. The King, while paying the money, observed that eggs must be very scarce in that part of the country. 'No, Your Majesty,' was the reply, 'eggs are plentiful enough, but king's visits are rare.'

Such cases will have been infrequent. The Swiss always knew how to turn an honest penny, but they were seldom as rapacious as some indignant foreign travellers made out. They gave value for money. The Lucerne steamship company from whom the *Winkelried* was chartered were at great pains to do the right thing, even disarmingly writing to the British Legation in Berne for enlightenment:

> ... we have been given orders for preparing English flags for the use of our steamers. However there have been several different opinions as to the colour & design. We don't know a better authority to apply to than Her Majesty's Embassy. Would you be kind enough to inform us if we are right to cause the Flag to be made of red stuff with the well-known cross at the left corner – or ought the whole Flag to be filled up by the cross as we found on our 'Tableau des Pavillons' under the name of Jack. You would greatly oblige us in setting us right on this point![118]

The Legation answered immediately, 'giving some account of English flags in use.'

Some of the Queen's people at Lucerne developed a pronounced taste for Swiss beer, but there was a breakdown in communications when it came to paying. Three months after the Queen's departure the British Legation received a forlorn letter from the brewer, saying he no longer knew where to turn for payment of his invoice for a prodigious amount of beer, since he had received only Fr. 114 instead of the full amount of Fr. 174. A postscript pointed out that he had considered it a matter of honour to supply the best beer of his cellar to Her Majesty at Lucerne.

Recognition for the guide: testimonial, in A. Hofmann's leather-bound book

8   The Final Week

At the beginning of September the Queen, by now well rested and invigorated by her Alpine excursions – and who knows, perhaps even fortified by best Swiss beer – was ready to make full use of her remaining days in Switzerland. She began with another outing to Engelberg – to please the children, as she put it. It was not a great success.

> *September 2*
> *... The heat of the sun was very great & the dust most oppressive. It is an unpleasant tedious <u>nervous</u> road, so rough & narrow. Brown, who is always so attentive & watchful, got out & walked near the carriage, whenever we came to particularly steep & precipitous parts.*

They took lunch under the shade of some rocks and the Queen sketched, enjoying the view of the mountains, but they found the valley *'dreary'* and so

Rowing boat on lake. Watercolour by Queen Victoria, 3 September 1868

'*shut in*' that none of them cared for it much.[119] – However, they differ from the vast majority of visitors, who always find this valley the opposite of dreary.

After spending most of the next day in the summer house by the pension, the Queen took a turn on the lake, where she thought it would be cool and refreshing on the water, and made the only visit of the holiday to a private house. This stood on a lakeside promontory called Hertenstein at the foot of the Rigi and belonged to a leading local family which was later to provide the honorary British Vice-Consul in Lucerne.

Ponsonby, writing to his wife about that evening, conveys an atmosphere of jollity that says much for the curative powers of Switzerland. The Queen was laughing heartily again.

> Tonight at dinner Jenner gave us his account of his expedition up the Rigi with Bauer.* I don't know why my remarks are supposed always to be facetious when they are not. I simply asked what the tourists thought of their relationship. He replied oh of course they thought she was Madame which created some laughter. Then he added the guide was very decided and made us give up the horses we rode up – and come down in a chair. 'What?' I asked 'Both in one chair' – Well there is nothing odd in that but everyone laughed then I turned to Mary Bids – she was purple. On the other side I tried to speak to Louise She was choking. I looked across to Jenner. He was convulsed. Of course this was too much I gave way – we all had a fou rire till the tears ran down my cheeks which set off the Queen. I never saw her laugh so much. She said afterwds it was my face. At last we got a pause when Jane to set things strait again began with 'Did you find it comfortable?' which started us off again. My laugh was at Jenner stuffing his napkin over his mouth to stop himself at Mary Bids shaking and speechless on my side, and at Bids' solemn face.[120]

The full-day excursion that followed took the Queen, Princess Louise, Jane Ely and Colonel Ponsonby south to the Brünig Pass, reached by way of a long and obviously enjoyable drive.

> *September 4*
> *The valley here is very wide & much cultivated. Next reached Sarnen, a pretty picturesque village, & the very lovely Lake of Sarnen, which is long, much reminding one of the Scotch Lochs in the West Highlands. Towering mountains rise, as one drives along the lake. Came to Sachseln,*

---

* Fräulein Bauer, Princess Beatrice's governess, large and of limited charm.

another small town, where we changed horses. By this time it had become overpoweringly hot. At Giswyl, the next small place, people offered us milk, water & fruit. The road then began to get very steep & we ascended the Kaiserstuhl, soon after which we came to Lungern, another pretty picturesque village, where many tourists & carriages were waiting. The pretty, long Lake of Lungern soon came in sight & after that commences the long Brunnig Pass, which is splendid, high bold rocks, with silver fir growing up into the rocks & along the road, which is extremely good, & was only finished 7 years ago. The Wetterhorn with its snowy peaks, suddenly burst upon us, at the top of the Kaiserstuhl. At the beginning of the Brunnig Pass 3 little girls walked by the carriage singing very prettily in parts. At 1/4 to 2 we reached the top of Pass, but had no time to go further. However from here one could see the Engelshörner, very curiously formed, peaked mountains, – the Faulhorn, the Wendelhorn, Zelgerhorn, & Willhorn, a small portion of the Rosenlaui Gletscher, the Wetterhorn & Plattenstock.

The guide Hofmann had done an excellent job of instructing the Queen in the names of the various mountains and in locating them, and she was clearly an apt pupil. It was standard practice for travellers to toss off the names of mountains at every opportunity, rather like a litany.

September 5
Breakfast out & writing in the summer house. – Settled to go to Selisberg in the afternoon. Lunched a little earlier & started afterwards in 2 carriages with our 3 children, Janie E. & Col. Ponsonby, for the steamer, taking our ponies & 2 hired horses on board with us. Steamed to Treib, where there are only a few cottages & here we landed. The road was dreadfully bad, a steep climb up a <u>paved</u> road with occasional steps, of a slipperiness not to be described. Poor dear 'Flora' went beautifully, but it made me feel very nervous. It took us 3/4 of an hour going up. At the top there are 2 Hotels, which were full of curious odd

Showing the tortuous road from Treib to Seelisberg

people, & 2 Churches. The view is fine, overlooking the Lake, & the mountains to be seen: the Frotenalp, the Nieder Ober Bauenstock, the fine Uri Rothstock, with its glacier, to which we seemed quite close, the Breitenstock, the Windgellen & above the Tell's Platte the Axenberg. We again bought some wooden things, which I always give as souvenirs, to those who accompany us. Got off & walked some way, riding again a little, but when it came to a particularly steep part, I preferred being carried in a chaise à porteur, which the men, who are daily in the habit of it, did very carefully.

This is how the Queen would have been carried down the steepest part of the Seelisberg

Writing to Princess Victoria, the Queen confided that she did not much like being carried down: '*it is a humiliating proceeding*'.[121]

… September 5
We met several ladies being carried up & much luggage on men's backs, also one poor dog carrying heavy packs. The sun set splendidly & Pilatus & the Schwytzer Mythen, were beautifully lit up in the Alpenglühen. It was late when we got down to the bottom & steamed off, as quick as we

Schwyzer Mythen. Watercolour by Queen Victoria, 5 September 1868

could. Had our tea on board, & only got home at 1/4p.8. – During dinner, the amateur singers of Lucerne serenaded us & very well. I went & thanked them afterwards, & while we were sitting gazing at the moonlit lake & landscape, they sang 2 songs with Yodeln. –

September 6
Fine, but very hot. – Breakfast out & writing till 12, when Mr. Duckworth held a short service. – Directly afterwards Louise & I made sketches of a girl from Engelberg. – Drove in the afternoon with Louise, & sketched in a field where we took our tea, a beautiful view of Pilatus. – Sitting out after dinner. –

The next morning the Queen wrote at length to Disraeli on the episcopal appointment to be made. And Jane Ely sat down to write Disraeli (at the Queen's request) a letter in which she was at pains to explain the logic behind recent dramatic developments in the Paris visit saga.

The situation had indeed been changing with bewildering speed. To begin with, there had been a Prussian outflanking manoeuvre launched soon after the Queen had agreed to visit the Empress in Paris. Jane Ely reported it immediately.

Woman in Unterwalden costume. Watercolour sketch by Queen Victoria

I am going to tell you a little secret [she wrote to Stanley on 3 September, with her punctuation letting her down even more than usual], which you must kindly keep for me as it is not even spoken of in the house. The Queen has heard from the Princess Royal of Prussia, that The Queen (Dowg)* is coming here, incognito, and the Queen intends to pay her Majesty a private visit as The Queen says she feels sure it will please and have a good effect in Prussia, I am sure it will and please them immensely. The Queen thinks it will do away with any bad effect, of the visit to Paris, I tell you this my dear Lord Stanley, because I mentioned

* The Princess Royal, i.e. Crown Princess Victoria, was referring to her aunt-in-law, the Dowager Queen Elisabeth of Prussia.

to you the other day, the Queen's dread lest what she did in Paris might create jealousy elsewhere. The Queen told me this yesterday, but told me not to mention it, in the household, as The Queen wished it kept quiet, but I feel you will like to know it and also know you will not mention it.[122]

Stanley was a man of honour. He waited a day before telling the Prime Minister. Meanwhile he confided to his diary his reaction to this cunning move from the north: *I hear from Ly Ely, privately, that the Queen, after having announced her intention to see no one at Lucerne, has now settled to receive a visit from the Queen of Prussia: that is, from the one person whose coming will be most distasteful to the French government.*[123]

Then, in his letter to Disraeli, Stanley showed that this new source of pressure on the Queen was making him see her behaviour in a new light. 'I hear on good authority that German, and especially Darmstadt influence has been at work to limit as far as possible the exchange of civilities at Paris, and that the refusal in the first instance was not the result of accident or whim, but predetermined.'[124]

There was more to tell in this letter:

All wrong again – but this time not by the Countess's fault. She agreed to call on Eugénie in Paris: now the latter objects to come up, and wishes the visit to take place at Fontainebleau – that is, in the early morning, after a night in the train, and after making a long road to get there. This the Queen will not do, and I really don't think she could be expected to do it. The original fault of the non-returned visit remains, but in the subsequent proceedings we have got ourselves in the right. The Empress will probably go off to Biarritz, and there the matter will end.[125]

So fate (with a little help from Prussia) was going to be kind to the Queen in Paris. Meanwhile, though, she had realized what she had let herself in for by agreeing so readily to the other visit (the one wished upon her by her kin in Germany), to the Dowager Queen of Prussia in Lucerne. She had first written to the Crown Princess that

I should much like to see her and think that I could manage to do it – if you would let me know the exact day of her arrival. I could manage to <u>go quite</u> privately <u>in my drive</u> to see her. Her case is really exceptional, and perhaps they would not put it into the German papers nor would I have it put into the English Court Circular.[126]

Three days later she was in a mood to call this visit off, having heard that the Dowager Queen would only arrive in Lucerne on the day of her own departure and having had time to reflect on other implications. 'As the Dwr. Queen only arrives on the 9th I cannot go & see her, & it wld be best to explain that,' she wrote to the Crown Princess. '– Indeed as I have had some trouble with the Empr. & Empss of the F. it wld be better I shld not go to see her – as it wld leak out.'[127]

A day later Prussia was on again but Paris was off.

This, then, was the state of affairs which the Queen was now asking Lady Ely to lay before the Prime Minister, who might by now have been more than somewhat confused by the zig-zag march of events. Taking a deep breath, she bravely set to, her anxiety to explain and justify rather at odds with the length of her sentences.

You will no doubt have heard ere this, that The Queen's visit to the Empress cannot take place. The Queen said she really could not stop at Fontainebleau on her way to Paris, that Her Majesty had been invited by the Grand Duke and Duchess of Baden, if the Queen changed her route, to rest for a night in a Palace belonging to them, & The Queen had declined saying she went no where. The Queen desires me to tell you, that Her Majesty has written to the Empress herself, to express all her regrets, but to say, Her Majesty had given up paying visits now, & had declined going to her own relations, but hoped at some future time, when she passed through Paris to call & see The Empress. I am sure that the Queen's letter will go far to allay any soreness that is felt. The Queen has been much troubled about it, she showed me your letter to her & said you had written so kindly & nicely. The Queen also desires me to say to you, Her Majesty had desired the Morning Post should not put in articles or notices about Her Majesty's movements, & they had promised only to insert what was sent to them by Her Majesty's orders; since the Queen has been here, they have not adhered to that promise & Her Majesty would be so much obliged to you, if you could have something done about it, to prevent the repetition of this annoyance, to the Queen. ... She is very sorry to give you so much trouble. ... The Queen always speaks of you in the kindest & nicest manner & is constantly saying how considerate you are & that you understood her.[128]

The prospect of losing Disraeli if the Conservatives were defeated in the coming election must have clouded the Queen's enjoyment of her holiday, but being a constitutional and not an absolute monarch she was conditioned to a certain degree of reticence where party politics were concerned. A more immediate anxiety, of course, was to keep her forthcoming meeting with the Prussian Queen from leaking out and putting herself and her country in the dog-house as far as the French were concerned.

She now had only three days left in Switzerland and was determined to make the most of them. Ponsonby was going around singing the praises of a little-known church he had discovered not far from Lucerne. He had written to his wife about it:

> I drove with Duckworth and P. Leopold this afternoon to my favourite little drive of Herrgotteswald. I have taken everyone there now except the Queen. It is only about 1 1/2 hours off. Thick woods, a deep ravine high hills & in front Pilate rising grandly before you. An ascent of a wooden staircase about 1000 steps or more brings you to the church. Most curious. The whole ceiling covered with crests or mottoes. Really good figures of about 20 saints etc. But the views magnificent. Pr'aps I've told you all this before. But I am always full of it – & there is nothing in the guide books about it, & the guides don't know it.[129]

Now Ponsonby talked the Queen into going to see for herself.

> *September 7*
> *The time for going away, is fast approaching. – … In the afternoon drove with Louise, Leopold & Janie E. to see a curious old Church below the Schwartzenberg, & in fact close to Pilatus, from whence the view was very fine. After we had gone a little way beyond Reuzlach we stopped & got on our ponies. Rode through one of those curious covered bridges, overlooking a ravine. Gradually the path became very steep & slippery & I got off & walked, but it was very trying, as I am a bad climber & had not tried it for 6 years. The view of Pilatus on one side & of the lake below was perfectly beautiful. Passed a sort of farm house, below which stands the curious old Church Herrgotteswald. We walked down to &*

From Herrgotteswald.
Sketch by Princess Louise,
7 September 1868

Drawing by Queen Victoria, 7 September 1868. She captioned it: '*Ach geben Sie mir ein kleines boutönchen oder so etwas*' (Spare a copper, lady).
Since her bereavement, the Queen had hardly sketched people, but only places. Here was a sign that she was recovering some of her old verve

into it. Then looked about for a place to take our tea, & found one just above a small inn. Here Louise & I afterwards sketched a little. The Alpenglühen was again very lovely but very quickly over. Began our descent, Brown helping me & holding me up, else I should have never succeeded in getting down over that bad ground, my knees being very weak & rheumatic. When we came to the bend, remounted my pony & rode on to where the carriage was waiting. It was fast getting dark, & we made Benz drive quickly home. – Sitting out after dinner. –

September 8
The sun very hot. – Breakfast out & sitting writing in that nice summer house. – Settled to go out early, alas! for the last time, for it is sad to be leaving such beautiful scenery, though I shall be glad to go to my own dear Highland home.

Two days earlier the Queen had already written to Princess Victoria in similar vein: 'I shall remain the 12th and 13th at Windsor & start on the night of the 14th for dear Balmoral where I shall be glad to be again on account of the air & the quiet & the dear people whom one misses shockingly here.'[130]

Yet it almost looks as if in spite of this the Queen was finding it difficult to tear herself away from Switzerland. This excursion was to be the last, but in the event she took two more 'last' drives the day after, right up to her departure in the evening. Gone were all those earlier pleas of exhaustion and malaise that had so bedevilled the earlier part of her holiday.

... September 8
Started after luncheon with Baby, Janie E. & Mary B. for the steamer,

steaming up to Brunnen. It all looked so beautiful, that the thought of no longer seeing that glorious scenery made one quite sad. We landed and got into our carriage, which we had brought with us. It was a holiday, many of the peasant women being out in their smart costumes. Drove a short way along the Axenstrasse and then turned up a totally new road, safe & good, though very steep. It was beautiful, under splendid rocks & through fine fir trees, & gradually the most glorious view of the Lake & mountains opened out. Came to the small village of Marschach, close under the highest points of the Fronnalp, with Châlets, trees & valleys, one of the finest spots we have yet been to. It took us an hour to get up to the very top of this road, where a large Hotel is being built, & where the air is beautiful. Got out for a moment to gaze at the magnificent view, which was perfectly clear, the sun setting over Pilatus, but unfortunately we could not wait to see it actually go down, as darkness comes on so quickly, without hardly any twilight. Got down easily & at once got on board the steamer & steamed off, taking our tea, as we went. It was quite dark by the time we got back, though very starlight, & Lucerne looked extremely pretty lit up. – Some singers again came to serenade us whilst we were at dinner.

Now came the day of departure.

September 9
Breakfast out & then took a lovely drive with Louise, our <u>last</u>, along the beautiful lake, through the town, & back by the Kreuzbuche. So glad to get the last & most beautiful view of all the mountains, in the soft vapoury morning light, all so clear. – Took another little drive in the afternoon & when I came back gave Hoffmann a pin with my cypher & Bentz also a pin, he making me a speech of thanks, also for taking his daughter Elise or Lisele to England as housemaid. She has been acting as such here & was good & active. – At 1/4 to 7 we left with <u>real</u> regret the dear comfortable, cheerful little home of Pension Wallis, where we had spent quiet & very pleasant days, & where all had lived like a family together. Drove with our 3 Children down to the station & waited a few moments in the waiting room, where I saw the Dowager Queen of Prussia whom I had not seen for 23 years, when all was bright & happy for us both & our dear Husbands were well, & my beloved one so young! They were both taken the same year! The Queen is grown very old but I should have known her again, & she was most kind. She had expressed such a wish to see me, that she had offered, though only just arrived at Lucerne, to come up to see me this afternoon, but the house was in too great a state of confusion to allow of that.

A railway station was – to put it mildly – not quite the place for such a meeting. The Queen knew it and was at pains to explain it away to the Crown Princess:

> She only arrived in the afternoon but <u>most</u> kindly shewed so much wish to see me – that she offered to come up, or to meet me at the Station, & as our little Home with <u>all</u> the packages carrying out by the <u>only door,</u> was totally <u>unfit</u> for her to come to – I agreed to the latter. She was so very kind & herzlich that I was much touched by it.[131]

> *... September 9*
> *I only remained about 10 minutes talking, while everything was being got ready, & then entered the train, taking leave of good Hoffmann from the window of the saloon.*

In France – En Route Back Home

It was Emperor Napoleon III's saloon train, the same as on the outward journey, that was now rattling its way towards Paris on the way back. But whereas then, in early August, the Queen had not been able to sleep at all, now she *'got a good deal of sleep during the night'*,[132] and Lady Ely wrote to Disraeli from the British Embassy, where they spent the day, that the Queen 'seems ... not in the least tired after her journey'.[133]

But the heat of the city, and probably the prospect of having to return to everyday life, gave her a headache, which was not made better by her going on a sentimental journey to the Palace of St Cloud where she had stayed on her triumphal visit in 1855.

> *September 10*
> *At 1/2 p. 5, after taking tea, drove out in Ld. Lyons' carriage, with him, Louise & Janie E., the 2 Children with Frl. Bauer & Col. Ponsonby, following in another carriage. We went through the Champs Elysées, past the Arc de Triomphe, which I recognised well, through the Bois de Boulogne, which looked dull & dreary at this time of year, – through the small town of Boulogne, – over the bridge to St. Cloud, which I much wished to look at again, in remembrance of the happy days spent there with my dearest Albert in 55. Drove into the quadrangle, where we stopped for a moment at the door, but being tired, & having little time I did not get out. Besides, the idea of seeing those rooms again, now uninhabited & triste, would have been too painful for me. But I*

recognised all & was able to look through the open door at the great
Staircase, where there is now a picture, representing our arrival in 55.
Drove round the garden, which looked bright, but the fine avenues &
silent house made a very dreary & sad impression upon me. It was dull,
hazy & oppressive.

Back at the Embassy, she complained that

a Café Chantant, at the end of the garden, outside, made such a noise
that I could get no rest. Such a contrast, to the quiet little house at
Lucerne.- Dined alone with Louise. The room opened on to the garden,
& the fountain made it pleasant & look cool. Started at 10 for
Cherbourg, Ld. Lyons accompanying us to the station.[134]

A day in Paris had left the Queen's incognita distinctly frayed at the edges.
In the afternoon her every move – even the way she looked through the
windows of St Cloud during her visit there – had been closely followed by
the press, albeit with benevolent eyes. *Galignani's Messenger* wrote:

Her Majesty was so greatly affected that she could not enter the apartments,
and remained for some time at the entrance. It was merely through the
windows that the Royal visitor cast a look full of tenderness on those rooms
which she had occupied so happily in company with the Prince Consort during
their visit to Paris. The Queen walked in the gardens, but still, from time to
time, glanced at the interior.

Nothing highlights the contrast between the simplicity of Switzerland and
the pomp of Paris better than the spectacular arrangements for her departure,
cordial though they were. Her departure in the evening as duly reported in
La Presse and relayed later in *The Times*,[135] could almost have passed for the
end of a full-blown State Visit; only the flowers and the Imperial Family were
missing.

The St. Lazare station changed its physiognomy during two hours of Thursday
evening. The arrival quays of the Normandie Line were enlarged and carpeted,
as was also the great waiting room that communicates with the court of exit.
The rooms and the line were brilliantly lighted up. A special train, composed of
the Emperor's saloon carriage and of ten first-class carriages with luggage vans,
kept its steam up in the middle of the line. The company's chief officers, in
black coats and white cravats, were there collected, the Secretary-General
replacing the director, who is away from Paris. Those officials who were to go
on duty with the train were all in full dress, as was also Dr. Bergier, the
company's chief physician, who took his seat in a carriage with his instruments
and medicaments. At half-past 9 the persons composing the suite of the Queen
of England began to occupy the places assigned to them by the majordomo.
Soon afterwards a closed landau and pair brought her Britannic Majesty, her

two daughters and her son Leopold to the entrance of the large waiting room. The Ambassador's carriage followed. The Queen, preceded by a chamberlain of her Court, advanced first towards the imperial train, surrounded by her family; the English Ambassador followed, bareheaded. There was profound silence; all the persons who had been admitted into the station took off their hats. The Queen wore a black dress and a black lace bonnet. Everybody remarked the simplicity of her attire and the modesty of her attitude. Out of respect for the Queen's mourning and her incognita, the railway administration had not put flowers in the station as is generally done at the departure of Sovereigns. The Queen got into the carriage first, without any assistance. The two young Princesses and the Prince followed, and the chamberlain shut the door. Lord Lyons stood at the door of the waggon, hat in hand, on the side on which his Sovereign was seated. The Princess Louise, who was opposite to the Queen, exchanged a few words with the Ambassador. When the whistle sounded for the departure, the august traveller waved her hand to Lord Lyons, who bowed low, and the train started at full steam on the line for Cherbourg. ... On Friday morning at 6.30, the train reached the military port of Cherbourg, where the Queen left the railway for a yacht, which was like leaving one apartment for another, the arrangements there being admirably adapted for the transition.

The Queen's day in Paris had seen the dénouement of the long drawn-out drama that had developed out of her famous refusal to return Empress Eugénie's call when she first passed through Paris in August. After all those weeks of recrimination, cajoling and manoeuvring, the Queen – having finally been cornered into agreeing to return the call on her way back – now managed to turn the tables on her tormentors and avoid making the call after all. With great tactical skill she had lulled the opposition into a false sense of security when outnumbered at Lucerne, bided her time and was then saved from an unexpected quarter: the Empress for various reasons found herself unable to be in Paris on the day the Queen was there. The whole business ended with an exchange of friendly messages. Although Queen Victoria had risked a worsening of Anglo-French relations by meeting the Dowager Queen of Prussia in Lucerne at the last moment, she had managed to keep this meeting from leaking out. For the Queen it was victory on all fronts: she had done the decent thing by her German relatives, she was discreetly fostering diplomatic relations with Prussia without at the same time jeopardizing those with France and she was off the hook in Paris, spared having to make a formal visit.

So honour was in the end satisfied and the Queen set sail for England not only refreshed by her month in Switzerland but victorious in her dealings with her Ministers and diplomats.

On 11 September 1868 *The Times* had another leading article (to match that of 7 August) to celebrate the Queen's return to her realm and round off her stay in Switzerland.

LONDON, FRIDAY, SEPTEMBER 11, 1868

The stream of returning tourists has this year a splendid addition. Queen VICTORIA has had the enterprise and the good sense to see what every one of her subjects sees if he can, and has accomplished a few of the most familiar, most accessible, and, it may be added, most beautiful objects in Switzerland. In so doing she has put an end to one reflection which rises to everybody's lips in the grandest spots of a progress through that country. It is a thought of pity for Royalty that, whatever it may see in palaces, parks, and Scotch Highlands, it cannot see Switzerland. The clerk or the curate scrapes up his 50£ and forgets his cares in Switzerland; the newly married couple, the master of a small competency, the father of the daughters to be brought out in the world, the elderly folk released from ties, and the solitary cast on the world, all meet there, and are in heaven for a time. Small people become great people, and great people small, once on their legs, or on mountain horses, or asking admission to crowded hotels a good mile above the clouds, or seeking a place at the dinner-table, or inquiring for a guide. There is no such happiness in this sublunary sphere – indeed, it is not felt to be sublunary, and in that rarefied atmosphere even extortions, mistakes, and long bills are soon forgotten. The struggle to rise, which takes a lifetime in England, and is not there achieved without many downfalls, takes a few hours, and by noon, if you are early enough, the world lies below your feet. Thence, after a brief rest, an easy descent to dinner and bed. Tomorrow you resume. Every day the traveller sees as many of his fair, intelligent, or well-to-do compatriots as he is likely to see in a twelvemonth in a country seat or a country town. Learning is there an involuntary process and memory indelible. It is impossible not to notice and to remember. The stream of life is human, and therefore with the usual well-known drawbacks of humanity, but it is a little disguised. It is the world in a grand picnic, mankind glorified in a mountain ballet. Nature somewhat diminishes the scale of life, and tones down even the strong features of the Great Briton. But how could we subsist so many centuries without Switzerland? This mitigation of our sad insular lot was only discovered, one may say, about fifty years ago; but since that it has become a necessity. The SOVEREIGN was the only one in the realm denied the common joy. There are those who affirm, believe, and certainly feel that the mountains of Scotland, not to say of Wales and of the Lakes, are superior to those of Switzerland in beauty of form and colour; that they excel in the shades of the foliage and in the lights of the atmosphere; that the air of a Scotch valley is purer than that of a Swiss. But, nevertheless, even with that horrid sea to cross and recross, and with a thousand miles to be done between this and the Alps, costing 25£ a head the move to and fro, our people still turn their steps to Switzerland with an instinct as common and irresistible as that which directs a shoal of herrings or half the birds of this island in their annual migrations.

The conditions of Royalty have prevented what is called a tour, and have confined HER MAJESTY to a few points within reach of Lucerne. But the selection has been judicious, and the QUEEN has been enabled to see some things that everybody has seen, some things that very few have seen, and fair specimens of every kind of Swiss scenery. Everybody knows the quaint mediaeval city of Lucerne, its marvellous and almost too scenic combination of lakes, and the Righi, which is pretty nearly all Switzerland and a good deal more at one view, the beautiful ascent of the St. Gothard road, the lofty desolation of the Furka Pass, the huge glaciers of the Rhone, and the innumerable objects comprised in these titles. But very few have visited Engelberg and the ascents of the Tittlis, said to have no equal in beauty. Very few comparatively go up Pilatus, though a much grander mountain than the Righi, and commanding, if not so extensive a view, yet one more sublime and purely Alpine than that from the Righi Culm. Lucerne is the only point where so many various objects of interest are within easy reach, and where life would be very tolerable even if the weather should prevent mountaineering. The loyal regret, or the disloyal self-gratulation, will still return at a few other points of that charmed region. There are Grindelwald and Chamounix, the upper end of the Lake of Geneva, the Gemmi, the Grimsel, Zermatt, and the eastern mountains and valleys of Switzerland, where the most inveterate tourists are now finding grander and more picturesque scenery than any they saw before. There is the one view of Mont Blanc from the summit of the old diligence road from Dôle, whence the mountain, fifty miles off, is seen in the skies, and the intervening Lake of Geneva far below one's feet. But it is necessary to tear one's self away from the well-remembered scenes. The QUEEN is still young, happily strong, and with sufficient enterprise. She may return to Switzerland another year. Her subjects, who feel an intense and inexhaustible curiosity to know or imagine how anything strikes the eye of Royalty, will amuse themselves for some time in speculating whether Scotland holds her own against Switzerland, whether outline and colour tell against bulk, or whether eternal snow has the same fascination for Sovereigns as for citizens. We believe it to be almost everybody's experience that the great upper land of Europe, midway between nations and the sky, and the very paradise whence spring north, south, and east the three great rivers of the continent, is a new creation, and brings a new nature, if it may be said, to every mind at all open to new impressions. It is a return to youth; a new start in life and feeling, a softening of the past, a brightening of the future, and the opening of fresh springs of feeling and of thought.

Well, HER MAJESTY has had this rare fortune for Sovereigns, so common to even the "lower middle" class of her drudging and generally stay-at-home subjects. We confess ourselves well pleased that her circle should be widened, and that she should see more than is visible in a periodical oscillation between Osborne and Balmoral. Anything to interrupt an inveterate habit and break the spell of sorrowful and saddening recollections. Why else were these marvels of creation given us, these glimpses of a new heaven and a new earth! There are few, if any, who do not require, at least once in their lives, to have the train of thought turned by some sweet violence into a more practical and salutary direction. Since new duties cannot be made, or new persons started into existence, new scenes are the appointed method, and no balm is more soothing or effective. Often and often are returning tourists found to aver they do not come home rested in body, or certainly better in physical health; but that in the fund of new impressions and the passing away of old troubles they feel the certainty of returning health and strength and a new lease of vitality. Having thrown herself, with a laudable effort, into the great European stream of tourists, even for a few days, the QUEEN will feel herself once more in the living, moving world. There, in the presence of a more than human majesty, and in a court higher than that of any earthly realm, she has seen a gathering of all nations assembled to offer at least the secret service of their souls. It is an occasion and a spectacle to open the heart long locked in private contemplation, to revive the sympathies, and to reduce to its due proportion everything that is exaggerated and engrossing. The QUEEN now shares with her subjects many of the grandest recollections that nature can supply, and that can at once elevate and bring into unison the souls of all that have them. In this way she is more at home with us, and a sharer of thoughts and pleasures almost domestic in their character. She has felt that touch of Alpine nature which makes us all kin. The beauties of Switzerland are household words in this country, and at every fireside where they are known and remembered the Royal tourist will now be, in thought, a fellow-traveller and self-invited guest.

PART

Three

9 Aftermath

The Queen was clearly the better for this Swiss interlude – perhaps more than she realized, or indeed admitted to herself. True, it had not wrought a miracle cure for her nerves or for her underlying state of mind; some years were to elapse before she finally found the strength and inner balance that enabled her to crown her long reign with thirty years of glory. Yet this first break with her recent past did initiate a change.

She was now finally emerging from the depths of her mourning. She had had the complete change and quiet she had been seeking for so long, as well as the stimulus of excursions to places far and wide. She had not needed to be at odds with the outside world – indeed there had been no conceivable cause (except, for a few days, the weather). Affairs of state had been routine, hardly anything contentious, apart from ecclesiastic appointments and of course the great Paris visit fracas. She had ventured into a totally new environment where in a close family circle she could be herself, untrammelled by Court ritual or public pressure. Whether or not the seeds of her later reconciliation to her fate were sown during these both peaceful and stimulating weeks, they will have given her a gentle kick-start for a new phase in her life. Henceforth her desolation was less settled than it had been.

Meanwhile, it was back to everyday life. Once she stepped ashore at Portsmouth on 11 September after crossing the Channel, the Countess of Kent became the Queen of England again. A brief stay at Windsor plunged her back into the thick of public affairs. On arrival she found a letter from Disraeli, the grandiloquent flourish with which it begins barely concealing his anxiety to get the Queen back to business as usual: 'He begs permission to offer his humble congratulations to Yr. Majesty on Yr. Majesty's return to Yr. Majesty's dominions, & trusts, & believes, that the visit to Lucerne will have given tone both to the spirit, & the frame, of Yr. Majesty, & will always be remembered with salutary gratification.'[136] Disraeli then 'proposes to avail himself of Yr. Majesty's most gracious permission to be in audience of Yr. Majesty on Sunday next, at three o'clock, as there are matters of great moment to be submitted to Yr. Majesty & the Council Day wd. be scarcely convenient for that purpose.'[137]

These were matters he had not wanted to bother the Queen with at Lucerne, particularly the politically sensitive appointment of a new Bishop of Peterborough. Being a past master in the art of combining flattery with cajolery, he had taken the precaution of broaching the subject in a letter to the Queen just after she had returned to Lucerne from her stay on the Furka pass:

> Mr. Disraeli with his humble duty to your Majesty ... He is sincerely gratified, that the expedition to the Furca was successful. It is a great thing to have seen the glacier of the Rhone; greater to have walked upon it. This visit alone would repay your Majesty for much exertion and some suffering. When these are passed and forgotten, the recollection of beautiful and striking scenery remains; and adds to the aggregate of those pleasing memories, that make life interesting ... Since Mr. Disraeli wrote last to your Majesty, a long impending vacancy in the Episcopal Bench has occurred. There is no necessity to precipitate the appointment, and the final decision can await your Majesty's return ... On the nomination to the see of Peterborough in the present temper of the country, much depends ...[138]

Now at Windsor, the very next day after this private audience with Disraeli, the Queen held a Council at which it was decided to prorogue Parliament further until 26 November. The Queen was in the thick of formality again and the Court Circular for 14 September reflected it:

> The United States' Minister arrived at the Castle this afternoon, and was introduced to Her Majesty by Lord Stanley, Secretary of State for Foreign Affairs, and presented his credentials.
>
> Her Majesty held a Council this afternoon at 3 o'clock, at which were present the Duke of Marlborough, the Right Hon. Benjamin Disraeli, the Earl of Devon, Lord Stanley, and the Judge-Advocate-General.
>
> Previous to the Council the Duke of Marlborough and the Judge-Advocate-General had audiences of Her Majesty.
>
> Mr. Helps was Clerk of the Council.
>
> Viscount Bridport and Colonel Du Plat, Equerries in Waiting, were in attendance.
>
> The Queen, accompanied by Princess Louise, Prince Leopold, and Princess Beatrice, left the Castle this evening at a quarter before 7 o'clock for Balmoral.

The journey north – with the immensely long Royal train occupied by a powerful contingent of the Royal Household – was a far cry indeed from the simple style the Queen had been keeping in Switzerland. It was reported in *The Times* in meticulous detail.

Her Majesty, on quitting the Castle, drove to the Windsor station of the Great Western Railway, where Prince and Princess Christian of Schleswig-Holstein and Prince Christian Victor had arrived. The public having, by the courtesy of the railway authorities, been admitted to the terminus, the platform was consequently thronged by a large assemblage of spectators, all of whom were attracted by the prospect of seeing the Queen leave for Scotland. Many arrived at the station early and remained a considerable time before the hour fixed for the Royal departure. There they passed the time by inspecting the special train with its handsome saloons fitted with sleeping appliances. The Royal train numbering some 14 carriages, had been despatched from the Euston station of the London and North-Western Railway under the care of Mr Bore, the superintendant of the carriage department, and reached Windsor shortly after 2 o'clock. Her Majesty and the Royal family on alighting at the Windsor station were received by the principal officers of the Great Western and London and North-Western Railways, and the illustrious travellers at once took their seats in the saloons. Her Majesty and Princess Louise occupied the Royal saloon, which was placed in about the centre of the train and was the seventh vehicle from the engine. Prince and Princess Christian, with Prince Christian Victor and the nurse, sat in a double saloon in front of the Queen, between which and that occupied by their Royal Highnesses was another double saloon, containing the Queen's personal servants and the dressers. Behind Her Majesty's saloon was one with her Royal Highness Princess Beatrice, governess, and maid, while the next to that contained Prince Leopold and his attendants. Sir T.M. Biddulph and Lord Bridport had the next saloon, the directors and Prince Christian's attendants riding in the adjoining carriages. The rear of the train was brought up by the Queen's fourgon and a break van. The rest of the carriages in front of the Royal saloons were allotted to Her Majesty's dressers, pages, and upper servants. The length of the Royal train was 401 ft., not including the engine, and the Queen's saloon and the other carriages were fitted throughout with Mr Martin's system of electrical communication between passengers and guards. The Royal train quitted the Windsor station at 6.50 p.m., under the care of Mr Tyrrell, the Superintendant of the Great Western line, Her Majesty's route being by way of Reading and Didcot to Oxford, where the train arrived at 8.6 p.m. A stay of 5 minutes was made here and at 8.11 the trip was resumed.[139]

And so on, right up to the Highlands, all stopping places with times reached and mileages (even fractions of a mile) being proudly set forth. Balmoral was reached at 2 p.m. the following afternoon.

During the Queen's autumn residence there, troubles both public and private once again beset her. There were Church appointments still to be made, with a government in pre-election mood looking at the political leanings of the candidates more than suited the Queen. There was the increasingly fearsome prospect of a General Election – not only the first since the Second Reform Bill of 1867, but one which might well sweep the Conservatives from office and her congenial Prime Minister Disraeli into the political wilderness, to be replaced by the far from congenial Gladstone. And there was all-round trepidation at the implications of Prince Alfred's determination to marry a Russian (or Greek as it was then called) Orthodox Princess – and the daughter of the Czar, Alexander II at that. Prince Alfred had in his way been a problem son before. Now he had come up with something that was not only a personal headache for the Queen, but a constitutional one for the government.

This had already been the subject of confidential correspondence during the Queen's stay in Switzerland. Sir Thomas Biddulph had written to Disraeli in early September: 'The Duke of Edinburgh, as is usually the

Disraeli as a fox making up to Queen Victoria, with Gladstone sharpening his knife in the portrait behind. Cartoon by Richard Doyle

case with young men in love, presses the Queen for an immediate answer.' There was apparently an early opportunity for the Czar and the Czarina to be asked whether Prince Alfred might become their daughter's suitor. The Queen wanted the government's opinion before letting this happen. 'It is certain,' Biddulph continued, 'that there is little choice of bride for the young Princes, and the Duke appears to have picked out this young lady for himself. If he could settle himself it would no doubt be a great point gained.'[140] This was a covering letter for a confidential memo written on behalf of the Queen.

The Queen has desired me to write to you very confidentially on a subject of great interest to Her Majesty, and of considerable political importance....

Her Majesty has long wished that the Duke of Edinburgh might make a suitable marriage, but up to this time H.R.H. has shewn no disposition to form any allegiance. Within however the last few weeks, he has had the opportunity of meeting the Emperor of Russia and his family at Darmstadt. It appears both the Emperor & Empress have treated him with marked kinship, and the acquaintance he has made with their only daughter, the Grand Duchess Marie, has produced such an impression on his mind, that he asks the Queen's leave, before going abroad on his cruize, to request the Emperor & Empress to allow him to renew his acquaintance with their daughter on his return, and in short at that time to become a suitor for her hand. I should observe that the Grand

Duchess Marie is at present under 15 years of age, and that therefore some time must elapse before, under any circumstances, a marriage could take place, but the Duke fears that during his absence, should he leave without giving any intimation of his intentions, some other arrangement might be made.

The account which the Queen hears of the personal qualifications of the young Princess are very favourable, and on this score, Her Majesty has no reason whatever to object, but the question on which Her Majesty desires your opinion is whether the fact of the Grand Duchess belonging to the Greek Church would legally or politically present an insurmountable obstacle.[141]

This request stuck in the throat of the government, who saw various obstacles and put them to the Queen. As late as 5 October the Lord Chancellor expressed his concern that at this crisis time for the government a political act such as this should be taken by the Cabinet. 'English feeling is on such matters highly sensitive & highly uncertain. A section of our Church wd probably hail the alliance as a means of promoting the union of Churches which they have in view: & just in the same proportion it wd become unpalatable to another section.' In the end (in 1874) Prince Alfred married his chosen one, but only after a good deal more political and ecclesiastical agonizing.

As if the Queen had not had her fill of wrangling with Disraeli over Church appointments, now – quite unexpectedly – none other than the Archbishop of Canterbury died, which plunged the Queen yet again into a trial of wills concerning the nomination of his successor. She stuck to her guns and got her candidate through.

Foreign affairs also gave the Queen cause for concern soon after her return from Switzerland – not only as a mother with children in Germany, but as Queen of a country whose maxim of non-interference in Continental affairs was under growing strain. Belgium was feeling threatened and asked for a British guarantee of help if it was attacked by France. The Foreign Secretary, Lord Stanley, thought this should not be given. The Queen could not overrule this political position, but she had her own recipe and at the end of September instructed General Grey to convey it to Disraeli:

I have written by her command to the King of the Belgians stating Stanley's reasons for thinking such interference as the King asks for, would be inexpedient at the present moment at all events.

But Her Majesty does not think the Belgian govt. can be blamed for feeling suspicious of French designs. – A powerful party amongst French official men have never concealed their wish to effect the annexation of Belgium – and we cannot forget the readiness which Bismarck expressed, at one time at all events to assist that wish.

It was to prevent the danger of a combination between France and Prussia to effect an object which, if attained, would be so fatally injurious to English Interests, that the Queen has always urged the expediency of making it clearly understood both at Paris and Berlin that England would never stand quietly by, & see the Independence of Belgium attacked. – She did not wish any official diplomatic action to be taken in the matter. – But there are always ways of letting a determination be known which are equally effective.[142]

The General Election in mid-November brought the expected swing in favour of the Liberals, who had a majority of about 120. The Queen recorded in her Journal on 23 November that the defeated Disraeli asked her '... *what did I wish them to do? Whatever he thought was the best, I answered.*[143]

Normal parliamentary practice would have been for the Prime Minister and his Cabinet to be ejected from office on the first meeting of the new Parliament. But in view of this decisive result, Disraeli created a precedent and resigned almost at once.

The Queen now had the – for her – unhappy task of sending for Gladstone and charging him to form a Cabinet. This brought with it the appalling prospect of having to deal with some of the people he might choose.

... she owns she is haunted by the fear of want of consideration from the new ones [she wrote to General Grey on 23 November]. She feels very depressed at the trials before her, but she will meet all except having people who are insolent and rude to her. She has only heard this evening from Princess Mary how insolent & bitter & even impertinent Lord Clarendon is. The Queen will not have him; she could not stand it. Another who the Queen would wish should not be brought in close contact with her & for whom she has a great personal aversion, for she knows him to be very sarcastic & unkind, is Mr Lowe. He must not be a Secretary of State. Anything short of this. Now tho' Mr Bright is very violent he has always shown the kindest feeling for the Queen & publicly on 2 occasions spoken very feelingly when the world spoke unfeelingly & ungently. The Queen is sure that Lord Halifax can do a great deal.[144]

Once the new Cabinet had been appointed, the great hand-kissing ceremony had to be got through. With Liberal zeal they all wanted to come at once. The Queen appealed emotionally to General Grey for mercy:

The Queen is terrified at the amount of people (from a mistaken idea of convenience) who are coming to-day, nothing tires the Queen more than that.

'The new ones' – the
Gladstone Cabinet of
1868

'The new ones' – the Gladstone Cabinet of 1868

Rather <u>several</u> days than <u>one long one</u>. It is not the least necessary to bring everything before the Queen goes to Osborne. The Officers of State could kiss hands on <u>Saturday</u> without any Council & the Queen could <u>easily</u> have a Council on the 21st or 22nd at Osborne for <u>any</u> other appointments which require it, or to receive any other people who had to receive <u>white</u> Wands. The Queen dreads today's work <u>very</u> much. <u>Quite</u> alone; not <u>one</u> of her Sons even by her side! General Grey will feel for her. Time does not make this <u>less painful</u>.[145]

The painfulness was to plague the Queen for some years yet. It occasioned even more serious Parliamentary and press criticism than in 1868 and led not only to renewed talk of abdication, but to republican sentiments being expressed in the House of Commons. These ceased after 1872 as the country rallied in support of the monarchy and as the Queen came to terms with her condition and the painfulness faded.

The Queen found it difficult to warm to Gladstone. Almost a year after he became Prime Minister she commented tersely to Princess Victoria: 'I cannot find him very agreeable. He talks so very much. He looks dreadfully ill.'

So Queen Victoria's holiday in Switzerland was only an interlude. But without this respite, an eventful and anxious year might have become an intolerable one for her, with dramatic consequences.

As for the Queen's own health, even her now firmer, clearer handwriting showed that her physical condition and state of mind had certainly taken a

Once a Week.]   'June 6, 1868.

THE RIGHT HON. W. E. GLADSTONE.

turn for the better as a result of her stay in Lucerne – although, as usual, the Queen was the last to admit that Switzerland had done her nerves good. In some of her references to Switzerland there are words such as 'relaxing'[146] and 'southern climate'[147]; that difficult mid-August week – without bracing air – had definitely left its mark.

But so had the more positive aspects of her stay. Towards the end of it she had told Lord Stanley that she was much pleased with Switzerland and was contemplating coming again another year.[148] And on the journey back to England she wrote to Princess Victoria:'I am sorry that our pleasant quiet visit to that splendid country Switzerland is over – which was so very successful – without one single contretemps and without one single entirely bad day! And yet I am glad to go home. We were never kept in once.'[149]

Hardly had she arrived at Balmoral a few days later than the Queen was complaining about the weather they were having in Scotland – a belated tribute to the Swiss weather, showing that she remembered more than the Föhn and its ravages: *A dull, raw, chilly day, rather a trying contrast after the great heat, – & cloudless sky we had so long.*[150]

Next day she thought of Switzerland again: ... *drive in the Balloch Bhui ... No sun shone, but the country looked fine, wild and peculiar, when one does not try to compare it with the immense height of the Swiss mountains, or the marvellous forms of that ideal country.*[151]

In Lucerne the Queen had commissioned paintings from the well-known Swiss landscape artist J.J. Zelger, to whom she had been recommended by the German artist F.X. Winterhalter, portraitist of royalty. Two are reproduced on pp. 67 & 109. Of the six large oil paintings (at Sfrs. 1,000 each) and two watercolours (at Sfrs. 100), no less than three oils were to depict the view from the Pension Wallis – in the morning, at noon and in the evening. When the pictures arrived in England (in good time for Christmas) the Queen returned one of them because she found the sky 'so unfriendly'.[152] An amended painting was accordingly sent to the Queen, to her full satisfaction.

In the months and years to come, as she travelled around her realm and other countries, Queen Victoria was to note down many a resemblance or

contrast to what she was seeing and what she vividly remembered of her weeks in Switzerland – a lake here, a valley or a mountain contour there. Recording a trip in Scotland a year after her Swiss visit, she noted in her Journal that *we at once got into our celebrated sociable, which has been to the top of the Furca in Switzerland.*[153] In fact, she had an ever-present reminder of Switzerland engraved on a plaque and placed on the back of the box, so that facing her as she sat in the sociable driving around in the Highlands she could see the names of some of the Swiss places to which she had been in it. Nor did she fail to add a footnote to a Journal entry about riding her pony Sultan: *I rode him up to the top of the Righi (nr Lucerne) … in 1868.*[154]

And in 1879, when staying in Italy at Baveno on Lake Maggiore (the northern shores of which are in Switzerland), she rounded off an account of a boat trip by writing in her Journal: *We had a delightful expedition, which reminded me of our pleasant Swiss excursions, & I only wish I had more such.*[155]

Queen Victoria never returned to Switzerland, although she twice passed through by train on her way from France to Germany (in 1885 and 1890). Both occasions were duly recorded in her Journal.

Locarno, as the Queen
would have seen it on
her last excursion on
Lago Maggiore

1885

April 22

… Our first stop was at Bellegarde, on the Swiss frontier, & then on to Geneva, before reaching which we suddenly saw Mont Blanc, quite without a cloud, rising above the town & the other mountains in its spotless whiteness. Emily Peel* with her son & 3 younger daughters was at the station, & they gave me beautiful nosegays. Directly after leaving Geneva, we came upon the Lake, which is very broad & almost like the Solent. The shores at this end, are very flat, but we soon saw Mont Blanc again, this giant, with its surrounding peaks. The afternoon was brilliantly fine, & frightfully hot. Made a short stop at Nyon, & also at Lausanne. All the fruit & chestnut trees were covered with blossom, which had a lovely effect with the snow mountains in the background. By degrees the light faded away & the mountains stood boldly out against the crimson sky. It was a glorious sight. I do so admire the beauties of Switzerland, & was so glad to get this glimpse of it again after 17 years. It was quite dark when we got to Fribourg, where we waited about 2 hours, & had dinner. It had grown a little cooler, which was a great relief.

Five years later to the day Queen Victoria was once more on her way through Switzerland on the same route, again without setting foot on Swiss soil. But this time she was given a rousing reception at Lausanne.

1890

April 22

… By the time we reached Geneva it was raining heavily. Mr. Barton & a Deputation of the English were at the station, & presented me with an address, & Ly.Emily & her daughter Mrs. Barton (my godchild) gave us beautiful flowers. After leaving we took some tea. Alas! the beautiful mountains & Mont Blanc I had so much enjoyed seeing 5 years ago, were not to be distinguished, & we might as well have been in Holland, as in Switzerland. By the time we reached Lausanne it was quite dark. There another Deputation presented me with an address, & a sweet little 3 year old girl, daughter of the British Vice Consul, gave me a bouquet. A Band played & the station was decorated with Chinese lanterns. We had some dinner, & after it, Beatrice stepped out & brought in Alphonse Mensdorff's 2nd daughter Sophie Kinsky,† with her 3 daughters & only son…. They remained about 10 minutes & then left. There were great crowds,who cheered, & sang 'God save the Queen'.

---

* Lady Emily Peel, daughter of the eighth Marquess of Tweeddale. One of her daughters, Victoria, married Daniel F.P. Barton who was to become British Consul in Geneva.

† Queen Victoria's cousin once removed.

On another occasion Queen Victoria passed through Switzerland en route between Italy and Germany, stopping at Lucerne, where she saw the stalwart guide Antoine Hofmann, who had done so much to provide her with varied and successful expeditions in 1868. Alleged sightings of the Queen at other times and in other parts of Switzerland were reported, but resulted from the presence at various times of a variety of Empresses, Queens and Princesses named Victoria, the name being confusingly popular in royal and aristocratic families. There were also legends, the most persistent of which – firmly anchored in French-Swiss folklore – tells of Queen Victoria having been given an islet off the southeastern shore of the Lake of Geneva and having returned it smartly to its Swiss donors when they served a tax demand (a disgraceful insinuation). Diligent searches have been made in many an archive, but none have yielded a shred of evidence.

On her many further travels abroad, the Queen continued to use the device of travelling incognita, which had served her so well in Switzerland. But 'Countess of Kent' was no longer available after 1874, when the Duke of Edinburgh, her son Prince Alfred, married. Since the title Earl of Kent was one of his, she had been free to use it as long as he was unmarried. But his wife now became Countess of Kent as well as Duchess of Edinburgh – and going abroad as her own daughter-in-law was not the Queen's idea of fun. For her first visit to Italy in 1879 she chose the name 'Countess of Balmoral', and she continued to use this name on her increasingly frequent visits to Italy and France.

But with the passing of time the effect wore off, so that on her later appearances in France in the 1890s she was given royal welcomes by enthusiastic crowds and treated as Queen by the authorities. Colonel Ponsonby's son, the later Sir Frederick Ponsonby was a member of the Queen's Court accompanying her on her visits to France in the 1890s. His memoirs contain an account of one of these, starting with the Queen's arrival in France after crossing the Channel.

> On the pier was a beautiful red velvet and gold lace tent for her to sit in, with a guard of honour of the French Army, while a host of Generals, Admirals and officials hoping to be presented were drawn up near the tent. What with the band playing and the crowd continually cheering vociferously, it was difficult to hear anything … we travelled comfortably by train across France … At Nice the whole town turned out and lined the streets from the station to the hotel. There were four regiments of infantry and a battery of artillery to keep back the ever enthusiastic crowd. At the station the Préfect, the Mayor, the General and a host of men in evening clothes and tall hats were assembled.[156]

By this time, though, the Queen could accept such formalities on her journeys abroad. Incognito had done its work.

Art.Anst.J.A.PREUSS Zürich.

Axenstein. The pavilion
marking the spot where
the Queen admired the
view on 8 September
1868

10   Echo in Switzerland

Queen Victoria's visit in 1868 echoed far and wide throughout the land. For the Swiss, this was the visit that launched a ship – and much else besides. The new steamship *Victoria* started plying the Lake of Lucerne in 1871, while all over Switzerland hotels called 'Victoria' were mushrooming. The fashion for English-sounding names had started before the Queen's visit, but her presence accelerated it. Astute hoteliers were well aware of the pulling-power of this name. One hotel did not even have to change its name to mark its connection, because it was the only hotel (apart from the Pension Wallis) in which the Queen herself had stayed – the inn on the Furka. For the hymn-writer Frances Ridley Havergal a stay there in 1871 was worth writing home about:'The Inn here was very small, but is being enlarged. We have a very comfortable little room with a table and sofa, and are royally lodged, for here the Queen slept when she was in Switzerland, in this very room! Hitherto, being the only English we have been taken into the best rooms at once.'[157]

The Queen's visit to Hertenstein on the Lake of Lucerne on 3 September 1868 is commemorated by a memorial stone with a Latin inscription set in the

The steamship *Victoria*
on the lake of Lucerne

Stone inscription at Hertenstein, where Queen Victoria walked in September 1868

highest point of the grounds where the Queen walked. The spot is called 'Victoria Hill' and, sure enough, a hotel was established nearby.

Not only hotels played on the Queen's name and its connotations. When the British Consul in Geneva sponsored a new concert hall there in the 1890s it was, of course, named Victoria Hall.

The Queen's Diamond Jubilee in 1897 was celebrated in Switzerland not only by the considerable British colony but with the active participation of large numbers of Swiss – and the Swiss press noted especially that the British flag was flying from the Pension Wallis.

There were whole columns about the celebrations taking place in the British Isles and Empire, emphasizing the enormous popularity and loyalty the Queen enjoyed (to say nothing of her enormous family: nine children, forty grandchildren and thirty great-grandchildren, making a grand total of seventy-nine direct descendants). Erudite articles dwelt on the depth and strength of Anglo-Swiss relations, for example recalling with gratitude how swift British diplomatic action had saved the Swiss Confederation at its birth in 1848 from interventionist

Goblet presented by Queen Elizabeth I in 1560 to the Zurich reformer H. Bullinger

threats on the part of its neighbours. During a glittering reception in Zürich the British Consul-General handed around a silver and gold goblet (filled for the occasion with wine) which had been presented in 1560 by Queen Elizabeth I to the reformer Zwingli's successor Bullinger, in recognition of the way Zürich had harboured English and Scottish Protestants exiled by the Counter-Reformation. Two years later the new English Church of St Mark's at Lucerne was consecrated and it did not pass notice that the Queen had contributed to Anglican church funds at the end of her visit.

In 1968 the centenary of the Queen's visit was marked in Lucerne by a commemorative exhibition in the Swiss Transport Museum there, with the Balmoral Sociable, lent for the summer by H.M. Queen Elizabeth II, as its

Commemorative tablet unveiled in 1968 on the Gütsch, near the former Pension Wallis

IN REMEMBRANCE OF HER BRITANNIC MAJESTY QVEEN VICTORIA, WHO SPENT A HOLIDAY ON THE GVTSCH FROM AVGVST 7TH TO SEPTEMBER 9TH 1868

ZVR ERINNERVNG AN I.M. KÖNIGIN VICTORIA VON GROSSBRITANNIEN DIE VOM 7.AVGVST BIS 9.SEPTEMBER 1868 ZV EINEM FERIENAVFENTHALT AVF GVTSCH BEI LVZERN WEILTE

centrepiece. At a simple ceremony the Mayor of Lucerne and the British Ambassador to Switzerland unveiled a memorial tablet on the Gütsch near the Pension Wallis (the house still stands but is now divided into apartments).

All this because, in 1868, the Queen of England took another name and escaped to a haven on a hill in a small country where she found not only breathtaking scenery but also the complete change and repose and above all the simple family life she had been vainly seeking for many a tormented year.

References

Abbreviations used:

RA   Royal Archives
PRO   Public Record Office
HHS   Hessische Hausstiftung
Disraeli MSS   Hughenden Papers, Bodleian Library

The source for all quotations from Queen Victoria's Journal is the transcript (made by her youngest daughter, Princess Beatrice) which is in the Royal Archives, with the exception of a few extracts which are taken from printed sources as indicated below.

 1 RA, Queen Victoria, Journal, 31 August 1868
 2 *'Lord M'*, David Cecil (Constable, 1954)
 3 Grey Papers, Durham, 25 January 1863
 4 Grey Papers, Durham, 5 February 1863
 5 Grey Papers, Durham, 4 September 1863
 6 Grey Papers, Durham, 28 August 1865
 7 Grey Papers, Durham, 29 August 1865
 8 Grey Papers, Durham; 29 August 1865
 9 Grey Papers, Durham, 30 August 1865
10 Grey Papers, Durham, 1 September 1865
11 *Early Years of the Prince Consort*, C. Grey (London, 1867) pp.154-5
12 Grey Papers, Durham, 17 December 1863, Viscount George Byng Torrington to General Grey (Queen Victoria file 4)
13 Grey Papers, Durham, 4 September 1866
14 Grey Papers, Durham, 5 September 1866
15 Queen Victoria to Lord Russell, 22 January 1866; from *Queen Victoria in her Letters & Journals*, sel. Christopher Hibbert (John Murray, 1984) p.192
16 RA, Queen Victoria, Journal, 6 February 1866
17 Grey Papers, Durham, 13 June 1867
18 Grey Papers, Durham, 14 June 1867
19 RA, Add A/15/1103, Major Elphinstone to Queen Victoria, 11 August 1867
20 RA, Queen Victoria, Journal, 4 August 1867
21 RA, Add A25/204, 27–8 August 1867
22 RA, Add A25/205, 6 September 1867
23 RA, Add A15/1137, 25 October 1867
24 Ibid.
25 Grey Papers, Durham, 29 January 1868
26 Grey Papers, Durham, 2 February 1868

27 Disraeli MSS, Bodleian, 6 May 1868
28 Disraeli to Queen Victoria, 12 May 1868, *Letters of Queen Victoria*, 2nd series, vol. 1, ed. Buckle (Murray, 1926)
29 Disraeli MSS, Bodleian B/XIX/A/48, 14 May 1868
30 Queen Victoria to Mr Theodore Martin, 14 May 1868; *Letters of Queen Victoria*, 2nd series, vol. 1, ed. Buckle (John Murray, 1926)
31 Grey Papers, Durham, 22 May 1868
32 Disraeli MSS, Bodleian, B/XIX/A/52, 22 May 1868
33 *Idem*
34 Grey Papers, Durham, 26 May 1868
35 Queen Victoria to Princess Victoria, HHS, 26 May 1868
36 Crown Princess Victoria to Queen Victoria, 2 June 1868, from *Your Dear Letter*, ed. R. Fulford (Evans Brothers Ltd, 1971) p.195
37 Queen Victoria to Princess Victoria, 8 June 1868, from *Your Dear Letter*, ed. R. Fulford (Evans Brothers Ltd, 1971) p.195
38 Queen Victoria to Princess Victoria, HHS, 15 June 1868
39 Queen Victoria to Princess Victoria, HHS, 20 June 1868
40 RA, Queen Victoria, Journal, 22 June 1868
41 Ibid.
42 Queen Victoria to Crown Princess Victoria, HHS, 25 October 1867
43 *Early Years of the Prince Consort*, C. Grey (London, 1867), pp.154-5
44 *The Queen thanks Sir Howard*, M.H. McClintock (John Murray, 1945) p. 107
45 Grey Papers, Durham, 24 March 1868
46 Disraeli MSS, Bodleian B/XX/Ca/28a, 8 April 1868
47 Crown Princess to Queen Victoria, 2 June 1868, from *Your Dear Letter*, ed. R. Fulford (Evans Brothers Ltd, 1971) p.195
48 Queen Victoria to Crown Princess Victoria, HHS, 8 June 1868
49 Politisches Archiv des Auswärtigen Amtes, Bonn, Dépêche No. 115, 30 May 1968
50 Queen Victoria to Crown Princess Victoria, HHS, 15 June 1868
51 Disraeli MSS, Bodleian, B/XIX/D/62, 1 July 1868
52 Disraeli MSS, Bodleian, B/XX/Ca/39, 5 July 1868
53 Queen Victoria, Journal, 7 July 1868
54 Disraeli MSS, Bodleian, B/XIX/D/66, (undated) July 1868
55 Derby Papers, Liverpool, Disraeli to Stanley, 31 July 1868
56 Derby Papers, Liverpool, Diary, 17 June 1868
57 Derby Papers, Liverpool, Diary, 2 July 1868
58 PRO, FO 100/165, No. 43 (Draft), 30 July 1868
59 PRO, FO 192/57, No. 43, 30 July 1868
60 Ibid.
61 PRO, FO 100/170, 27 July 1868
62 RA, Queen Victoria, Journal, 10 September 1873
63 Queen Victoria to Crown Princess Victoria, HHS, 6 July 1868
64 Queen Victoria to Crown Princess Victoria, HHS, 15 July 1868
65 Queen Victoria to Crown Princess Victoria, HHS, 8 July 1868
66 Queen Victoria to Crown Princess Victoria, HHS, 10 July 1868
67 Crown Princess Victoria to Queen Victoria, HHS, 7 July 1868
68 Queen Victoria to Crown Princess Victoria, HHS, 10 July 1868
69 Queen Victoria to Crown Princess Victoria, HHS 29 July 1868
70 Queen Victoria to Crown Princess Victoria, HHS, 1 August 1868

71 Queen Victoria to Crown Princess Victoria, HHS, 22 July 1868
72 RA Add. A25/232, 25 July 1868
73 RA Add. A25/232, 4 August 1868
74 Queen Victoria to Crown Princess Victoria, HHS, 25 July 1868
75 RA Add. A/36/27, 5 August 1868
76 Derby Papers, Liverpool, letter to Lord Lyons, 25 July 1868
77 Derby Papers, Liverpool, Diary, 6 August 1868
78 Disraeli MSS, Bodleian, B/XIX/A/90, 7 August 1868
79 Derby Papers, Liverpool, Diary, 8 August 1868
80 Disraeli MSS, Bodleian, B/XIX/A/82, 7 August 1868
81 Ibid.
82 Queen Victoria to Crown Princess Victoria, HHS, 8 August 1868
83 RA, Queen Victoria, Journal, 8 August 1868
84 The Note-Books of Samuel Butler (A.C. Fifield, London, 1919), p.342
85 RA, Queen Victoria, Journal, 10 August 1868
86 Queen Victoria to Crown Princess Victoria, HHS, 12 August 1868
87 RA, Add A36/28
88 PRO LC 11/194, for Quarter to 30 September 1868
89 Disraeli MSS, Bodleian, B/XIX/D/83, 13 August 1868
90 Derby Papers, Liverpool, Diary, *passim*
91 Derby Papers, Liverpool, Diary, 9 August 1868
92 Queen Victoria, Letters and Journal, *passim*
93 RA, Queen Victoria, Journal, 6 August 1868
94 RA, Queen Victoria, Journal, 7 August 1868
95 Queen Victoria to Crown Princess Victoria, HHS, 15 August 1868
96 Derby Papers, Liverpool, Diary, 16 August 1868
97 Disraeli MSS, Bodleian, B/XIX/A/93, 20 August 1868
98 Queen Victoria to Crown Princess Victoria, HHS, 19 August 1868
99 Disraeli MSS, Bodleian, B/XIX/A/83, 17 August 1868
100 Queen Victoria, Journal, 17 August 1868
101 Disraeli MSS, Bodleian, B/XIX/A/83, 17 August 1868
102 PRO 192/58, 21 August 1868
103 Queen Victoria to Crown Princess Victoria, HHS, 19 August 1868
104 Disraeli MSS, Bodleian, B/XIX/A/94, 23 August 1868
105 RA Add A36/29, 24 August 1868
106 Queen Victoria to Crown Princess Victoria, 30 August 1868, from *Your Dear Letter*, ed. R. Fulford (Evans Brothers Ltd, 1971) p.206
107 RA, Queen Victoria, Journal, 30 August 1868
108 Derby Papers, Liverpool, Diary, 15 August 1868
109 Disraeli MSS, Bodleian, B/XIX/A/86, 31 August 1868
110 Derby Papers, Liverpool, Diary, 1 September 1868
111 Derby Papers, Liverpool, to Lord Lyons, 1 September 1868
112 Disraeli MSS, Bodleian, B/XIX/A/96, 2 September 1868
113 Derby Papers, Liverpool, Diary, 1 September 1868
114 Disraeli MSS, Bodleian, B/XIX/A/96, 2 September 1868
115 RA, Queen Victoria, Journal, 1 September 1868
116 PRO FO 100/170, 14 July 1868
117 Derby Papers, Liverpool, to Disraeli, 29 August 1868
118 PRO, FO 192/59, 12 June 1868
119 RA, Queen Victoria, Journal, 2 September 1868

120 RA, Add. A 36/30, 3 September 1868
121 Queen Victoria to Crown Princess Victoria, HHS, 6 September 1868
122 Derby Papers, Liverpool, 3 September 1868; B24, 128
123 Diary, Derby Papers, Liverpool, 4 September 1868
124 Disraeli MSS, Bodleian, B/XIX/A/98, 5 September 1868
125 Ibid.
126 From Queen Victoria to Crown Princess Victoria, HHS, 3 September 1868
127 Queen Victoria to Crown Princess Victoria, HHS, 6 September 1868
128 Disraeli MSS, Bodleian, B/XIX/A/88, 7 September 1868
129 RA, Add. A 36/30, 3 September 1868
130 Queen Victoria to Crown Princess Victoria, HHS, 6 September 1868
131 Queen Victoria to Crown Princess Victoria, HHS, 10 September 1868
132 RA, Queen Victoria, Journal, 10 September 1868
133 Disraeli MSS, Bodleian, B/XIX/A/89, 10 September 1868
134 RA, Queen Victoria, Journal, 10 September 1868
135 *The Times*, 14 September 1868
136 RA A37/51, Disraeli to Queen Victoria, 10 September 1868
137 Ibid.
138 RA, A 37/50, 31 August 1868
139 *The Times*, 15 September 1868
140 Disraeli MSS, Bodleian B/XIX/A/76, 3 September 1868
141 Disraeli MSS, Bodleian B/XIX/A/77, 3 September 1868
142 Disraeli MSS, Bodleian B/XIX/D/69
143 RA, Queen Victoria, Journal, 23 November 1868
144 Grey Papers, Durham, 23 November 1868
145 Grey Papers, Durham, 9 December 1868
146 Grey Papers, Durham, 23 December 1868
147 Queen Victoria to Crown Princess Victoria, HHS, 6 September 1893
148 Derby Papers, Liverpool, 23 December 1868
149 Queen Victoria to Crown Princess Victoria, 10 September 1868
150 RA, Queen Victoria, Journal, 16 September 1868
151 RA, Queen Victoria, Journal, 17 September 1868
152 Zelger family papers 302, 303; R Löhlein to J.J. Zelger 10 December 1868 and 2 January 1869
153 RA, Queen Victoria, 1 September 1869 (in *More Leaves from our Life in the Highlands*)
154 RA, Queen Victoria, 4 September 1869 (in *More Leaves from our Life in the Highlands*)
155 RA, Queen Victoria, Journal, 17 April 1879
156 *Recollections of Three Reigns*, Sir Frederick Ponsonby (Eyre & Spottiswoode, 1951), p.53
157 F.R. Havergal, *Swiss Letters and Alpine Poems* (J. Nisbet, London, 1881), 3 July 1871, p.131

Illustration Sources

Index

Entries in italic type refer to illustrations

Photoshop CS

A *to* Z

The essential visual reference guide

Peter Bargh

ELSEVIER

AMSTERDAM • BOSTON • HEIDELBERG • LONDON • NEW YORK • OXFORD
PARIS • SAN DIEGO • SAN FRANCISCO • SINGAPORE • SYDNEY • TOKYO

Focal Press is an imprint of Elsevier

Focal
Press

Words and design: Peter Bargh
Produced using Adobe's InDesign DTP program – it's awesome!
All photographs: Peter Bargh
e-mail peter@bargh.co.uk

Focal Press
An imprint of Elsevier
Linacre House, Jordan Hill, Oxford OX2 8DP
200 Wheeler Road, Burlington MA 01803

First published 2004

British Library Cataloguing in Publication Data
A catalogue record for this book is available from the British Library

Library of Congress Cataloguing in Publication Data
A catalogue record for this book is available from the Library of Congress

ISBN 0 240 51957 4

For information on all Focal Press publications visit our website at:
www.focalpress.com

Thanks to:
Will Smith and Tracey Johnson for their invaluable assistance on ePHOTOzine.
All the musicians in the world who provide me with great sounds.
This week I have mostly been hearing Bjork, Sigur Ros and Tricky.
And a special thank you to everyone who made
Photoshop 5.5, 6.0 and 7.0 A to Z a huge success.

Words of the day: Kumquat, Aardvark, Plop, Whatever
Saying of the day: Candle in the eye

Printed and bound in Italy

Contents

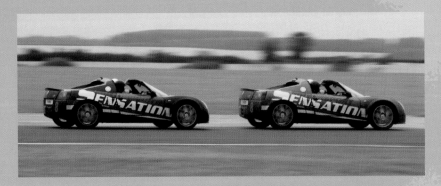

Introduction

Photoshop is, arguably, the most complex image editing program sold, but it's equally the most versatile when you become familiar with its tools and functions. Many of the reference books written about Photoshop are as complex as the program, but they don't have to be. Photoshop CS A to Z has been produced to present the program in a visual way and in a logical order.

It's too easy to get lost wading your way around a 300 page book trying to find out how a certain feature works. In this book you look up the mode, tool or filter, presented in a logical A to Z order, to find a visual reference with handy tips and quick keys.

The book can be used as a helpful guide to keep near your computer, giving you nuggets of essential information as you work. It will also give you plenty of ideas to try out on your own pictures.

It's really important when working with a program like Photoshop that you set it up to work better for you. To do this there are a selection of preferences that are used to take the program off the original settings and customize it to your liking. I've included an explanation of all these in the appendices, along with an area where you can make notes of filter settings that work well so you can refer back to them when using the filters again.

Because of the logical steps Adobe have made with their upgrades, this book is also suitable for owners of earlier versions of the program; there's a comparison of all the versions of Photoshop, including LE, and the budget program from Photoshop called Elements in Appendix A. Those wondering what happened to version numbers, this is really version 8.0, but Adobe have decided to replace the version number with CS, which stands for Creative Suite, and forms part of a new family of Creative Suite programs.

As an English author I would naturally prefer to use English spellings, for example colour instead of color, but as the book will be sold throughout the world I've adopted the US spelling for the word color. This ensures the book is consistent with the Photoshop users' manual and interface.

In the first three books I used Apple Mac screengrabs throughout, simply because I'd used a Mac for years in favour of the PC. I've recently switched to PC so many of the screengrabs are now from the Windows XP platform. Essentially Photoshop runs the same whichever platform you work on. The main difference is when a keyboard shortcut includes the Command key on a Mac you would use the Ctrl key on a PC. Similarly when the Option key is used on a Mac the Alt key should be used on the PC, and the Return key on the Mac is Enter on the PC. You'll also see subtle differences in the look of palettes on a Mac over a PC, but all the options are in the same place. Enjoy!

Pete Bargh

Peter Bargh, 2004

Actions

MENU   WINDOW →
              ACTIONS
QUICK KEY **F9**

An action is a way of automatically applying a technique to an image using a pre-recorded series of commands, or a script,

You can turn part of an action on or off, as well as record, play or edit new or existing actions.

that is triggered by pressing one or a combination of keys. Many actions are already supplied with Photoshop and can be found at the bottom of the Actions menu by clicking on the arrow at the top right of the Actions palette. They can also be found

in the Presets folder. An action can be as simple as opening a new canvas or as advanced as creating a drop shadow on an existing picture or, as in our example (left), making snow.

     You can also create your own Photoshop actions using the Automate mode, so if there are techniques you find particularly fiddly or ones you'll want to use again, record the commands as you run through them and assign the action a shortcut key.

     To record a new action open an image and select New Action from the hidden menu or click on the page icon at the bottom of the palette. This displays a new palette. Name your action, choose a destination folder, a shortcut key and a color for the button display.

     The shortcut can be a single F button or any combination of an F along with Shift and Control keys. Click on the record button and run through the various steps to produce the desired result. You'll see each step appear in the menu as it's recorded. When you've done click stop.

     Now when you want to apply the recorded effect just click on the designated shortcut key. Actions can also be applied to several images in one go using the Batch command or created into droplets. **(See Batch command and Droplets)**

Tips

● If a command cannot be recorded you can insert it manually using the Insert Menu command.
● If you make a mistake, keep going, you can edit the script later.
● Some settings may need modifying for different images. Clicking on the box to the left of the action will stop the script at that point and bring up the dialogue box so you can manually adjust before continuing the script.

Active layer

This is the layer that is currently selected. To select a layer click on the layer icon in the layers palette. The layer will become highlighted and when a filter effect or brush is applied it will only affect the highlighted layer.

Airbrush

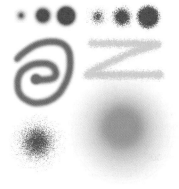

A painting tool that applies a color in much the same way as a real airbrush. The airbrush moved from the toolbar in Photoshop 7.0 and appears in the brush options bar. Now you simply choose airbrush as a style and select how you want it to work from the brush palette.

Hold down the mouse and drag it around to spray color evenly onto the canvas. Hold it in the same place and color builds up while spreading outwards. Covering an area that's already sprayed increases color depth.

As with all brush modes you can specify size, blending mode and opacity from the bar that appears at the top of the page when you click on a brush. There's also an option to adjust flow.

Adjustment layer

MENU   LAYER →
NEW ADJUSTMENT LAYER

An adjustment layer is a layer that you can apply effects to that will change all the layers below it in the stack. If you then turn off the eye icon next to the layer it will turn off the effects for that particular adjustment layer. It's great for hand coloring black & white pictures as well as controlling levels or curves.

You can delete these layers at any time to remove the effect.

A Hue/Saturation Adjustment layer was used to color this infrared black & white original. Make a selection of an area and save it as an Adjustment layer. You can then adjust the color of just that selection without affecting the rest of the picture, as illustrated here. At this stage I was trying out a violet colored temple.

The finished picture. Each of the 15 layers can now be changed to alter the color of individual elements within the picture. And as each layer has a mask you can change the area colored using the Brush and Eraser tools.

a

Align Linked

MENU   LAYER ➜
ALIGN LINKED   Feature introduced in Photoshop CS to make it easier to align items within layers. Select this option and one of the six align options to make objects on linked layers align to the top, centre or bottom edge in either horizontal or vertical directions.

Here Align to left edges has been selected and the three images have lined up to the left while maintaining their horizontal positions.

Anchor points

QUICK KEY J SELECTS IT
FROM TOOLBOX   The small square boxes that are placed around an object when you make a selection with the Pen tool. The points can be moved when they've been placed using the Direct Selection tool.

Apply image

MENU   IMAGE ➜
APPLY IMAGE   Used to blend one image layer and channel with another. The source and destination image have to be the same size. I found the effect works well using the same image with the blend option. It's very much a trial and error process but well worth the effort as seen here as I've appeared to change the time of day in one simple step. **(See Calculations)**

Alpha channels

These are ideal for saving selections separate from the RGB or CMYK channels. Carefully draw round a subject and choose Select➜Save Selection once you're happy with the selection. This is stored at the base of the Channels palette as a separate channel – the Alpha channel.

It can be recalled and the selection applied to the image at any time by calling up Load Selection from the Select menu. This saves you having to reselect a subject later. Up to 53 Alpha channels can now be added to an RGB image allowing you to produce very complex selections that can be recalled to make changes to a variety of detailed parts of the image at any time.

> **Tip**
> ● Alpha channels can be combined to add selections together.

Anti-aliasing

Aliasing occurs when the sharp edges of pixels appear jagged on the straight edges of an image or text.

Photoshop uses anti-aliasing to smooth out the edges by making the pixels semi-transparent so that they pick up color from surrounding pixels. It's useful when cutting or copying and pasting selections onto new backgrounds. Anti-aliasing can make the image look a little blurred when viewed close up.

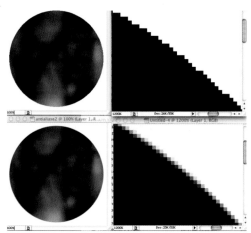

Pixels make round edges look jagged. Using anti-aliasing smooths the 'jaggies' by adding midtone pixels to the harsh edge. Here two circular selections have been made – one with anti-aliasing on (bottom) and one with it off (top). Then the selections were copied and pasted onto a white background. Notice how sharp the top cutout looks.

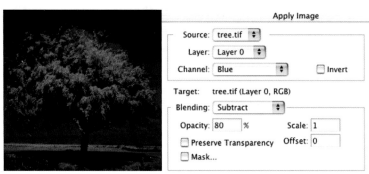

Moonlit scene, made possible by the Subtract Blend mode and green channel.

| | Brush: 21 | Mode: Normal | Opacity: 100% | Style: Tight Short | Area: 50 px | Tolerance: 0% | |

Art History Brush

QUICK KEYS **SHIFT+Y ALTERNATES BETWEEN HISTORY AND ART HISTORY BRUSHES** A feature first seen in version 5.5 that will appeal to artists as, with a little experimentation, it can create some stunning painterly effects.

> History Brush Tool   Y
> Art History Brush   Y

You choose from a variety of patterns and select the Blending mode and opacity before painting over an existing image. The more you paint over the same area the greater the effect. The larger the brush size the bigger the paint daubs and less realistic the effect.

Colorful images like this are suitable for the Art History Brush attack.

With a small brush and careful choice of the palette options paint effects can be quite realistic (above).

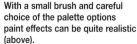

Choose too large a brush size and the effect could go completely wrong (left). You could use this sort of treatment as background to text, though.

Setting Fidelity to a low value produces brush strokes that have more color than the source point (left). A high value maintains the source color (right).

● Using one of the other custom brushes from Photoshop's Presets folder will produce more unusual results.

Here two of the Special effect brushes were used with Fade mode to create an oil paint style photograph.

You can also use the technique to paint around the head of a bride to create a pretty vignette/diffuser style effect.

a

Artifacts

Digital photography, like any form of image capture, can produce faults. In digital photography they're referred to as artifacts and can be caused by a number of problems including flare from the camera's lens, electrical interference or low resolution CCDs. Low resolution CCDs cause curved edges to appear jagged as the curve takes on the square edges of each pixel – known as Aliasing.

Blooming is less of a problem now but occurred on earlier CCDs when the electrical charge exceeded the pixel's storage capacity and crossed into adjacent pixels causing image distortion. We've all seen the TV presenter with the stripy shirt appearing as a strange colored pattern. The same thing happens on CCDs and it's known as color fringing.

This photo from a digital camera's economy mode, shows the high level of compression has caused the unusual artifacts in certain areas.

Artistic filters

MENU   FILTER →
ARTISTIC

Change your picture into a painterly image using this collection of filters that mimic natural or traditional artists' effects. Each filter has a selection of sliders which I'll explain for the Colored Pencil (below).

For the rest I've used the same image and included settings I made, but you should experiment with your photos, because each filter suits different images.

Also try using the Edit→Fade option with a Blend mode. **(See Fade)**

COLORED PENCIL
Produces a rough crosshatch effect by drawing in a pencil style over the original using the background color. Edges are retained and the original background image shows through the pencil strokes. Moving the pencil width slider to the left makes the pencil lines thin while sliding to the right makes them thick.

Stroke pressure controls the accuracy of the lines over the original image. Moving over to the left fills the image with color and to the right produces deep and defined lines.

The paper brightness slider affects the color of the pencil. Move it to the right for the maximum color. Moving the slider to the middle produces a progressively gray pencil effect and to the left it goes black.

Above left: Pencil Width: 9, Stroke Pressure: 4, Paper Brightness: 0
Above right: Pencil Width: 2, Stroke Pressure: 13, Paper Brightness: 49
Right: Pencil Width: 2, Stroke Pressure: 4, Paper Brightness: 25, Difference filter 70%

DRY BRUSH
Paints edges using a dry brush technique that appears midway between an oil and watercolor effect. The range of colors is simplified as the filter looks at nearby pixels and blends them into areas of common color.
Brush Size: 9, Brush Detail: 9, Texture: 2

CUTOUT
Builds up the image as though it's created by a collage of several pieces of torn colored paper. It has a similar look to a posterization effect.
Number of levels: 6, Edge Simplicity: 3, Edge Fidelity: 1

NEON GLOW
Adds a glow to parts of the image. The glow color is selected by clicking the glow box and choosing a color from the color picker.
Size: 12, Brightness: 15, Color: Green, Fade filter 95% with Linear Light blend mode

FILM GRAIN
Applies a pattern of grain that simulates real film. The higher you set the grain the more like fast film the effect becomes.
Grain: 8, Highlight Area: 13, Intensity: 1

FRESCO
Converts the image into a coarse stippled effect using short, rounded, quickly applied brush dabs. Good for a Classic painting effect. Brush Size: 2, Brush Detail: 6, Texture: 1, Fade filter by 59% and Darker blend mode.

ROUGH PASTELS
Makes an image appear as though it's on a textured background, covered in colored pastel chalk strokes. Stroke Length: 15, Stroke Detail: 8, Texture: Burlap, Scaling: 61%, Relief: 65, Light Direction: Right

a

PAINT DAUBS
A nice effect varied by altering the brush size to between 1 and 50, with a selected brush type that includes simple, light rough, light dark, wide sharp, wide blurry and sparkle.
Size: 6, Sharpness: 20, Brush Type: Simple

PALETTE KNIFE
Similar to cutout, but with more blurred edges to emulate a palette knife style of painting. Will only suit certain images.
Stroke Size: 10, Stroke Detail: 2, Softness: 3

PLASTIC WRAP
Create Terminator style morphing by coating the image with a shiny plastic effect that accentuates surface detail.
Highlight Strength: 13, Detail: 12, Smoothness: 7

SMUDGE STICK
Uses diagonal strokes to smudge or smear the darker areas and soften the image while lighter areas become brighter and lose detail.
Stroke Length: 8, Highlight Area: 14, Intensity: 5

SPONGE
This is supposed to give an appearance of the image being painted with a sponge. Hmmm!
Brush Size: 2, Definition: 1, Smoothness: 4

UNDERPAINTING
Makes the image appear with a textured background that shows through the surface.
Brush Size: 9, Texture Coverage: 8, Texture: Canvas, Scaling: 98%, Relief: 24, Light Direction: Top right

POSTER EDGES
Creates poster style effects by reducing the number of colors in the image and adding black lines around edges. Edge Thickness: 2, Edge Intensity: 7, Posterization: 0, No Fade 20% saturation.

Tip

● As with most filters and styles once the effect has been applied you can fade the result using the Edit → Fade command. Add a Blend mode to make the result very different than the original filter effect. Here's a couple of examples using the Artistic filters, but turn to the Fade page for more ways to use this excellent control.

Above Cutout and Plastic Wrap were applied in succession each using fade and a Blend mode. Right: Fresco faded followed by a duplicate layer with threshold command and Saturation blend, reduced to 70%. The key is experiment – you never know what will happen.

WATERCOLOR
Saturates colors and paints in a watercolor style by simplifying image detail. Can become too contrasty if you're not careful.
Brush Detail: 8, Shadow Intensity: 0, Texture: 2

Assign profile

MENU   **IMAGE →**
           MODE →
           ASSIGN PROFILE

An option that lets you select a color profile to your image so that it will always request being opened in this mode or will indicate that a different profile is being used.

Assign Profile

Assign Profile:
○ Don't Color Manage This Document
○ Working CMYK: Light GCR 340 UCR CMYK Euro Positi...
● Profile: ColorMatch 3.01 – SWOP Ink, Sheetfed, Coated

OK
Cancel
☑ Preview

Audio Annotation tool

If you have a microphone plugged into the audio-in point of your computer you can record short audio messages and place them on a picture. The annotation appears as a small speaker icon which, when clicked, will replay the recording. This is a great tool for designers who want to leave messages to the next person who will work on the image. It's also open to abuse!
(See Note)

Notes Tool   N
Audio Annotation Tool   N

Audio Annotation

Instruction
Press the Start button to begin recording by speaking into the microphone.

Start...
Stop
Cancel

Auto Color correction

MENU	IMAGE →
	ADJUSTMENTS →
	AUTO COLOR
QUICK KEYS	CTRL+SHIFT+B

An auto feature that first appeared in version 7.0. Clicking on the Options button from the Curves dialogue box calls up a window that allows you to preset the way that each of the auto correction modes works.

Selecting Enhance Monochromatic Contrast clips all channels identically to ensure the photo holds its color values while making highlights appear lighter and shadows appear darker. Applying Auto Contrast from the Image→Adjustments menu has the same effect.

Enhance Per Channel Contrast maximizes the tonal range in each channel. This produces a more dramatic correction, but as each channel is adjusted individually a color cast may be removed or added. Applying Auto Levels uses this algorithm.

Find Dark & Light Colors locates the average lightest and darkest pixels and uses these to maximize contrast while minimizing clipping. This happens when the Auto Color command is used.

 Tip

● Add the same effect as placing a color filter over the front of your camera, by altering the color of the highlights or shadows. Below left: Here I selected maximum red from the color picker, which has produced a lith style effect. If you looked at the channels now you would see that the green and blue channel thumbnails were black.
Below right: Here's the result of a blue shadow selection and a green highlights. Don't forget to reset to white or any future auto adjustments will come out wrong.

Auto Contrast

MENU	IMAGE →
	ADJUSTMENTS →
	AUTO CONTRAST
QUICK KEYS	CTRL+ALT+SHIFT+L

Auto mode that looks at the brightest and darkest parts of the image and adjusts the picture's highlights and shadows. It works well on some images, but it's often better to adjust the picture using Levels or Curves.
(See Levels)

BEFORE

AFTER

Auto Levels

MENU	IMAGE ➜
	ADJUSTMENTS ➜
	AUTO LEVELS
QUICK KEY	CTRL+SHIFT+L

Scanned images using the auto setting rarely turn out with correct color or density so you need to adjust brightness and contrast.

Auto Levels looks for the brightest and darkest points and adjusts contrast so both maintain detail. It's a quick and easy fix, but learning how to adjust Levels manually produces better results. **(See Levels)**

Using any of the three Auto modes from the Image ➜ Adjustments menu can provide a quick fix, but there are times when you have to choose the mode with care. The beauty with Photoshop is you can always undo an adjustment if you don't think it has worked well.
Here are two examples of when things can go wrong.
The first example (above left), of the couple on the steps, lacks contrast and has a slight warm color cast, so the obvious choice would be Auto Color, but this introduced a blue cast (above middle), Auto Contrast actually got it about right here (right).
The sunset picture (below) also looks a little dull, Auto Contrast did nothing, Auto Color did nothing and Auto Levels made a right mess of it (below middle). The only option here was to use Curves and adjust manually which has enriched the photograph (below right).

Automate

MENU	FILE ➜
	AUTOMATE

A series of pre-written auto tasks used to make contact sheets, multi-format prints, batch conversions and format pictures for your Web page.

b

Background color

QUICK KEY X ALTERNATES BETWEEN BACKGROUND AND FOREGROUND COLOR The default is white which appears in the lower box of the tools palette. You can change the color from white by clicking on this box and using the color picker to select a new one. One reason for doing this is when making gradient fills which

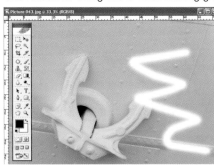

progress from the foreground to background color. Erasing part of an image leaves the background color. **(See Foreground color)**

Tip
● To fill a selection with the Background color press Command+Delete.

Background eraser

A feature that first appeared on version 5.5 that makes it much easier to make selections. Now you paint over the area you want to remove using the Background Eraser tool and the tool makes the area transparent. Then when you copy and paste to a new layer it will look more natural.

Discontinguous erases the sample color wherever it appears in the picture; Contiguous erases pixels that are connected and Find Edges preserves edge sharpness.

Tip
● Change the tolerance level when working on different areas of the image. A higher percentage can be selected when there's a definite variation between the edge of the selection and the subject.

Batch processing

MENU FILE ➜
AUTOMATE ➜
BATCH

If you've ever had to deal with a pile of images that all needed converting from one format or color mode to another you'll welcome this feature. Batch processing takes a selection of images from a folder and performs action sequences that you've pre-recorded in the Actions palette. You can specify whether you want the processed files to replace the existing ones or create new versions in a different destination folder.
(See Actions)

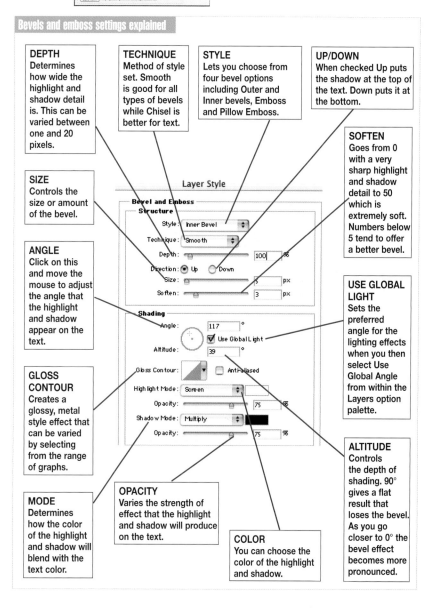

Bevels

MENU LAYER ➜
LAYER STYLE ➜
BEVEL AND EMBOSS

A mode that you can use to produce stylish type that will leap off your page. It can also be used on colored shapes to create 3D panels and buttons.

Using the Effects palette you can adjust the highlight and shadow of the bevel to create shallow or deep 3D effects.

Results vary depending on the resolution of your image so experiment with the settings to find a suitable effect. Turn Apply on so you can see the changes as you play. Here are several I made using a 7x3cm canvas with a resolution of 300ppi and 50 point text.

Just a few examples of some of the effects you can obtain using Bevel effects.

Bevels and emboss settings explained

DEPTH
Determines how wide the highlight and shadow detail is. This can be varied between one and 20 pixels.

TECHNIQUE
Method of style set. Smooth is good for all types of bevels while Chisel is better for text.

STYLE
Lets you choose from four bevel options including Outer and Inner bevels, Emboss and Pillow Emboss.

UP/DOWN
When checked Up puts the shadow at the top of the text. Down puts it at the bottom.

SOFTEN
Goes from 0 with a very sharp highlight and shadow detail to 50 which is extremely soft. Numbers below 5 tend to offer a better bevel.

SIZE
Controls the size or amount of the bevel.

ANGLE
Click on this and move the mouse to adjust the angle that the highlight and shadow appear on the text.

GLOSS CONTOUR
Creates a glossy, metal style effect that can be varied by selecting from the range of graphs.

MODE
Determines how the color of the highlight and shadow will blend with the text color.

OPACITY
Varies the strength of effect that the highlight and shadow will produce on the text.

COLOR
You can choose the color of the highlight and shadow.

USE GLOBAL LIGHT
Sets the preferred angle for the lighting effects when you then select Use Global Angle from within the Layers option palette.

ALTITUDE
Controls the depth of shading. 90° gives a flat result that loses the bevel. As you go closer to 0° the bevel effect becomes more pronounced.

Bézier curves

Curves created using Photoshop's Pen tool are called Bézier (bay-zee-ay) curves, named after French mathematician Pierre Bézier.

The shape of a curve is created by the position of anchor points and direction lines that can be moved to change its shape and direction. They're used to make perfect selections around smooth or curved objects.

Bicubic interpolation

Used to increase the image size by adding pixels based on the average of the colors of all eight surrounding pixels. It also boosts contrast between pixels to avoid a blurring effect that's usually evident from interpolation. It's the slowest of the three interpolation processes, but it's the most precise and gives the smoothest gradation between tones.

Photoshop CS has two new Bicubic additions in the drop down list – Bicubic smoother and Bicubic sharper. These are more advanced methods of resampling. Use Bicubic smoother when enlarging a photo and Bicubic sharper when making a photo smaller. (**See Interpolation**)

Tip

● To ensure one of the Bicubic options is selected as a default go to File→Preferences→General and pull the option down in the interpolation box drop down menu.

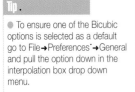

Bitmap image

An image made up of a grid of squares (pixels) also known as a Raster image and not to be confused with Bitmap mode. Bitmap images are resolution-dependent which means the number of pixels used to make up the image is fixed.

A bitmap is good at reproducing subtle colors, but jagged effects can occur when the image is enlarged.

Bitmap mode

MENU	IMAGE →
	MODE →
	BITMAP

Converts the picture into a grid of black & white pixels. The option won't be available if you're trying to convert a color image. Discard color first by selecting Image→Mode→Grayscale. Set output in the dialogue box to your inkjet printer's resolution.

ORIGINAL
This black & white image scanned and saved as an RGB image was converted to grayscale first using Image→Mode→Grayscale.

◀ PATTERN DITHER
Converts the image into a geometric pattern of black & white dots that produce a range of grays when viewed.

50% THRESHOLD ▶
Pixels with gray values above mid-gray convert to white and the rest become black resulting in a very high contrast, black & white image.

◀ HALFTONE SCREEN
Converts a grayscale image to simulate a printer's halftone dots.

DIFFUSION DITHER ▶
Produces a film-like grain that's useful for viewing images on a black & white monitor.

◀ CUSTOM PATTERN
First define your own pattern and then apply this pattern as a texture screen.

Blending modes

QUICK KEYS SHIFT & +/- TO SCROLL THROUGH LIST A range of modes selected from within the Options or Layers palettes. The modes control how the pixels in the base image are affected by a Brush, Editing tool or other Layer. You can use the keyboard's up and down arrows to go through each option when you've just selected one. Here's what happens when a photograph of the moon is placed on a new layer and blended with a sky.

Linear Burn ⌄
Normal
Dissolve
Darken
Multiply
Color Burn
Linear Burn
Lighten
Screen
Color Dodge
Linear Dodge
Overlay
Soft Light
Hard Light
Vivid Light
Linear Light
Pin Light
Hard Mix
Difference
Exclusion
Hue
Saturation
Color
Luminosity

NORMAL

COLOR DODGE

HARD LIGHT

As well as using the Blend mode for the obvious merging of objects within layers it can also be used to add creative coloring by blending two duplicate layers with different colors, as seen in this example of two boys who were asked to pull mean and moody faces. Top shows the two color layers with Normal blend set. Green is on the base and purple above. The middle version is set to Linear light and has become orange. The bottom version is set to Luminosity and has a green color.

b

To show how the Blend mode affects colors in the layers I've created this simple color swatch and placed the colored gradient over the top, set to an opacity of 60%.

COLOR
Shift+Alt+C
Produces an end color with the luminance of the base color and the hue and saturation of the blend color. It's a good mode for hand-coloring black & white images as it keeps the gray tones.

COLOR BURN
Shift+Alt+B
Merges the darker colors of the upper layer or paint with the base layer. Blending with white has no effect on the overall image. Can be too harsh for many applications.

COLOR DODGE
Shift+Alt+D
Uses the upper layer or paint to add color and brighten the color of the base layer. Blending with black doesn't affect the image. Has the opposite effect to color burn and is less useful.

DARKEN
Shift+Alt+K
Looks at the color in each layer and selects the darker of the base or blend layer as the final color. Lighter pixels are replaced, darker pixels stay the same.

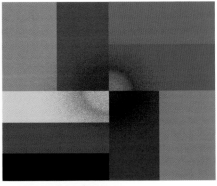

DIFFERENCE
Shift+Alt+E
Subtracts either the blend color from the base color or the base color from the blend color, depending on which has a larger brightness value. Base colors are inverted when blended with white, but blending with black has no effect.

DISSOLVE
Shift+Alt+I
When two layers are combined there's no effect unless the active layer has been feathered and then a splattering effect appears in the feathered area. Could be used for graphical illustration work but has little benefit for photographers.

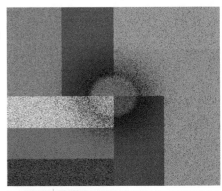

EXCLUSION
Shift+Alt+X
A similar, but lower contrast effect to the Difference mode. I've never found a suitable use for this blend mode.

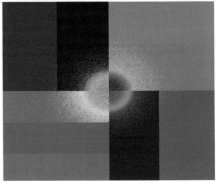

HARD LIGHT
Shift+Alt+H
Adds color together and, like Soft Light, lightens image areas lighter than 50% gray and darkens the Blend color if it's already darker than 50% gray. Painting with black or white produces pure black or white. A harsh overlay.

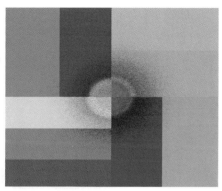

LINEAR BURN
Shift+Alt+A
A new option that appeared in version 7.0 that looks at the color values in each channel and decreases the brightness of the base color to reflect the blend color. Produces a less solarized result than color burn.

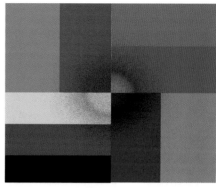

HARD MIX
Shift+Alt+L
A new Blend mode addition for Photoshop CS. This one works in a similar way to Vivid light but produces a very strong posterized color effect. I can't imagine it being used that often and it's hardly a benefit to CS.

LINEAR DODGE
Shift+Alt+W
First appeared in version 7.0 that looks at the color information in each channel and increases brightness in the base color to reflect the blend color. Blending with black has no effect.

HUE
Shift+Alt+U
Produces a combined color that includes the luminance and saturation of the base color and the hue of the blend color.

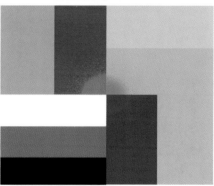

LINEAR LIGHT
Shift+Alt+J
New on version 7.0 and is similar to Vivid light, but it adjusts brightness to dodge or burn colors. If the blend color is lighter than 50% gray, brightness is increased to lighten the image. If it's darker than 50% gray, brightness is decreased to darken the image.

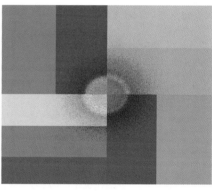

LIGHTEN
Shift+Alt+G
Looks at the color in each layer and selects the lighter of the base or blend layer as the final color. Pixels darker than the blend color are replaced and lighter pixels stay the same. There's no sign of our green layer in this one.

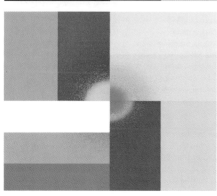

LUMINOSITY
Shift+Alt+Y
Notice how it's the base color that is strong here. That's because this mode mixes hue and saturation of the base color and the luminance of the blend color and creates the opposite effect of Color mode.

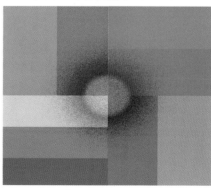

b

MULTIPLY
Shift+Alt+M
Painting over a base color with the blend color produces a darker color. Painting with black changes base color to black, white leaves color unchanged. Painting repeatedly over the same area produces progressively darker colors and is similar to coloring with a felt tip pen.

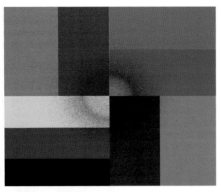

SATURATION
Shift+Alt+T
Takes the hue and luminance of the base color and blends it with the saturation of the applied color.

NORMAL
Shift+Alt+N
When the layer or brush is at 100% the pixels produce the end color with this default mode and are not affected by the base image. Change the opacity and colors blend and form an average.

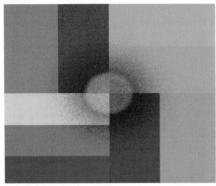

SOFT LIGHT
Shift+Alt+F
Similar to Overlay, but more subtle. If the blend color is lighter than 50% gray, the whole image will lighten. If it's darker than 50% gray, the image will darken. How much depends on the paint color used. When you merge layers you benefit from a lighter image.

OVERLAY
Shift+Alt+O
Similar process to Multiply, but Overlay holds onto the base color's highlights and shadows while mixing with the active layer to produce an image with more contrast. Use this mode with a Paintbrush to build up a hand-coloring effect.

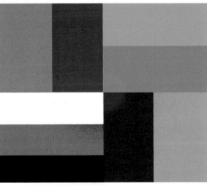

SCREEN
Shift+Alt+S
Opposite to Multiply with the end color always lighter. Painting with black leaves the color unchanged while white produces white. The active layer becomes lighter. This is a useful mode to use when you are making multilayer composites.

PIN LIGHT
Shift+Alt+Z
Replaces colors, depending on the blend color. Darker pixels are replaced when they are lighter than 50% gray, while lighter pixels are unaffected. Lighter pixels are replaced when the blend color is darker than 50% gray, darker pixels are unaffected.

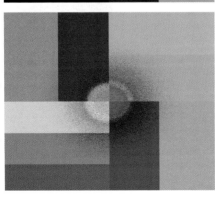

VIVID LIGHT
Shift+Alt+V
Appeared on version 7.0. Similar to Linear light, but adjusts contrast to dodge or burn colors. If the blend color is lighter than 50% gray, contrast is decreased to lighten the image. If it's darker than 50% gray, contrast is increased to darken the image.

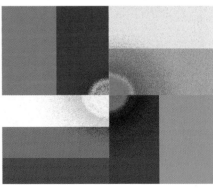

Blur filters

MENU   FILTER →
                BLUR →

A series of

effects accessed from the filter pull down menu and used to soften all, or part, of an image by reducing the defined edges between pixels. Quite silly really – you have a camera that's been carefully engineered to give razor sharp images that you're now going to make blurred! The beauty with a digital image is you can control how much and where the blur will occur. So consider having infinite control of depth-of-field or the ability to soften wrinkles and hide freckles while keeping the eyes sharp. Now you're thinking! Two new filters have been added to Photoshop CS bringing a total of eight options in the Photoshop filter menu. These include Average, Blur, Blur More, Gaussian Blur, Lens Blur, Motion Blur, Radial Blur and Smart Blur.

BLUR

Smoothes out color transitions in an image by averaging out pixels next to hard edges of defined lines and shaded areas. This is a good mode to help smooth out harsh looking pictures created using a digital camera.

The Blur filter seen in action here on a highly magnified section of a flower. The result can be controlled using the Edit→Fade option.

AVERAGE

This filter is new to Photoshop CS and takes the colors of all the pixels in a selected area and scrambles them to deliver an average color value. It can be

used to reduce noise, and also to find the average value of a group of pixels when the 5x5 square option of the eyedropper tool isn't enough. I haven't found a use for it for a photographic application yet, but I'm sure there will be one.

BLUR MORE

Similar effect to the Blur filter, but up to four times as strong. Helps reduce the effect of pixelation in digital pictures.

The original was taken using a Nikon Coolpix 990 digital camera. Top is before Blur More is applied and bottom is after. The result is soft so I sharpened the image and have enlarged the eye in each example so you can see the difference.

Before

After

Sharpened

GAUSSIAN BLUR

An adjustable blurring effect, controlled by one slider that adjusts the pixel radius in 1/10 pixels from 0.1 to 250. It adds low-frequency detail that can produce a hazy effect.

The picture in the preview window can be adjusted in size so you can watch the result on a localized area or the whole picture. The preview appears quicker if the area is highly magnified.

The screenshot above right shows the effect of setting a low radius and you can still see detail in the background. The below right picture shows what happens if a high radius is set – the whole background goes unnaturally blurred.

You should adjust the radius to suit each picture and the file size also affects the setting. A larger file size would need a higher radius to have any effect.

The first thing to do is make a selection of the area that you want to make blurred.

I find it easier to select the subject that you want to stay sharp and then invert this selection.

Draw around the subject using the Lasso tool, and use the Shift and Ctrl keys with the Lasso tool to add or subtract from this selection.

Once completed and with the selection inverted to the background I find it useful to expand by one pixel and feather by one to ensure a less harsh edge.

Tip

● To blur a background when there's a difficult subject to cut around, such as hair. Draw a very rough selection using the Lasso tool at a short distance from the hair and feather dramatically (150 pixels on this 5Mb image). Then when you apply blur it will look more natural and less like a cutout.

LENS BLUR

Another new Blur filter introduced with Photoshop CS and a very welcome one too. This offers a vast amount of control of blur making soft focus options far more controlable. This option can be used to control front to back subject sharpness, known as depth-of-field.

Digital cameras and wide-angle lenses deliver incredible depth-of-field. Sometimes this is so much, that even with the lens at its widest setting you cannot throw any of the subject out of focus. This new lens blur filter helps create the most natural out of focus points in the photo. In this example the rocks appear more three dimensional when the background is blurred. I've also used the new shadow/highlight filter to lighten the shadow areas in the rocks. The overall image is now much better.

PREVIEW
Make this active so you can see the effect of the filter on the image. You can choose whether to have a Faster or More Accurate preview. Working in Faster mode helps you see roughly if the effect's going to work without you having to hang around tapping your fingers. When you think the effect seems about right switch to Accurate for the best result.

IRIS
Simulates a lens iris, giving you control over its shape, size (radius), blade curvature and rotation. As you increase the number of sides and curvature of blades, the iris becomes rounder, so rotation is less important. If you have a straight-bladed triangle, Rotation is much more obvious in the highlights.

NOISE
When you blur an image, you blur the noise/grain. This lets you re-introduce noise to the blurred result to maintain a realistic look. If the image started out with minimal noise turn the Amount down. If you're shooting with high ISO settings, adjust these controls until you get a lifelike result. Look at the image at 100% magnification to make it easier to adjust these values correctly.

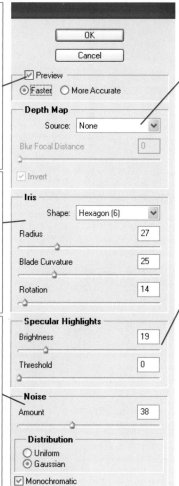

DEPTH MAP
Lens Blur uses an alpha channel or layer mask to create the Depth Map. This indicates what's in front of and behind the plane of focus. Black areas in the alpha channel represent areas closer than the point of focus and white areas are treated as if they are further than the focus point. Any alpha channel or layer mask you create appears in the Source drop down menu along with Transparency which can be used to make the layer get blurrier as it gets more transparent. Image layers or backgrounds that are solid and have no layer mask deliver the same results as 'none' where the blur is applied uniformly.

The Blur Focal Distance slider ranges from 0 to 255 and indicates the value in the Depth Map which in turn adjusts the plane of focus. Values less than the selected Blur Focal Distance indicate that the area is in front of the plane of focus, greater values mean the area is behind the plane of focus. The crosshair cursor sets the Blur Focal Distance from the value of the Depth Map at the point in the photo where you click.

SPECULAR HIGHLIGHTS
Blurring an image averages out the brightness values, which means completely white areas become grayer. To ensure the image looks natural, this control makes specular highlights remain white which is what they would be like if you used a soft focus lens on your camera. Threshold determines which of the highlights become specular and brightness adjusts how much to re-brighten these areas after blurring. This works well when, for example, you have sun reflecting off the body of a car, you can keep the reflections bright while blurring parts of the body. View at 100% for accurate results.

If you create a black to white gradient as the alpha channel you can click at any point in the image to blur in front and behind. This technique works really well on subjects like this illustration, where I clicked on a pillar to the left, landscapes, buildings from low angles and reclining figures etc.

MOTION BLUR

Recreates slow shutter speed effects by blurring adjacent pixels at user selectable angles through 360°. You can also control the intensity of the blur producing a streak with a length of between 1 and 999 pixels.

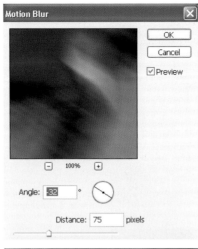

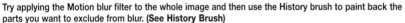

Try applying the Motion blur filter to the whole image and then use the History brush to paint back the parts you want to exclude from blur. (See History Brush)

Look what happens if the Motion Blur angle is changed. In the above example blur was applied in the same direction as the bike. Right: apply at right angles to the natural direction and the biker looks as though he's either pulling a wheelie or crash landing to earth.

RADIAL BLUR

Recreate zoom lens or rotating blurring effects with this mode. Ticking the Spin box makes the image look as though it's, wait for it, spinning. You then specify a degree of rotation by dragging the slider across while viewing a graphical representation of the rotation.

Tick the Zoom box to blur along radial lines and produce the same effect as adjusting a camera's zoom lens during a long exposure. You can adjust the depth from 1 to 100 pixels. You also have the option of Draft for fast, but grainy results or Good and Best for smoother results. Unlike in-camera effects you can also move the centre point of the effect off-centre by dragging the pattern in the graphic preview box.

Above: The Radial Blur filter can take ages to process, even on fairly high spec computers. Right: But the results can be worth waiting for. Time flies when you're having fun!

SMART BLUR

Smart Blur first appeared in version 4.0 of Photoshop and leaves edges sharp while blurring lower contrast parts of the image, often resulting in a posterization or watercolor style effect.

Radius and Threshold sliders are provided to control the blurring effect by the depth of pixels affected and their values. There's also a quality box that has low, medium or high quality blur options. And a final box to set the filter to work on the entire selection in Normal mode, or for the edges of color transitions using Edge Only and Overlay.

Edge Only produces a graphic black & white edge effect while Overlay Edge blends the graphical edge effect with the original image.

A careful blend of all four can produce some very creative images, but can also be used to reduce film grain or blemishes without affecting the overall result.

Smart blur produces lovely painterly images, but loses detail so use with care.

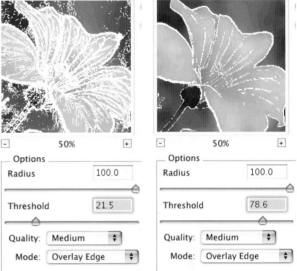

While in the Overlay Edge mode try adjusting the threshold and see how it affects the amount of edge detail that appears on the image. A higher threshold ensures more of the image appears beneath the edge effect.

● Turn off Preserve Transparency in the Layers palette to apply a Blur filter to the edges of a layer.

● Create pencil drawings by running the Smart Blur set to Edge Only mode (middle).

● Then Invert Image→Adjustments→ Invert to get a black sketch on white paper (right).

Borders

MENU   **SELECT →**

         MODIFY →

         BORDER

It's easy to add a border to your whole image or a selection. With an area selected choose the Border command and enter a width in pixels. The mode will be grayed out from the menu if you haven't made a selection.

The thickness of border is relative to the original image size – a 3 pixel border on a 300 pixel wide image will look twice as thin as one with a 600 pixel width.

When applied you'll have a second set of marching ants which you can fill using the Bucket tool or Edit→Fill command. Choose the color border you want and set this as the foreground color before applying the fill.

Tips

● Don't go mad! Black or neutral colors can look more striking than a vivid red or blue. You don't want all the attention on the border!
● Thin borders set a picture off – thick ones can be messy.
● Borders made using the Border mode always have a softer inner edge. To produce a sharp defined border use the Stroke command. **(See Stroke)**

Brightness

MENU   **IMAGE →**

        ADJUSTMENTS →

        BRIGHTNESS/CONTRAST

Adjust the intensity of the image using this slider control. You can go from −100 to +100, which gives the equivalent of about three stops exposure control that you'd experience using slide film.

While the Brightness control is a quick and easy option, it tends to clip the highlight or shadow detail and can result in a loss of valuable pixel information that cannot be returned once the image has been saved and closed.

It's better to use the Levels or Curves adjustments for more precise control of brightness and contrast. **(See Levels and Curves)**

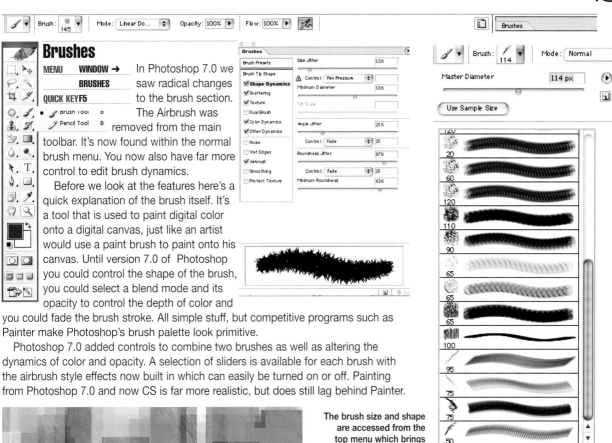

Brushes

In Photoshop 7.0 we saw radical changes to the brush section. The Airbrush was removed from the main toolbar. It's now found within the normal brush menu. You now also have far more control to edit brush dynamics.

Before we look at the features here's a quick explanation of the brush itself. It's a tool that is used to paint digital color onto a digital canvas, just like an artist would use a paint brush to paint onto his canvas. Until version 7.0 of Photoshop you could control the shape of the brush, you could select a blend mode and its opacity to control the depth of color and you could fade the brush stroke. All simple stuff, but competitive programs such as Painter make Photoshop's brush palette look primitive.

Photoshop 7.0 added controls to combine two brushes as well as altering the dynamics of color and opacity. A selection of sliders is available for each brush with the airbrush style effects now built in which can easily be turned on or off. Painting from Photoshop 7.0 and now CS is far more realistic, but does still lag behind Painter.

The brush size and shape are accessed from the top menu which brings down a scrollable list.

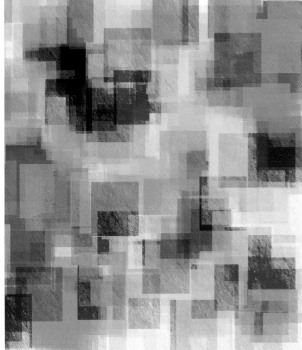

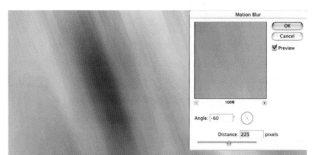

You can use the brushes to make creative backgrounds. Here a selection was made from an image. Then we created a custom brush using the Define Brush mode and started to paint. Saturation mode was used to create the colorful canvas, left, which was then treated to Motion Blur to create the background image above. **(See Define Brush)**

Brushes

(Cont.)

Photoshop 6.0 changed the way we saw brush options, version 7.0 took us a stage further. In previous versions you double clicked on the Brush tool to open the options palette and from there you could select the brush size, opacity and blend mode. Now a convenient bar appears across the top as soon as you click on any tool. This makes it much quicker to edit, once, of course, you become familiar with the new way of working.

The 65 brushes that appear as standard in this bar can be edited and added to. Where you used to double click on an icon to bring up an editing palette you now have a special Brush Presets palette where you can choose loads of editing options. Selecting Brush Tip Shape offers what version 6.0 had – control over the diameter, hardness and spacing of the brush along with the angle and roundness.

The diameter is selected in pixel width and can be anything from 1 to 999 pixels wide. Hardness determines how sharp the edge of the brush is and ranges from 0% to 100%. Spacing (see above right) varies the gap between each shape when you paint and can be set between 1% and 999%. A setting of 100% produces a shape that touches edge to edge, 50% overlaps by half so every alternate shape touches and 150% leaves a gap half the width of a shape between each shape. Got the idea?

The angle comes into play when you've changed the roundness and is great for creating calligraphy style brush strokes.

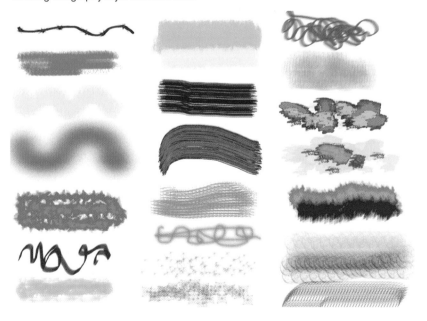

To illustrate the effect of the Spacing feature I first created an oblique-shaped brush and increased spacing in increments of 100% for each of the arrows I've drawn on the canvas.

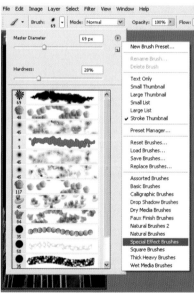

Photoshop CS has a selection of no fewer than 212 preset brushes in 11 groups. These can be accessed by clicking on the arrow to the right of the brush icon on the menu bar and then on the arrow at the side of the brush diameter slider from the brush palette.

From here you can also change how the brush palette displays the brush icons and load or save brushes.

Varying the size of a paint brush is essential when working with different images. Where a large background may suit a chunky brush, retouching a very small area would need a brush tip that may be just one pixel wide. This level of adjustment is made in the Brushes menu bar, which has a selection of pre-set sizes to

choose from, but custom sizes can be also be created. It's not just paint brushes that benefit from size – you can also adjust the Eraser, Smudge, Dodge & Burn tools, and, in this example, the Clone tool which made it much quicker to duplicate the boat. Its color was then changed.

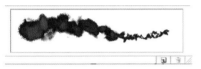

Almost any shape of brush is possible, created using the new Brush Presets palette normally found in the palette well. The palette can be dragged out of the Well and positioned where convenient on the screen.

Burn tool

QUICK KEY SHIFT+O A few of Photoshop's tools are based around conventional photo aids, the Burn tool being one of them. Drag this icon, shaped like a hand making an O, over the image to darken it – as you would in the darkroom using card with a hole cut out to let more light onto the paper.

You can choose which parts of the image the Burn tool affects and by how much. The photo (right) shows three areas that were painted over with the Burn tool using different settings.

Toggle between Burn, Dodge and Saturate using Shift+O. Use the opacity setting to vary the strength.

The Burn tool offers three options: Highlight darkens the light parts of the image (top), Midtones affects the mid-grays (middle) and Shadows alters the dark parts (bottom).

Button mode

This is a pretty looking interface that's an alternative to the normal Actions palette and is selected from the black triangle drop down menu.

Each Action is assigned a color, making it easy to group similar Actions. This mode is useful for less experienced users of the Actions feature, but scripts can't be edited so more advanced users should stay clear. **(See Actions)**

History	Actions	Tool Presets	
Vignette (selection)		Frame Channel - 50 pixel	
Wood Frame - 50 pixel		Cast Shadow (type)	
Water Reflection (type)		Custom RGB to Graysc...	
Molten Lead		Make Clip Path (selecti...	
Sepia Toning (layer)		Quadrant Colors	
Save As Photoshop PDF		Gradient Map	
Focal RGB.pct t... ⇧F12		Aged Photo	
Blizzard		Light Rain	
Lizard Skin		Neon Nights	
Oil Pastel		Quadrant Colors	
Sepia Toning (grayscale)		Sepia Toning (layer)	
Soft Edge Glow		Soft Flat Color	
Soft Focus		Neon Edges	
Soft Posterize		Colorful Center (color)	
Horizontal Color Fade (...		Vertical Color Fade (co...	
Gradient Map		Flourescent Chalk	

Calculations

MENU   IMAGE ➜
               CALCULATIONS

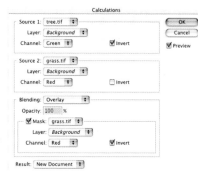

This mode lets you merge two channels from one or two images and save the result as a new channel in one of the existing images or create a new image. The Calculations palette gives you various options including Blend method and is useful if you want to combine masks or selections.

Calibration

The phrase 'what you see is what you get', or 'wysiwyg' (pronounced whizzywig) couldn't be more important. When you view an image on the computer screen you want it to appear exactly the same when it prints out – oh if life were so simple! Computer monitors can be wildly out – just like your neighbour's television, and a high contrast, vivid color image on screen is likely to be disappointingly dull when printed.

It's because the image on the monitor is an RGB file that's projected light, while the printed image is a CMYK version that you view by reflected light. To get round this you need to calibrate your system.

Adobe Gamma can be found in the **Control Panel** from the Start menu of a Windows PC.

Adjust your monitor using Adobe's Gamma file which should be located in your Window's Control Panel. Mac users can use the Apple utility that is in the control panel, or System Preferences on OSX. These easy-to-follow wizards help you adjust brightness, contrast and gamma to ensure life-like prints.

You also need scanner and printer profiles set up to ensure that the file keeps consistent color as it moves through your system.

Mac OSX gamma adjustments can be found in the display control panel in **System Preferences**.

Camera Raw support

Raw support was introduced halfway through the life of Photoshop 7.0 as an optional upgrade. It now comes free with Photoshop CS and allows you to open RAW files taken with more advanced digital cameras.

When you shoot in Raw mode the camera does no internal processing and gives you a file that cannot normally be read unless you use the manufacturer's own software. This plug-in allows Photoshop to read and process the file and has basic and advanced options.

Basic includes control over setting the white balance with preset options and a Kelvin scale for those who know more about color temperature. You can also adjust overall exposure,

shadow, brightness, contrast, saturation, sharpness and color noise reduction. You have the option to open as 8-bit or 16-bit color depth and adjust the file size and resolution.

Click on the advanced button and two more tabs appear offering control over individual RGB hue and saturation plus compensation for camera lens chromatic aberrations and vignetting.

As new cameras are introduced Adobe will make updates available on their Web site to support the cameras.

Even the best digital cameras currently suffer from distortion of color, known as chromatic aberrations, in the edges of the photo. The advanced options allow you to correct for this. Left is the Raw file which

displays slight red/ cyan aberrations. Above right is what happens if you adjust the R/C slider too far and right is the corrected version.

Canvas size

MENU **IMAGE →** **CANVAS SIZE** The canvas is the base to your digital photo, like an artist would add paint, you add pixels. When an image is opened the canvas size is the same as the image. If you want to extend to one side or to the top or bottom you need to increase the canvas size.

Here I've illustrated how to increase the canvas when you want more space for the sky, I would then add clouds. Click in the bottom middle of the Anchor grid of nine squares so that the extended area appears at the top of the existing canvas. I selected blue so you can see the effect (below

right). Ticking Relative allows you to enter the amount of extra canvas you want rather than a total when it's not ticked.

Channels

MENU **WINDOW →** **CHANNELS** Each file in Photoshop is made up of channels that store information about the image. A freshly created RGB file has a channel for each of the three colors, and a CMYK file has four channels, while Duotones and Index color images have just one.

You can add channels to store info about the picture. For example, Alpha channels can be added to save selections as masks. Then when you want to perform a similar cutout in the future you load the Alpha channel to bring the marching ants into play on the selected layer.

Channels can also be edited individually so you could blend certain ones, or fiddle with the color of just one channel – useful when you want to make a selection based on a certain color which would be easier to do in its own environment.

C

Channel Mixer

MENU   IMAGE →
      ADJUSTMENTS →
      CHANNEL MIXER →

The Channel Mixer is one of those tools in Photoshop that you come to once you have a little more experience. By adjusting the color of the individual R, G and B channels you can change the color of an element within the picture.

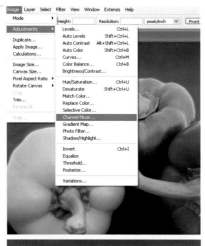

You could play around mixing channel colors all day! If you don't like the result, click on cancel and start again.

Try also converting the image to CMYK and adjusting the yellow, magenta, cyan and black channels for a completely different set of results

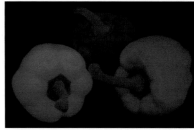

Tips

● Click on monochromatic filter and recreate black & white filter effects using the slides to adjust the colors in each channel. Experimentation is the key here!

Check spelling

MENU   EDIT →
      CHECK SPELLING

This feature, which was introduced in version 7.0, proves useful if you are using the type tool to work with text in Photoshop. This automatically runs through your work and finds anything that isn't spelt correctly or doesn't appear in its dictionary and suggests an alternative.

If, for example, it found grashopper it would suggest the correct grasshopper and you could then click on 'change' to have the word automatically substituted. This sort of feature is available with all word and DTP (desktop publishing) packages and is a welcome addition to Photoshop.

Clipping path

Puts an invisible path around an image to ensure the background is transparent when the image is dropped into an illustration or desktop publishing page.

To create a clipping path first draw around the subject to make a selection then click on the arrow at the right of the paths palette and select Make Work Path, then Save Path. Finally select Clipping Path.

Save the file as an EPS or TIFF which keeps the clipping path data which can then be read by the DTP software to allow a transparent background or text to wrap around the subject.

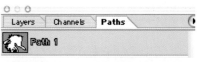

A clipping path was drawn around the wooden carving so it can be dropped into a DTP layout without a background, and text wraps around it.

Clone Stamp tool

Adobe followed most of the other software programmers in version 6.0 by giving the oddly named Rubber Stamp tool a more sensible title of Clone Stamp tool. This particular tool is responsible for many photographers taking up digital imaging.

The first time you see bits of rubbish being wiped right out of an image or spots and blemishes being removed from your partner's face you'll be in awe. All that's happening is the Clone Stamp tool is being used to pick up or sample pixels from one place and drop them somewhere else. It's one of the most used devices to remove or add detail to an image.

There are several ways to use it. For starters it acts like a brush so you can change the size, allowing cloning from just one pixel wide to hundreds. You can change the opacity to produce a subtle clone effect. You can select any one of the options from the Blend menu. And, most importantly, there's a choice between Clone align or Clone non-align.

To use it place the cursor over the sample point, hold down the Alt key and click the mouse. Then move the cursor to the point where you want the sample to appear and click the mouse to dump the pixels. If you hold down the mouse button and drag you'll paint from the sample area. Select Aligned from the Clone Stamp options palette and the sample cursor will follow the destination cursor around keeping the same distance away. When unaligned the sample cursor starts where you left off. Both choices have their advantages.

(See Pattern Stamp tool, Patch tool and Heal tool)

When cloning fine detail look around for similar areas and try to follow a path that will make the sample look natural. In this part I cloned from the arrow heads and followed their direction.

Removing fencing or cages is fairly easy if you're handy with the clone tool.

Here I sampled from the edge of the rock and followed up in the direction of the arrow.

You may think areas of sky would be easy to clone, but that's not always the case. As the tones subtly change you could easily end up with an obvious line. Sample from a point as near to the area that you are cloning over.

The face was fairly easy to clone over. Keep a steady hand and follow patterns in the wool when cloning.

The end picture, with a small amount of noise added and cropped at the right, to provide a more pleasing composition. Free at last!

C

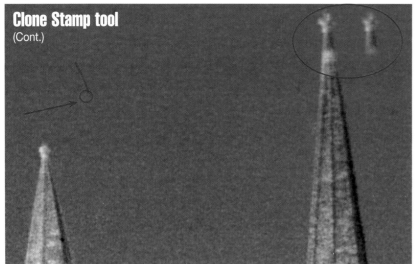

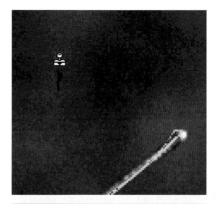

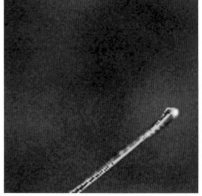

Clone aligned ensures the clone sample point stays at the same distance from the cursor as you move around cloning. This is useful when, as in our example above, you're cleaning up blemishes or dust in a sky. The sampling point (indicated by the arrow tip) will follow at the same distance from the cursor (cloning over the scratch) so the sampled pixels will usually be a similar color and texture. It's generally the best method to use and only falls down when, as in our example, it cloned the steeple when a blemish was just to the right. Here you would take a new sample to the right of the blemish.

Clone unaligned keeps the sample point where you left off so when you move the cursor it stays put. This is useful when you want to take a certain part of the image (sky in our case) and paint it in various other similar parts.

Play God and create new life. This started out with just four ducks!

Dust from scans of unclean transparencies can easily be removed. Select similar areas of color or pattern from nearby and sample from those to clone over the spot. Zoom in on screen and vary the brush size on different areas.

Some programs allow cloning to be applied at different percentages to produce a smaller or larger version of the original. Photoshop doesn't (right), but you can get round this by adding a new layer. Then take your sample point from the original layer and clone with the new layer active. Then use the Transform tool to rescale the cloned image.

You can take your sample point from one image and then reposition the cursor on a different one to clone onto it.

Clouds filter

MENU	FILTER →
	RENDER →
	CLOUDS

This useful addition to the Filters menu creates cloud effects that can be used as effective backgrounds to your pictures. Before selecting the filter make sure your background color is set to white and the foreground to the color sky you'd like. Blue creates natural skies while orange will deliver a sunset effect and black will produce a stormy sky.

Open a new canvas and set it to the size you want to end up with and select the filter. If you don't like the clouds that are created, try again – it's random.

Draw around your subject to make a selection, then copy and paste the selection onto an image created using the Clouds filter. Try experimenting with colors for unusual effects.

If the cloud effect is too harsh use Ctrl+ - key to reduce the image on screen. Then use the transform tool to stretch the clouds.

Go to Image→Adjust→Hue/Saturation (Ctrl+U), click on Colorize and adjust Hue to change color.

Use the Gaussian or Motion Blur filter to soften the effect.

You may wish to create a surreal sky. Simply select Hue/Saturation and adjust the sliders until the color you like pops up.

CMYK

When a digital image is printed it's converted from RGB into CMYK. CMYK is the standard method of printing and uses Cyan, Magenta and Yellow inks to make up the various colors.

A 100% combination of C, M and Y should produce black, but in reality it's a murky brown color so the Black ink (K to avoid confusion with the Blue of RGB) ensures black is printed where necessary.

Collage

Strictly speaking a collage is a collection of photographs mounted together, but Photoshop creates a perfect alternative by bringing several photos together to form one larger image that hasn't seen a drop of glue or sticky tape.

It's a great technique to use to create a family tree, group photo, promo, surreal image or, as below, a panel to go on a Web site or stationery header.

Using Layers makes the job much easier and more controllable. Here masks and blend modes allow lower layers to react with ones above. The binary text was created using the text tool and then distorted, skewed and stretched, to give it a forward look.

C

Color Balance

MENU	IMAGE →
	ADJUSTMENTS →
	COLOR BALANCE
QUICK KEYS	CTRL+B

Used to remove or create a color cast. The Color Balance palette has three sliders to control the color. Moving the top slider left adds cyan and reduces red. Move it to the right to add red and reduce cyan. The middle slider controls magenta and green and the bottom, yellow and blue. Precise values can be keyed in the top boxes. You can also select where you want the color to change, placing emphasis in the highlights, shadows or midtones. The final option is to Preserve Luminosity which maintains the original brightness when it's turned on.

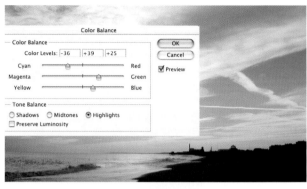

The above original lacks that extra something. Maybe a vivid glowing sunset. Applying lots of yellow and red gives a strong sunset that would make any shepherd delighted!

Or how about blue for a stormy winter sunrise effect? Almost anything's possible with the Color Balance sliders.

Daylight film is designed to produce a natural looking range of colors for outdoor photography or indoor shots taken with flash. Take a photo indoors without flash and you'll end up with a color cast. This will be green if the light source is fluorescent or orange if it's tungsten light.
Some flashguns are so harsh that they create a blue color cast. The walls in a room can also reflect light to add a color to your subject. Any color cast can be removed, or added, using Photoshop's Color Balance mode.

Color burn
(See Blending modes)

Color Channels
(See Channels)

Color dodge
(See Blending modes)

Color Range

| MENU | SELECT → |
| | COLOR RANGE |

Photoshop's Color Range is a versatile tool to help you select and change the color of a part of your picture. This could easily be a model's lipstick, car paint work or, as in this case, red pupils.

With the picture open call up the Color Range palette. To make it easier to see what you're doing click on Selection at the bottom of the palette to turn the preview window into a grayscale image. For this exercise also select Sampled Colors from the menu at the top of the palette.

Now click on the left-hand Eyedropper tool and position your cursor over a part of the red pupil and click once. You'll see areas of white appear on the grayscale preview. These are red pixels that are similar in color to the red you've just clicked on. Adjust the Fuzziness to control the range of reds that are selected.

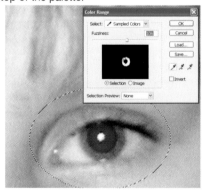

The Fuzziness slider above the preview window controls the range of reds either side of the one you picked. Adjusting the slider to the right increases the selection, and to the left decreases the selection.

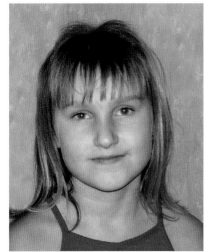

WHICH MASK?

The Color Range palette also lets you choose which type of mask to put over the image as you work. We've been using None, but the menu box, labelled Selection Preview at the bottom of the palette, has four other options. Grayscale makes the image look like the palette's preview. Black Matte (above) shows the unselected area black. White Matte makes the unselected area white. Quick Mask puts red over unselected areas.

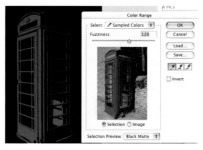

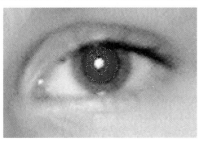

Another method is to let Photoshop pick the color you want to change. Go to the Select menu and pull down the Red option. Now you'll see the Fuzziness scale cannot be adjusted and everything that's red in the image has been selected. You can also use this method to select highlights, midtones or shadows. It couldn't be used in this example though because the girl's top would also be highlighted. Now turn to the Patch tool to see how we get rid of wrinkles.

Tip
● Press CTRL to change the grayscale preview to the color image or click inside the preview box.

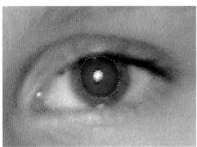

Color Replacement tool

QUICK KEY **J** Appears as the third option under the Heal and Patch tools in Photoshop CS's toolbar.

This is used to replace the color in the photograph with the foreground color selected and acts like a paintbrush to change the color. If you set the foreground color to black and the mode to hue it acts like a desaturation brush (below). You could previously do this by changing a photo from color to grayscale and then back to color, setting the History to the grayscale state and painting in with the History

brush. Using the Color replacement tool is a much quicker way.

It goes one stage further by working like the Magic eraser where it only replaces the color of pixels within the same tolerance range as the first sampled point. You can chose Hue, Saturation, Color or Luminosity modes.

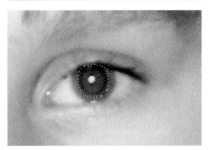

Each eye was selected using the + Eyedropper in the Color Range window and fuzziness was set to ensure all the red area was selected. Then hue/saturation was used to turn the eye to a suitable color.

C

Colorize

MENU   **IMAGE →**
ADJUSTMENTS →
HUE/SATURATION

Turned on in the Hue/Saturation palette to create a monocolor image. If you want to tone a black & white image first convert it to RGB, Image→Mode→RGB Color. Adjust the Hue slider and watch the image go from blue through the colors of the rainbow and back to blue. Stop when the image is the color you like and save. Use lightness and saturation sliders to vary color further.

I've included a range of examples here using a black & white infrared photograph with the various settings made. You could use these as starting points to colorizing your own photographs. The color tonal range is displayed below the rainbow color bar in the preview window.

Tick the preview box to ensure you see the effect as you adjust the sliders.

Original grayscale image

35

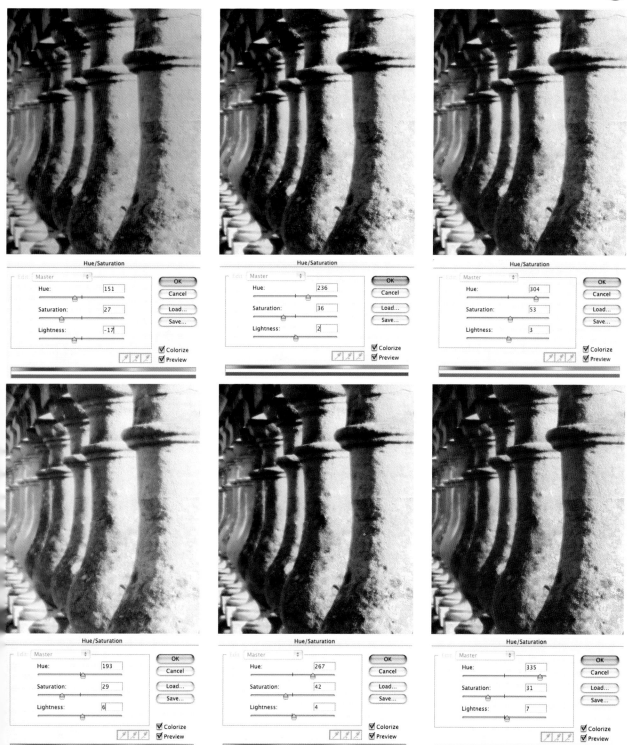

C

Color Sampler tool

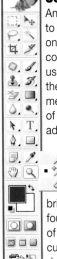

An Eyedropper tool that is used to place up to four sample points on the photo so you can compare color and density of each spot using measurements displayed in the Info palette. A second set of measurements appears at the side of the current values, showing the adjustments you make when using controls such as levels, curves, contrast and brightness. In this example I placed four samples in the highlight areas of the waterfall so I could adjust curves and ensure there was still detail in most parts.

Color Settings

MENU   EDIT →
        COLOR SETTINGS

Allows you to set up color profiles so that images you open up use a pre-selected color space. Spend some time setting this up correctly and you'll maintain consistent color when the image is displayed and printed. Mac OSX users will find the item under the Photoshop menu not the Edit menu.

Compression

Digital images can have huge file sizes. A 10x8in RGB image with a resolution of 300ppi, for example, has a file size of 21Mb. A few of these will start to fill up your computer's hard disk and a quick calculation finds you'll only ever fit 30 on a CD. It doesn't have to be this way. There are several file formats that change the data to reduce the file size – a method known as compression.

Two types exist – Lossy and Lossless. Lossy removes data for good, Lossless keeps it all safe. JPEG is the common storage format used by most digital cameras and Kodak's Picture CD. JPEG is a Lossy version and can affect the picture quality if it's highly compressed.

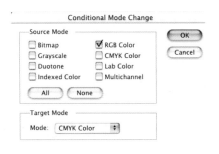

Conditional mode change

MENU   FILE →
        AUTOMATE →
        CONDITIONAL
        MODE CHANGE

Add this to an action to keep the color mode of a file the same when the action is being performed.

Contact sheet

MENU   FILE →
        AUTOMATE →
        CONTACT SHEET

Photoshop has a neat conversion that takes a collection of images and turns them into low resolution thumbnails that are positioned like a contact sheet.

It's a good way of keeping a record of your images and also to submit with CDs so the client can have a rough visual of what's included in the package.

You can choose the size of sheet and the number of pictures displayed across the page. The quality is a bit disappointing, but it's quick and easy to use.

Contact Sheet II

Source Folder
Choose... F/ BACK UP:Backup PIX on CD :Petespix10 :Infrared pics:
☑ Include All Subfolders

OK
Cancel

Document
Width: 8.268 inches
Height: 11.693 inches
Resolution: 240 pixels/inch
Mode: RGB Color
☑ Flatten All Layers

Thumbnails
Place: across first
Columns: 5   Width: 1.637 inches
Rows: 6   Height: 1.295 inches

☑ Use Filename As Caption
Font: Arial   Font Size: 12 pt

The pictures appear on the contact sheet in the same way that they have been saved. It's a shame you can't preview and rotate the pictures before you save the contact.

AlportIR750   bradfieldchurch.tif   CastleskyIR750   cambIR750.tif   cornwall.tif

FenceIR750   hillsborough par...   Infraredbench.tif   IvyIR750   IvyNo IR

JapanIRSFX   LakesIR750   library.tif   PassIR750   park2.tif

SheepIR750   ShelterIRHIE.tif   Stones2IR750   Stones3IR750   StonesIR750

TreeIRHIE.tif   treepond.tif   WhirlowcafeIRH...   WhirlowIRHIE.tif   WhirlowIRHIE3.tif

Contiguous
(See Magic wand)

Contrast

MENU   IMAGE → ADJUSTMENTS → BRIGHTNESS/ CONTRAST

The range of tones between black and white, or highlight and shadow.

A high contrast image is one where there's dark and light tones, but not much in between. Shots taken into the sun, or with the sun high in the sky are often high contrast.

A low contrast image is one that doesn't have many tones in the lightest or darkest areas so it looks quite gray and flat. Pictures taken in mist or dull conditions are often low contrast. In the traditional darkroom contrast is controlled using special variable-contrast paper – in the digital lab you simply adjust the sliders and watch the preview.

This is a very basic method of tonal adjustment and can cause the image to lose detail, which could be saved if you adjust contrast using the more advanced Levels or Curves.
(See Levels and Curves)

This photograph was taken with a Nikon D1X and was incorrectly set to underexpose so the image came out very dull and lacking contrast. Look at the Color Sampler tool values in the Info palette and see what happens to the highlights when contrast is raised using the Brightness/Contrast control.

C

Contrast

(Cont.)

Here's what happens when you adjust contrast of a black & white print. I adjusted the slider in 15 point increments going from –75 to +75.

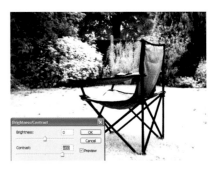

Adjusting contrast in a color image makes colors look dull and subdued when contrast is decreased (left) or vivid when contrast is increased (right). Edges can become overtly enhanced so the result looks very digital.

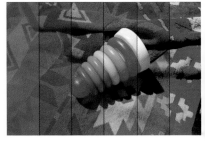

Convert to profile

MENU   **IMAGE →**
         MODE →
         CONVERT TO PROFILE

This changed from its previous title of Profile to Profile in version 5.5. It lets you convert a picture into a different color space so you can ensure a more accurate result when viewing or printing.

For this book I was given a CMYK profile by the printer which I used to convert all the RGB images before sending them to be printed.

Crop & Straighten

MENU   **FILE →**
         AUTOMATE →
         CROP & STRAIGHTEN PHOTOS

This feature, new to Photoshop CS, appeared a few years ago on flatbed scanners from the likes of Canon. It automatically detects the edges of a photo, that may have been scanned in with too much surroundings, and crops off the waste pixels. It also rotates if the picture was scanned at an angle like this example.

Tip
● Use this to tidy up screengrabs when you want a crop that's just around a palette. Do a rough crop using the crop tool to eliminate other parts of the desktop and leave the automated feature to remove the area around the palette.

Crop tool

Use this to be more creative with your composition and cut out wasteful surrounds. Click and hold down the mouse to draw a frame around the subject. Then use the handles to resize or reposition. When you've included everything you want click in the centre to make anything outside the frame disappear.

Photoshop 6 introduced a new version of the crop tool that masks all the area surrounding the crop frame in a colour and opacity of your choice. It's factory set at 75% black which gives a useful gray mask. This is much clearer to work with than previous versions and gives you a far better indication of the effect the crop will have on the image.

A tighter crop on this shot above adds emphasis to the face The Crop tool darkens the surrounding area to make it easier to judge the crop.

You can also click on perspective to allow the Crop box to be adjusted to straighten out perspective problems and badly squared shots, like this boat example, or off-vertical scanned images.

C

Cursor

The cursor is where all the action is. It's the point of the brush, the insertion point, the Cloning source, etc. and is controlled by the mouse or keyboard arrows.

The way it appears can be changed by going to File→ Preference→Displays & Cursors.

Paint cursors can be set to Standard, Precise or Brush Size. The brush or tool icon appears when the cursor is set to Standard, a crosshair appears on Precise and a shape the size of the brush being used appears with Brush size. Which you use is a matter of personal preference and may vary depending on the work you're doing. Try all three in different circumstances and pick whichever works best.

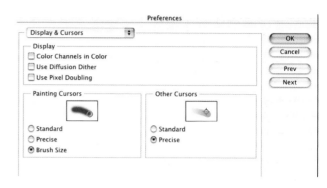

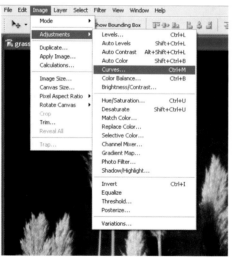

Tip

● The standard cursor shows an icon of the tool you are using. It's much better if you change to the precision or brush size icons.
(See Appendix D)

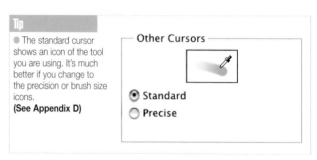

Curves

MENU	IMAGE →
	ADJUSTMENTS →
	CURVES
QUICK KEYS	CTRL+M

Curves is an advanced tonal control that offers the most accurate contrast, color and brightness adjustments of any Photoshop feature.

Its palette has a graph with vertical and horizontal scales representing input and output brightness.

When you first open this you'll see a straight line running through the graph at 45° from the bottom left to the top right. The bottom left represents the shadow area, top right is highlights and the midpoint is midtones. You can drag the line by clicking on it and holding down as you move the mouse. Moving the midpoint up has a lightening effect and down darkens the image. Use the Eyedropper tool and Ctrl+click anywhere on the image and its brightness value will appear as a point on the line. You can then move this point up or down to darken or lighten that part of the image. The picture will look natural, providing you create either a straight line or an arc. The best results are usually achieved with a very shallow S shaped curve, and is the reason why it's called Curves.

You can reverse the graph if you prefer the shadow detail to be at the top right and the highlights at the bottom left by clicking on the arrow on the horizontal bar.

Tips

● If you know what shape curve you want. Select the Pen icon and draw the line in the box. This can be quicker than dragging the line around.

● Hold down the Alt key and click on the grid to make it finer.

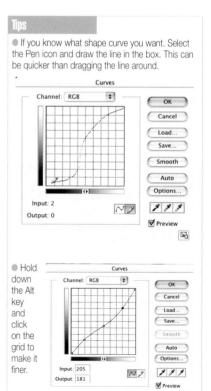

Dragging downwards from a point in the middle of the line darkens the midtones without clipping detail from the highlights or shadows.

Dragging upwards from a point in the middle of the line lightens the midtones without clipping detail from the highlights or shadows.

Tip

● A new feature, first introduced in Photoshop 7.0, lets you enlarge the Curves palette by clicking on the icon in the bottom right of the box. This helps you have more precise control of the curves graph. When you've done click on the icon again to reduce it.

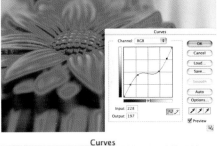

Harsh curves can create posterization. Keep them smooth!

The usual Curve to make is a slight downward direction of the 3/4 shadow areas and a slight upward movement of the first quarter highlight areas, creating a very gentle S shape. This gives a boost to contrast without clipping shadow or highlight detail that could occur when Levels or Brightness/Contrast is used.

Tip

● If you want extremely accurate control over your image, scan in or convert to 16-bit, instead of 8-bit, giving you a total of 48-bit color in an RGB image. Photoshop doesn't have layers in a 16-bit image, but you can edit the curves using this file and then compress back to 8-bit once you have a perfectly corrected image.

Tip

● If you need to make complex selections that require layers and masks and you are working with the 16-bit image, make a duplicate of the image Image→ Duplicate and save this as 8-bit. Work up the selection on the 8-bit image and save this selection Select→Save Selection. Then go back to the 16-bit version and load the saved selection Select→Load Selection. Now perform your curves adjustments.

C

Curves
(Cont.)

Curves can be used to make minor or major color adjustments. In this example I have selected the blue channel and pulled the highlight area upwards which intensifies the blue in the highlight area. This has made the flowers look a more vibrant blue without affecting the darker areas noticeably.

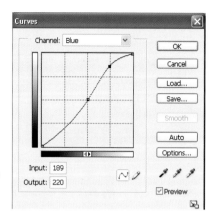

Better black & white

● Curves can be used to enhance your black & white pictures. Simply open up the picture and the Curves palette. First set up target white and black points for the Eyedropper (see Setting White and Black points). With targets set, click on the left-hand Eyedropper tool in the curves palette and, using your mouse cursor, place the Eyedropper icon on the darkest part of the image that you still want to contain minimal detail (deep shadow areas) and click. Do the same with the right-hand Eyedropper on the brightest area that you want minimal detail in (bright highlights) and click to produce an image with a more satisfactory tonal range. You must also choose the area that you click on with care as you could clip detail from the image if you select an area that's lighter or darker than necessary.

The original has a bad color cast.

Saturation is reduced so it becomes monocolor.

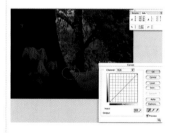

The shadow area is picked using the Eyedropper.

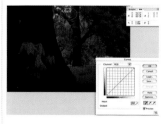

And then the highlight point selected which was in the bright sky area.

A duplicate layer was then made and Gaussian Blur was applied. Then the layer was blended in Overlay to finish off the improved infrared feel.

Curves
(Cont.)

Right: Pull the left part up from the bottom to top and the right down from top to bottom and totally reverse the image into a negative. Then drag the highlight area across to the right to wipe out all the detail and make the background white.
Below: You can also select up to 15 points on the line and pull them in either direction to create snake patterns and very interesting results. This is a mode to experiment with, especially if you enjoy creating surreal effects. If you stumble across a style you like you can save it to reuse on other images later.

Custom color table

Images produced to be used on the Web need small file sizes. Photoshop reduces the number of colors from millions down to just 256 when it saves files as GIFs and the colors that are used can be saved as a custom table. This photo of canal boats would contain these 256 colours when reduced.

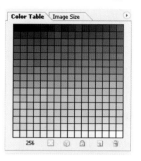

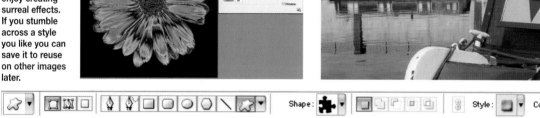

Custom Shape tool

Custom Shapes are selected from the toolbar and when selected they allow you to draw vector shapes that have editable path outlines. They can also be resized without any loss in definition as they are resolution independent.

Shapes can be filled with colors, patterns or images. You can also distort using the

Rectangle Tool	U
Rounded Rectangle Tool	U
Ellipse Tool	U
Polygon Tool	U
Line Tool	U
Custom Shape Tool	U

Transform tool and save as a selection which can then be saved as a clipping path.

The hand shape was selected here and a gradient fill was applied on top, along with a drop shadow and rounded bevel.

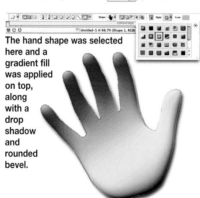

The Jigsaw piece Custom shape was selected and its path made into a selection. Then the new image was pasted into the selection – Edit→Paste Into. This creates a new layer with a layer mask that can then be edited.

Click on the arrow to the right of the Custom Shape palette to access the groups of custom shapes (right). The full selection of 249 Custom Shapes that come with Photoshop CS are seen below.

Darken mode
(See Blending modes)

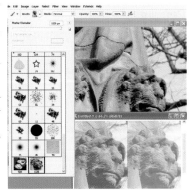

Define Brush

MENU   EDIT →
          DEFINE BRUSH PRESET

A useful feature hidden
away within Photoshop's
brush edit menu is the
Define Brush mode.
Selecting part of any
image, followed by
Edit → Define Brush Preset, converts the selection into a preset
that can then be used as a brush shape. The new brushes
appear in the Brush palette and can be adjusted in size like any
other brush. Copy a whole object and you can paint like you

would using Picture Tubes in Paint
Shop Pro.
    You can also create your own simple
graphics and use them as a brush
preset. **(See Brushes)**

Use the brush to simulate a 3D photo. The
lion statue was selected and turned into a
brush preset. Then red was selected and a
single click made on a fresh canvas using
the lion brush creates a red lion. Repeat with
green but slightly offset so it's out of register
with the original red lion. The picture looks
bad, but when you now view through red/
green 3D glasses you'll see a 3D shape.

Define Pattern

MENU   EDIT →   This is similar to define brush, but requires
          DEFINE PATTERN   you to make a rectangular selection
and then save this as a pattern using the Edit→Define pattern
option. Your saved pattern appears in the pattern group of
presets and can then be used to paint a stitched pattern on a
canvas using the Pattern Stamp tool. **(See Pattern Maker)**

A sample area was selected from the
rocks and then, once defined, the
pattern was selected from the drop
down menu (left) and used to paint
the rocky pattern (below). Use this to
make effective backgrounds.

d

Defringe

MENU   **LAYER →**
               MATTING →
               DEFRINGE

No matter how hard you try, when cutting round a subject you usually leave a few pixels from the old background. When you paste the cutout to the new background the unwanted pixels may stick out like a sore thumb. This orange flower, for example, cut out from a typical green foliage background has a few dark green pixels around the edge that show up when it's pasted to its new blue background.

The Defringe command changes these green pixels to orange to produce a cleaner effect. Like most commands, you can enter a pixel value, in this case, a width of between 1 and 200 pixels, depending on the nature of your original selection.

The above left is the straight cutout and above right is after a defringe value of 50 was applied to the pasted image. Below is the full version. I tidied up the centre as well by Cloning out the stray petals.

De-interlace filter

A filter used to smooth moving images captured on video.

Desaturation

MENU   **IMAGE →**
               ADJUSTMENTS →
               DESATURATE
QUICK KEYS **SHIFT+CTRL+U**

This mode takes all the color out of an RGB image, changing it to black & white without you having to convert it to grayscale. This is useful if you then want to add a color tone.

You can also desaturate an image by dragging the Saturation slider to the left in the Hue/Saturation mode.

Deselect

MENU   **SELECT →**
               DESELECT
QUICK KEYS **CTRL+D**

Removes the 'marching ants' selection from the image. Ctrl+Z would put them back again.

Despeckle filter
(See Noise filter)

Difference mode
(See Blending modes)

Direct Selection tool

QUICK KEYS SHIFT+A This is used to pick up Anchor points on a Path made by the Pen tool and either move the entire path, change a point or create a Bézier curve around the subject.

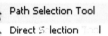

Dissolve mode
(See Blending modes)

Distortion filter

MENU   **FILTER →**   A collection of   **DISTORT →**   filters that distort the image. If you have an older computer be patient, some of these filters are memory intensive and apply to your image at a snail's pace.

Use them with care. If applied to a full image, like the main example, the result may look naff. They are illustrated like this so you can compare the affect of each on the same photo.

Use them creatively on selections within an image and the filters can be much more valuable. Below are a few examples of things to try.

Above: A window created through an archway using the Glass Distort filter. Below: Distorted ripples in the water using the Shear filter. Above right: An oval selection around the flower was inverted and the background was then treated with the Wave filter. Below right: The Zigzag Pond Ripple used was in a selection of just the water.

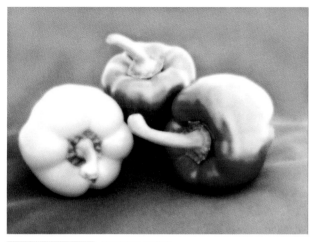

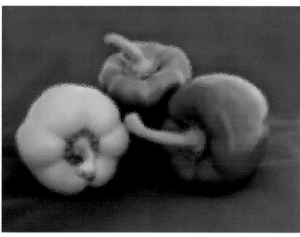

DIFFUSE GLOW

Creates an effect similar to looking through a soft diffusion filter by adding see-through white noise to the image and a glow, fading from the centre of the selection. Can be used to simulate infrared film effects. The palette has sliders to control the graininess, amount of glow and clear amount.

GLASS

Applies a distorted effect that looks like the view through a bathroom window. There's a choice of four styles and others can be created and loaded manually.

The palette has sliders to control the distortion level, smoothness and scale which can then be viewed in the preview window.

DISPLACE

Changes the image into a pattern that's previously been saved as a Displacement Map. These can be created from your own images or you can use one of the 12 supplied in the Displacement

Maps folder within Photoshop's Plug-Ins folder. The palette has options to tile a Displacement Map that's too small for the image you're applying it to or stretch it to fit. A tiled Map is the same image repeated to fit to the edges. The stretched version creates interesting effects and can be varied by changing the percentages in the horizontal and vertical scales.

OCEAN RIPPLE

Similar effect to the Glass filter, offering two sliders to control ripple size and magnitude.

d

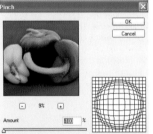

PINCH
A slider that varies from –100 to +100 to make the centre of the image appear to expand like a balloon or squeeze in like an hour glass.

RIPPLE
Another effect like Ocean Ripple that creates a water pattern on the selected area.

The slider controls the amount of ripple and a pull down menu has three ripple sizes.

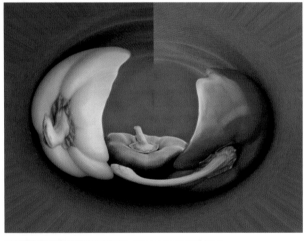

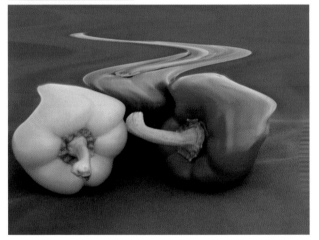

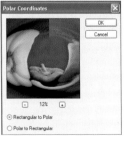

POLAR COORDINATES
Unusual effect with two options to convert the image from either rectangular to polar coordinates or vice versa. Can be used with text to stretch it round an image, or combined with a few other filters to create strange backgrounds.

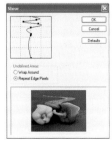

SHEAR
Displays a grid and a straight vertical line that you pull around to make a curved shape. This shape transfers to the selected image, distorting it along the curve.

SPHERIZE
In Normal mode it produces a similar effect to Pinch. In Horizontal Only the image becomes thinner or thicker as you adjust the slider and in Vertical Only it becomes shorter or taller.

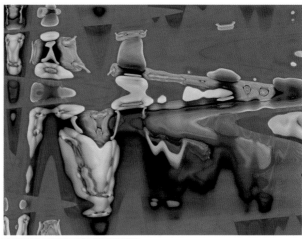

WAVE
An advanced version of the Ripple filter with seven slider and five buttons to choose from that control the number of wave generators, the distance between waves, the height and the type. Experiment at your leisure or press the Randomize button and let it choose a value.

TWIRL
Creates a spiral effect similar to the way water goes down a plug hole. It works in a clockwise or anti-clockwise direction depending on where the slider is set.

ZIGZAG
Another Ripple style distortion but one that includes the realistic Pond Ripple option. Apply this to water and it will look just like you've thrown a pebble in before taking the photograph.

d

Document Size

Click on the small arrow in the bottom left-hand corner of the image to show a five line menu. One option is Document Size that displays two values. The first is the size of the file if it's flattened to remove Layers data. The second is the value including Layers data and Channels.

Dots per inch (dpi)

This is the measurement used to determine output resolution of a printer or monitor and is often confused with PPI (pixels per inch) which is the capture resolution of cameras and scanners. A 200dpi print means there are 200 dots laid down across every inch of the paper. The latest 2880dpi printers are capable of placing 2880 dots of ink in an inch, but several of these are used in each pixel to ensure the highest color accuracy and that's where the confusion lies. It's understandable to fall into the trap of thinking that you need to create an image with 2880ppi to get the best results from a high spec printer when generally no more than 300ppi images are necessary.

When viewing on a monitor you need even less, as the typical resolution of a monitor is just 72dpi.

Dodge tool

Works like the darkroom dodging device. Hold the paddle over your image and the areas it covers will become lighter.

The palette's options include a menu to set for dodging midtones, highlights or shadows, along with an opacity setting to vary the strength of the dodging effect.

The dodge tool has been used on the background of this image to produce a misty appearance. I also lightened the shaded areas of the pagoda.

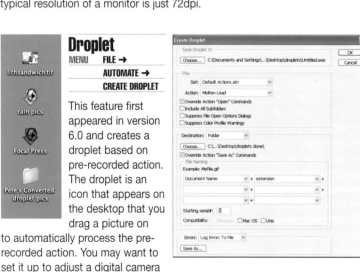

Droplet

MENU   FILE ➜
      AUTOMATE ➜
      CREATE DROPLET

This feature first appeared in version 6.0 and creates a droplet based on pre-recorded action. The droplet is an icon that appears on the desktop that you drag a picture on to automatically process the pre-recorded action. You may want to set it up to adjust a digital camera picture. Here you could pre-record an action that changes the resolution from 72ppi to 240ppi, adds a faint orange hue to give a feeling of warmth and a touch of Unsharp mask to improve the digital image.

Drop shadow

MENU   LAYER →
       LAYER STYLE →
       DROP SHADOW

Photoshop 6.0 introduced this to create drop shadows more easily. All you do is make a selection, go to the filter and apply the shadow. From the palette menu you can choose the Blend mode,

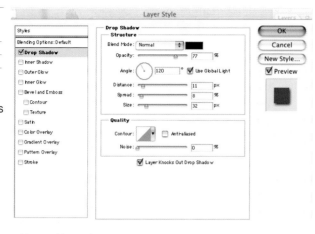

opacity, angle, distance, blur and intensity – play around until you're happy with the results. When you're happy you can apply the effect to your image and save the shadow for use later.

I often use the Drop shadow feature on a small selection of photos placed on one canvas to create a feeling of several pictures being laid down on a piece of paper. The shadow makes them look raised from the canvas.
Here's how it's done.

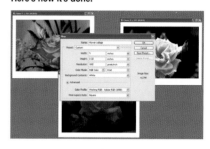

A selection was made around the statue, which was then copied and pasted onto a new layer and a drop shadow created on that new layer.

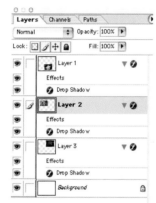

First open the pictures you want to use. Then resize them so they all fit on the new canvas. Now select one and copy it. Going to File→New produces a canvas the same size as the copied photo. Adjust the size so that it's about two centimetres larger in height and width than the total of the photos, and paste the first one that's still in the clipboard. It will appear in the middle of the canvas. Use the Move tool to get it into the right place. Now copy and paste the remaining pictures, moving each into place. Apply the Drop Shadow on one of the images and then drag the Shadow Effects onto all the other picture layers in the layers palette.

After gently rotating each image, I took advantage of the Pattern Stamp tool to paint the sand and marble textures for a natural background.

Duotone mode

MENU   **IMAGE →**

        MODE →

        DUOTONE

Grayscale images display up to 256 shades of gray, but a printing press only reproduces around 50 levels per ink. Grayscale images printed with black ink look coarser than ones printed with two or more inks.

Duotones are images with two colors that increase the tonal range of a grayscale image and look stunning when subtly applied. When black is used for shadows and gray for midtones and highlights you produce a black & white image. Versions printed using a colored ink for the highlights produce an image with a slight tint that significantly increases its dynamic range.

You need to be in grayscale mode before you can enter the world of Duotones (Image→Mode→Grayscale). Choose a Duotone preset by clicking on Load and locate it in the Presets folder, or create your own color by clicking on the colored ink squares to call up the color wheel.

Ink 1 Black Ink 2 None

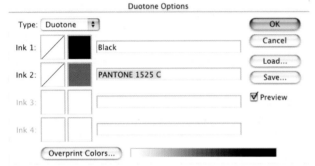

Select a color you like and watch the bar at the base of the palette appear as a range of hues from black to white. If you stumble across a Duotone color effect you'd like to keep click on save and put the *.ado file in a folder. It can then be called up from the Load option when required.

If you're new to color tone adjustments and only intend printing out on an inkjet printer it would be safer to use the Variations edit mode, which is far easier to adjust and can be applied to RGB files. **(See Tritones and Quadtones or Variations)**

Ink 1 Black Ink 2 Pantone 292c

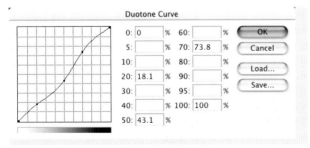

You can edit the duotone curve by clicking on it to bring up a new dialogue box. Moving the curve right makes colors print heavier in the shadows while moving it to the left makes colors print lighter in highlights.

Ink 1 Black Ink 2 Pantone 1525c

Ink 1 Black Ink 2 Pantone 129c

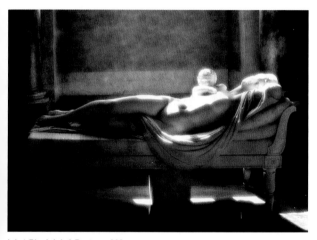

Ink 1 Black Ink 2 Pantone 362c

Ink 1 Black Ink 2 Pantone 246c

Duplicating images

MENU	IMAGE →
	DUPLICATE

Opens up an identical copy of the image and keeps the original open. You can also use the drag and drop method to duplicate one image onto another and avoid using up any RAM. Just click on the image you want to copy, hold down the mouse and drag the cursor over to the destination canvas. If, as in this example, you drag a color image onto a black & white one it will be automatically converted.

Tip

● The Duplicate image mode is helpful if you work with 16-bit files and find the missing features a handicap. Simply duplicate the image, save as an 8-bit file and anything you do on this can then be transferred back to the 16-bit version. This is useful when want to make complicated selections. If you make a selection using a Quick Mask in the 8-bit copy and then hold down the Shift key as you drag the selection from the 8-bit image to the 16-bit image it ensures the selection is in register on the 16-bit version.

Duplicating layers

MENU	LAYER →
	DUPLICATE LAYER

Adding a duplicate layer in the same image is useful when you want to produce complex multi-layered images using Blend modes. Layers can also be duplicated from one image into another using the same drag and drop technique, as described in duplicating images, or copied and pasted.

Tip

● Hold down the Alt key as you duplicate the image to add 'copy' automatically to the end of the title.

Dust & Scratches filter
(See Noise filter)

Edges

An edge is formed where adjacent pixels have high contrasting values. Photoshop has a number of filters that detect these and apply contrast reducing or increasing effects to soften or sharpen the image accordingly. **(See Find Edges filter)**

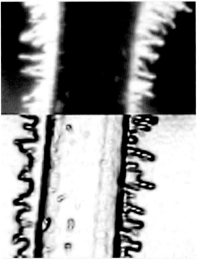

The top half of the picture (left) is an enlarged part of the stem of the plant in the picture above.
The Find Edges filter picks up all the areas of edge contrast and produces an almost posterized version that highlights these edges.

Elliptical marquee tool
(See Marquee tools)

Embedded profile mismatch

This box appears when you open a picture that has an embedded profile that is different to the one you use for your working color space. You then have three options. For best results you should select Convert providing you have set up your color management correctly.

Emboss filter
(See Stylize filters)

Equalize

MENU   **IMAGE →**
              ADJUSTMENTS →
              EQUALIZE

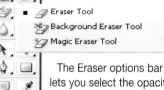

A quick fix that can help brighten up a dark scanned image that cannot be improved using Auto Levels. When you apply the Equalize command Photoshop redistributes the brightness values of the image's pixels so that they more evenly represent the entire range of brightness levels. It does this by finding the brightest and darkest values in the image and then adjusts the levels so that the brightest value is white and the darkest value is black. It then equalizes the brightness by distributing the intermediate pixels evenly throughout the grayscale.

You can also equalize just a selected area of an image by using one of the selection tools before you go to the equalize menu. In this mode you also have the option of applying the values within that selected area to the whole photo.

Equalizing picture A produces B. This is because the photo has dominant light tones which caused the process to overcompensate. If you make a selection of a representative area, picture C, and choose 'Equalize entire image based on selected area' you get a better result, as illustrated in picture D.

Eraser

Use this to remove pixels, replacing them with the background color, or to a previous state using the Erase to History option, or to an underlying layer.

Eraser Tool   E
Background Eraser Tool   E
Magic Eraser Tool   E

The Eraser options bar lets you select the opacity of the Eraser and can be set to gradually fade out in a selected number of steps.

You can choose from three brush styles including Paintbrush, Pencil and Block (users of version 6.0 please note that the Airbrush is now selected from a separate icon) and also vary the size of these from the Brush options box.

The Paintbrush has a Wet Edges option that produces a stronger effect towards the edges of the brush stroke.

The Erase to History option was selected here with a point before desaturation took place. Then when you erase you bring back the original color.

Tip

● Shift+E rotates through the various brush options.

Exclusion mode
(See Blending modes)

Exif data

Most digital cameras now capture and store information about the picture such as exposure details, properties, etc. This data, known as Exif data, stays with the picture and is read by Photoshop. It's useful when you are learning photography to compare pictures and exposure data to see what works and what doesn't.

In Photoshop 7 the info was found under the Exif tab of the File info window. In Photoshop CS it's split into a basic version showing main camera info or a huge list of recorded data under an advanced tab. Exif data also appears within the Metadata section in the File Browser.
(See File Browser and File info)

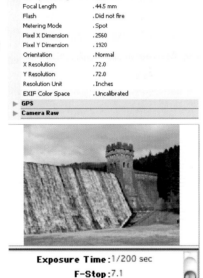

The illustrations above show the level of Exif data that's accessed from the File Browser. The two below show data that's accessed via file Info.

Exporting files

MENU   FILE ➔
         EXPORT ➔

Photoshop comes with two plug-in modules to export files to GIFs (using File➔Save for Web or, using File➔Export, you can save Paths to Adobe Illustrator. Paths to Illustrator converts Photoshop paths created with the Pen tool into Illustrator files.

Exporting from clipboard

As with most programs that handle pictures and text, when you copy an item it is saved in the program's clipboard. Photoshop is just the same, so pictures can be copied and then pasted into other programs.

Exposure correction

When an image is too dark or too light, caused by either poor scanning or a badly exposed original, it can be corrected using several Photoshop features. Brightness is the most basic but easiest to understand, Levels adds slightly more control, but Curves is the more advanced method of exposure correction **(See Levels, Curves and Brightness)**

Levels were used to lighten this image shot on a Fujifilm Finepix S2 Pro.

Extract

MENU	**FILTER →**
	EXTRACT
QUICK KEYS	**CTRL+ALT+X**

This feature, introduced in Photoshop 5.5, makes selecting objects from their background easier and is especially useful on complex cutouts such as hair.

You first draw around the edge that you want to cut out using the Edge Highlight tool. Then fill the inner area with the Fill tool. When you click 'preview' the command goes to work and produces a foreground cut out on a transparent background.

If you're happy with the preview cutout click on OK and the extraction is applied. In a few moments you are delivered a cutout that can then be dropped onto another background.

Version 6.0 introduced a few extra features to make the selection process even easier. Draw around the edge using the Smart Highlight tool and it calculates how easy it is to select the object and adjusts the thickness of pen to suit. If the edge detail is complex it makes the pen line thicker and if the edge is well defined the pen line becomes thinner.

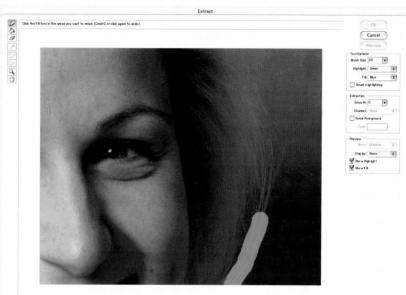

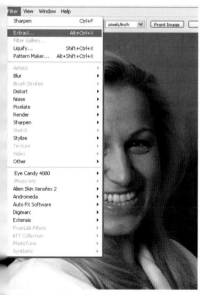

Cutting round the hair on this photo could be really difficult to do using one of the normal selection tools.

Paint over the edge that you want to cut round ensuring foreground and background areas are both covered by the highlighter. Use a larger sized highlight brush to paint over areas that aren't easy to define such as the hair where fine strands appear. Select a smaller size brush for the definite edges such as this girl's blouse.

The Smart Highlight tool, introduced on version 6.0, automatically adjusts pen thickness as you draw around the subject you want to extract.

When the selection is complete click in the centre, using the bucket/fill tool and then click on preview to see the extraction take place.

Depending on the speed of your computer's processor and the size of the image this could take a few minutes, or longer, to perform the task.

Extract
(Cont.)

The extracted image can be viewed in a number of ways. The preset version appears with a transparent background, but you can also select a gray, white (above middle) or black matte (above right) which are often more useful to display how good the cutout is. You can also select your own color, using the color picker. Version 6.0 even has an option to view the cutout as a mask (left).

It helps to look at the preview in the mask mode when using the new Clean Up and Edge Touch up editing tools. Both are used after the preview has been made to improve the accuracy of the extraction.

Tip

● When you've made an extracted selection it's often better to tidy it up using the clean-up tools in the extract box. In this example I've erased some of the straddling hairs to tidy up the cutout.

Once you have your extracted subject you can either drop the picture onto an existing canvas or create a new one with an interesting background. Here the green canvas effect (right) was achieved in Photoshop using the Clouds filter, followed by Contrast adjustment, Gaussian Blur and a dark vignette. You could also use one of your own photos as a ready-made background as I have done here with the picture of an old leaded window frame (above).

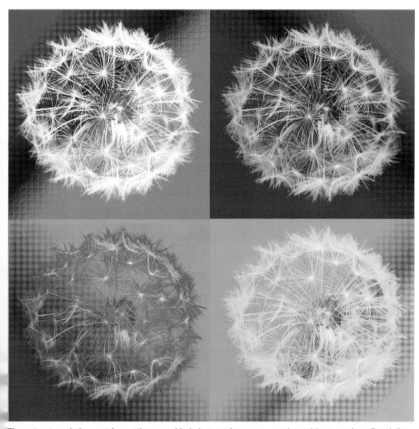

Eyedropper

This tool is normally used to select the foreground or background color and the only control you have is selecting the sampling area which can be accurate to one pixel, 3x3 or 5x5. Simply position the dropper end over the area you want to sample and click the mouse to take the sample which becomes the foreground color.

Eyedropper Tool   I
Color Sampler Tool   I
Measure Tool   I

Holding down the Alt key when you click selects the background color. The Eyedropper also appears in several other palettes, including Replace Color, Color Range, Levels, Curves and Hue/Saturation.

The extract mode is great for cutting round hair, but not for more complex subjects such as Dandelion Clocks. This example was brushed over using the Magic eraser before being pasted into this grid of color. If the Extract tool had been used I would have had to paint within all the inner areas of the seeds and it would have taken for ever!

Tip

● Some areas of the image that you wanted to keep may have been erased. If this happens set the History brush onto the stage prior to the extraction and paint back the missing pixels.

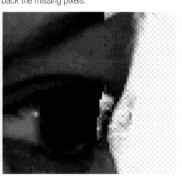

Tip

● Hold down the Alt key while using the Airbrush to convert it into an Eyedropper.

f

abcde**f**ghijklmnopqrstuvwxyz

Fade command

MENU	EDIT →
	FADE
QUICK KEYS	CTRL+SHIFT+F

The fade command allows any filter or color change to be reduced in strength using this fade control. The effect can also be adjusted using the fade with a Blend mode making the filter appear as though it's on a separate layer to give a completely different feel. Definitely one to experiment with. The Fade command moved to the edit menu on version 6.0. Version 5.5 users will find it in the filter menu.

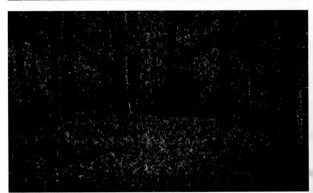

The Fresco effect from the Artistic filter menu has created a moody oil painting (middle). The Fade command, set to Luminosity Blend mode, gives added sparkle in the greens which is further enhanced by increasing brightness and contrast (bottom).

The Pencil effect from the Artistic filter menu has created a weak pastel result (right). The Fade command, set to Multiply Blend mode, increases contrast to give more vibrant coloring (below).

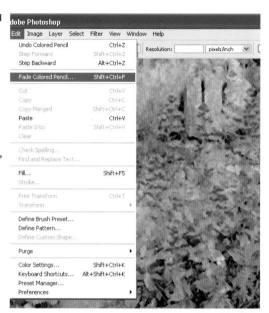

Here's what happens when the Fade is used after an artistic filter has been applied.

Two extreme effects of using the Fade option with a Blend mode.

Taking the fade mode a stage further, I've applied a few filter effects to this photograph of an osteospermum flower and then used the Fade command and various Blend modes to show what affects can be achieved. Turn the page for a visual feast.

62

f

Fade command
(Cont.)

The first stage was to play around with the Channel mixer to get some alternative colors, and then I faded the effect using Linear Light blend to really make the colors fly.

The Radial Blue filter was applied followed by Fade with Luminosity Blend.

The Graphic pen filter was applied followed by Fade with Luminosity Blend.

The Graphic pen filter was applied followed by Fade with Exclusion Blend.

The Neon Glow filter was applied followed by Fade with Difference Blend.

The Neon Glow filter was applied followed by Fade with Luminosity Blend.

The Neon Glow filter was applied followed by Fade with Pin Light Blend.

The Neon Glow filter was applied followed by Fade with Linear Burn Blend.

The Extrude filter was applied followed by Fade with Hard Light Blend.

The Extrude filter was applied followed by Fade with Lighten.

The Emboss filter was applied followed by Fade with Color Blend.

The Emboss filter was applied followed by Fade with Overlay Blend.

f

Feathering

MENU	SELECT →	Useful feature
	FEATHER	that's used to
QUICK KEYS	CTRL+ALT+D	soften the edge

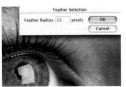

of a selection before you cut out or add a filter effect.

You control the pixel width of feather from the selection area inwards and outwards. The result is a gradual softening rather than a harsh edge.

A small feather of one or two pixels is all that's needed to make a cutout appear less obvious when pasted on a new background. A large feather of around 30 is better when you're adjusting the brightness, contrast or color of a selection within an image. The size of feather you choose depends on the number of pixels in the image. As with most features it's best to try several settings before committing the image to disk.

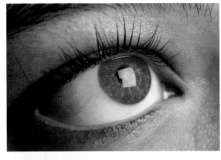

Feathering can be used to remove red-eye caused by flash or to color the pupils. Left top is what happens if you don't feather the selection. Left middle has a large feather so the red has bled into the white. In this example a +20 feather gives the best result with, apart from the choice of color, a realistic feel. A feather of +20 will not always be right, it depends on the total size of your image. Start at +20 and repeat stages until the ideal most effective size is discovered.

Feathering is ideal for wedding and portrait photography where a vignette is required. Simply make a selection, feather, then paste onto a new white canvas. Below left: selection made with no feather. Below middle: 50 feather, the edge is still quite hard. Below right: 150 feather and now although the effect is about right, you can see the edge of the print. A 100–120 feather would be perfect.

Fibres

MENU   **FILE →**
         RENDER →
         FIBRES

A useful background creating filter, introduced with Photoshop CS that produces a fibre style effect from the foreground and background colours. Once created you can adjust the pattern using blur and transform tools, as seen here.

It may come in useful for producing scratched metal effects, worn wood and

various cloth styles, making it suitable as another background creator.

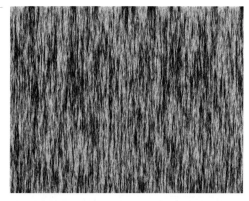

● Once you have created your Fibres go to Filter→Blur→Motion blur and add a horizontal blur. Then add Gaussian blur and Noise to create a weathered look.

File Browser

The File Browser was introduced in Photoshop 7.0. It looks much like a Windows Explorer interface, with folders on the left that open up on the right when you double click on them to view the contents. Select a folder of images and the contents appear as easy to view thumbnails that can be changed in size.

The layout can be changed so you can view small, medium or large thumbnails, and text alongside the pictures. Clicking on a thumbnail creates a large preview back on the left with information about the photograph. If you have pictures taken with digital cameras and haven't changed format it will also show details of the camera used and full exposure details.

You can also rename thumbnails in the browser, which alters the name of the original in its folder. You can also alter the orientation from horizontal to vertical or vice versa and when you next open the image in Photoshop it will automatically rotate to the correct format.

Photoshop CS sees the addition of an advanced Keyword database and a Metadata search, making it function more like a basic cataloguing program.

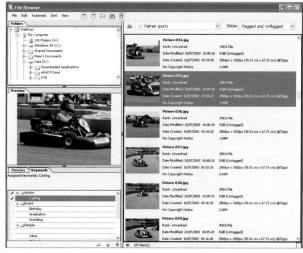

Bottom right: The browser seen in Large Thumbnail view. Bottom left: In Medium Thumbnail view. Above: Showing file info using Details option.

f

File conversion

Photoshop files can be converted into other formats suitable for different uses. When you save an image, select File→Save As and pull down the Save As menu bar in the palette to see a list of file formats to choose from. Then drag the cursor over the one you want to save in that format. Help screens will appear where necessary.

File format

Digital pictures can be saved in numerous formats, each having distinct advantages, well most do! The JPEG format is one of the most popular, so is TIFF, EPS, GIF and not forgetting Photoshop's very own PSD format. **(See the entries of individual file formats)**

File info

MENU **FILE → FILE INFO** A dialogue box with several pages completely rewritten for Photoshop CS. The first has spaces to add a picture caption, headline and special instructions that can be saved and used on future projects. The second and third pick up recorded exposure data from the camera. Next is the category file, then History and Origin with detailed Exif data and metadata in the last Advanced section. You can scroll through the pages using the up and down arrow keys. **(See Exif Data)**

File optimizing

You should always optimize pictures when saving them for Web use. The idea is to remove any color that can't be seen by a Web browser as well as resizing to suit the viewing conditions (usually Mac or PC monitor) and saving it all in the most suitable format (usually JPEG or GIF). This is made easier when you use the Save for Web option in Photoshop. **(See Save for Web)**

Filling color

MENU **EDIT → FILL** Works like the Bucket tool and drops color into the selection. Choose to fill using the foreground or background color in the palette. You can also adjust opacity and select a Blend mode to vary the result.

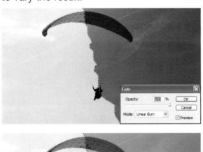

A rough selection was made around the black & white bottle neck. Then a green fill was applied. Left is unfeathered selection, right has a 5 pixel feather to smooth the fill and make the result look more natural. The close up inset pictures are taken from a point near the top of the neck.

Fill Layer

MENU **LAYER →**
NEW FILL LAYER →
A time saving feature that was introduced with version 6.0. Lets you fill a layer with a solid color, gradient or pattern. Fill layers do not affect the layers underneath them, but can be used in a composite picture to add a color, gradient or pattern to an image which becomes more effective when the fill layer's opacity is reduced.

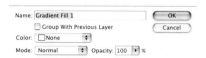

This old tower ruin gives you some more examples of what can be done. Setting the foreground color to black will introduce a dark and moody gradient (below left), while orange gives a sort of sunset effect (right). You could also add a pattern fill (below)...but maybe not for this shot!

Here I set the fill layer to gradient and added an orange gradation. Notice how the layer blocks the layer below. I then selected Multiply from the Blend mode menu to allow the layer below to come through. The original blue of the lower layer has now blended with the yellow in the fill layer to create a green band.

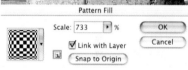

Filters

These are effects that change the look of the photograph by altering the pixels. There are many

filters supplied with Photoshop, but many more can be added from third party developers. Filters are found in the, surprise, surprise, filter menu and are listed individually in this book. The filter effect, and time taken to apply it, will vary due to the number of pixels in the picture. A low resolution picture (above left) will process quickly, but the effect may be very harsh, whereas a high resolution image (above right) delivers a more subtle result.

Tip
● Some filter effects are very memory intensive and can take ages to apply. There's nothing more annoying than waiting for an effect to materialize and then be disappointed by the result. To save time make a selection of a key part of the image and apply the filter to this small area.
If the effect works undo it by clicking on the previous state in the history palette or use the Undo (command+Z) shortcut.

f

Filter gallery

MENU   FILTER →
FILTER GALLERY

This feature is new to Photoshop CS and groups all the filters into one area where you can apply a filter quickly to see what effect it will have on your photo. You can also apply several filter effects using the layers option within the filter gallery and turn these on and off or rearrange the order. The palette is a little slow to load up, but once in place, the creative doors open wide!

Find and replace text

MENU   EDIT →
FIND AND REPLACE TEXT

Another word based feature that was introduced with version 7.0. This is used to search through text and replace one word, punctuation or sentence with another. Just key in what you want to replace in the 'Find What' box and what you want to change it to in the 'Change To' box. Then click 'Find Next'. The program searches for the words and highlights the first example it comes to. You then can change just the found words or change all occurrences or change the found one and then let it find the next.

Some filter effects are very memory int and can take ages to apply. There's noth annoying than waiting for an effect to m o be disappointing by the result. To sav make a selection of a key part of the im apply the filter to this small area. If the undo it by clicking on the previous stat palette or use the Undo (command+Z)

Fit image

MENU   FILE →
AUTOMATE →
FIT IMAGE

An automated feature that resizes the image so that it will fit within a certain predetermined canvas space. If, for example, you have the measurements set to 680x480 and apply the Fit image command to a 600x600 picture it would reduced it to 480x480. This helps when you need to resize pictures to suit a newsletter or catalogue format with predetermined picture boxes.

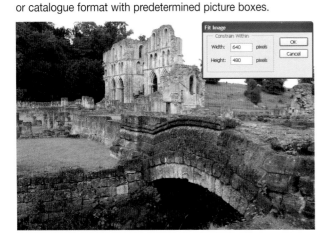

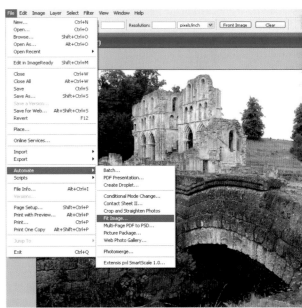

Here a landscape format of 640x480 pixel measurements was selected to suit viewing on a basic monitor. This reduced the height of the portrait format picture to 480 pixels.

Flatten image

MENU **LAYER →**
FLATTEN IMAGE Images with individual

layers can only be saved in the Photoshop PSD file format and need to be merged (flattened) if you want an alternative format. Merging layers reduces the size of the file so it's worth doing if you're totally happy with your results.

In this example eleven layers are used which result in a 25Mb image (above). When merged the file size becomes just 5.72Mb (right).

Tip
● If you want to keep the image with layers but need a version in another file format, choose File→Save a Copy to create a flattened duplicate.

Foreground color

QUICK KEYS **SHIFT+X** The foreground color is used to paint, fill and stroke selections and appears as the upper square in the toolbox. You can change the color by either sampling from an image using the Eyedropper, clicking on the colored square to call up the color picker, or choosing Window→ Show color to bring up the Color palette.

Freehand Lasso tool
(See Lasso tools)

Freehand Pen tool
(See Pen tools)

Fuzziness setting

A similar feature to Tolerance that determines how many colors are selected by the Eyedropper tool in the Color Range mode. Sliding the control to the right increases the fuzziness and allows a larger range of colors to be picked.

Tips
● Avoid high fuzziness levels – they create blurred edges and settings too low can cause jagged edges and missing selected pixels.
● Keep your finger held down on the mouse button as you move around the preview image with the Eyedropper icon. This will continually adjust the selection.

In this example I have taken a sample from the grass using the Eyedropper tool and a high fuzziness setting of 130. The preview shows that the selection includes all the grass and avoids picking up background pixels.

The same example with a higher fuzziness setting of 192 picks up all the grass, but also much of the background too.

g

Gamut warning

MENU   VIEW ➜
        GAMUT WARNING
QUICK KEYS SHIFT+CTRL+Y

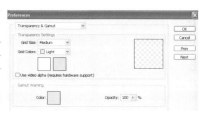

The range of colors a computer monitor can display is known as the gamut and the monitor's gamut has a larger range of colors than an inkjet printer can often output. If you don't watch out the vivid colors you've been editing will appear looking dull and lifeless. The Gamut warning's job is to prevent disappointment when you work in RGB mode. It does so by highlighting all the pixels that are out of gamut so you can modify the color before printing. Go to File➜Preferences➜ Transparency & Gamut to adjust the color used as a warning.

A small exclamation mark also appears above the color in the Color Picker and Color palette when a color is out of the printer's gamut. You should adjust the saturation to reduce

the areas indicated in the warning to a minimum using the Sponge tool or saturation control. **(See Saturation and Sponge tool)**

The rich red colors of the group members' tops are beyond the gamut of a printer and when the warning is set, in this case to display out of gamut colors as yellow, the picture is washed in yellow (left).

Pressing the keys Shift+Ctrl+Y while viewing the color picker will also show you the out of gamut range of color using the preselected color, in our case yellow. Move the Eyedropper outside this range to ensure a safe printable color.

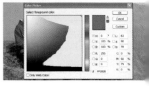

Gaussian blur
(See Blur filter)

GIF format

A GIF (Graphics Interchange Format) is an image with a reduced palette of 256 colors or less that's ideal for viewing on the Web. Photoshop files can be converted to GIFs using File➜Save As or File➜Save for Web which brings up the options displayed here on the right.

GIFs can be saved as normal or interlaced versions that appear gradually on screen as they download from the Web. The format works better with illustrations – jpeg is a better format for photos.

Glass filter
(See Distortion filter)

Global light

MENU	LAYER ➜
	LAYER STYLE ➜
	GLOBAL LIGHT

Several layer effects, such as Drop Shadow and Inner Bevel, give you control over the angle of lighting. Selecting Global lighting ensures that all the layer effects have the same lighting angle so the result looks more natural. If you don't want all the layer effects to be uniform go into the effect you want to have its own light and turn off the use global lighting option.

Glow effect

MENU	LAYER ➜
	LAYER STYLE ➜
	OUTER/INNER GLOW

A glow effect looks particularly effective when produced around type and can be made to appear from inside or outside the selection in any color. The mode is great for creating fancy headlines for Web sites or newsletters.

Glow can be used on text (right) selections around images (left) or vector art (below right). You can control the opacity, blur and intensity of the glow along with the Blend mode from within the Effects palette.

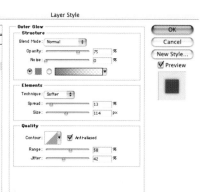

g

Gradient tool

QUICK KEY G   Interesting skies, colorful backgrounds and rainbows are all easily created by selecting the Gradient icon from the toolbox. This brings up a choice of five gradient patterns, from the options bar, that include Linear, Radial, Angular, Reflected and Diamond – each designed to create a smooth blend from one color to another.

As with most Photoshop tools you can adjust the opacity and Blend mode to control the effect the gradient has on the base

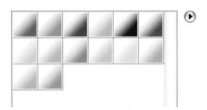

■ ▨ Gradient Tool	G
◇ Paint Bucket Tool	G

image. There's also a decent range of preset color gradients to choose from, or you can edit your own by double clicking on the icon to bring up a Gradient Editor dialogue box. **(See Gradient Editor)**

The Gradient tool has a selection of presets that can be loaded. The set above is Pastels and there are seven other sets to choose from including color harmonies 1 & 2, metals, noise, simple, special effects and spectrums.

Adjust the Editor to create a rainbow style color. Apply it on a new layer using the Gradient tool. Set the blend mode to soft light with an opacity of about 80%. Use the Transform→Distort tool to reposition the rainbow into a natural position and soften using Gaussian blur.

Gradient Editor

The Gradient Editor appears when you click on the gradient currently displayed in the options bar (top of page). From the editor you can select any of Photoshop's predesigned gradients and edit these or make your own from scratch. You can select any color and adjust its position on the ocala. Tho bottom sliders control the position of the color and the top ones the strength, or opacity, of the color. Click on the top of the bar to bring up a marker, which can be dragged to position and you change the opacity using the box below.

Tip

● Use the metal preset with the radial gradient option to create a halo on a new canvas. Then add Gaussian blur, followed by Noise, followed by Motion blur to create an interesting background effect. Use the Hue/Saturation sliders to change the color.

Gradient Fill

MENU LAYER →
     NEW FILL LAYER →
     GRADIENT

The Gradient Fill is placed on a new layer so it can be edited without affecting the underlaying layers. You can select any of the five gradient styles and adjust the angle and scale. This cannot be done using the gradient tool unless you undo and draw again so it makes it more versatile.

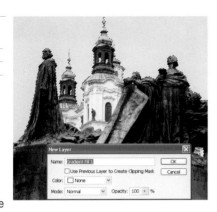

To create the Gradient Fill just click on the image at the desired start point, drag to the end point and release to flood the image with color. In this example I selected the sky so that the fill didn't affect the statues. If you don't like the effect Undo (Ctrl+Z) and start again.

The Gradient Fill appears in the channels box as a Gradient Fill Mask when it has been applied over a selected area.

Tip

● To have more control of where the gradient begins reduce the picture so you can draw the gradient line outside the picture area. In this example it's made the gradient less harsh.

A blue/transparent gradient was used on this already heavily edited image. You control how much of the image is affected by dragging the mouse across the picture at different lengths. Top to bottom: long, medium and short drag.

Tips

● Ticking the Dither box prevents any banding in the gradation.
● The Gradient tool doesn't work on Bitmap or Index color images.

g

Gradient Map

MENU   **IMAGE →**
       ADJUSTMENTS →
       GRADIENT MAP

This converts a color image to grayscale and then lets you apply one of the pre-selected gradients to replace the gray tones with new, posterized colors. You can edit the gradient and watch the preview to help achieve the desired result. The left color replaces blacks, the right one replaces whites and any in the middle will replace gray tones. It's like having full control of posterization.

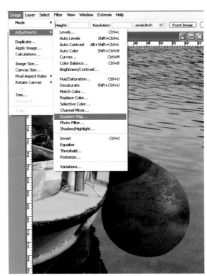

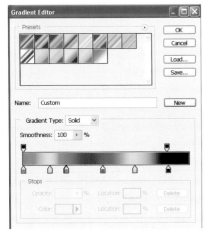

When you select a gradient from the editor your image is instantly turned into a graphical color display. Thousands of combinations can be created easily and then you can go off and change colors using Hue/Saturation or, as below, copy the layer, add a new style and blend.

There's no limit to what you can do. Left is a shiny sphere from the special effects set. Then, using fade with hue blend, I created the version below left. Below middle is a complex version using rainbow gradient, duplicated layer and Gaussian blur, motion blur and hue saturation applied to the upper layer. Below right is a posterized style effect using the new Hard mix blend mode.

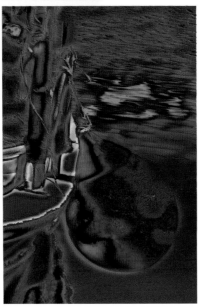

Gradient Mask

MENU **LAYER** ➜
ADD LAYER MASK ➜ Adding a Gradient
Mask to a layer
makes the image take on the gradient
when blending with other layers. This is
useful for complex image creation.

The mask can then be edited to
change the shape of the gradation by
adding or subtracting from it.

(See Layer masks)

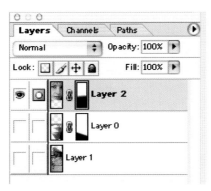

Use the Radial
Gradient tool
to add a dark
vignette.
This is a useful
tool for low key
vignettes on
wedding and
portrait photos.

To show how the Gradient Mask can be put to use I've merged three photographs – a portrait, sculpture and metal girder. The metal girder was first rotated to suit the angle of the neck on the sculpture, then a black to transparent mask was added to the sculpture layer so that the image fades to transparent. This was repeated on the girl layer and now you can't see the joins.

Grain

Film-like grain can be
added to pictures using
either the Noise filter
or the Diffuse Glow
with the Glow slider
turned down and Grain
increased.

You could also try
creating your own grain
pattern and add it as a
new layer using a Blend
mode.

(See Noise filter)

Graphic tablet

A graphic tablet such as the Wacom Graphire II has a special pen that replaces the computer mouse to control the on-screen cursor. Using a pen gives you much more natural control and makes it much easier to draw or paint and trace around objects when making cutouts.

Photoshop has support for most tablets and using one opens up some extra features such as pressure sensitivity when using the airbrush. These appear on the options bar along the top of the image. The pen can often be reversed so the other tip can be used as an eraser.

Tablets can go up to sizes as large as A3 which are used by designers. There's even one available that displays the image so you can draw around the actual picture.

This Wacom tablet, like many others, has a transparent sheet that lifts so you can place a photo or artwork under and trace around this to draw a replica on screen.

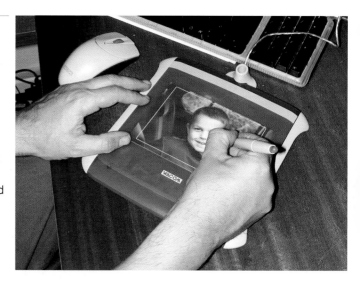

Grayscale mode

MENU	IMAGE ➜
	MODE ➜
	GRAYSCALE

Produces an image made up of 256 gray tones from black to white. You can't adjust Hue or Saturation in this mode, but Brightness and Contrast can be controlled. Use this mode to convert original color images to black & white.

Tip
● An image converted from color to grayscale may look a little flat. Adjust levels to brighten up the tones.

Tip
● Before converting to grayscale have a look at the tonal range in each channel. You may find that the tones in one channel look better than the other two and if you covert to grayscale while in this channel it will use the brightness values of just that one channel.

Two variations using selected channels. Top is blue, bottom is red and green.

Grid

MENU	VIEW →
	SHOW →
	GRID
QUICK KEYS	Ctrl+'

A non-printing grid of horizontal and vertical lines that's used to arrange elements symmetrically within an image and to straighten up sections, making it perfect for use with the Transform→Perspective feature.

Selections snap to the grid so it's easier to create and align the same sized boxes.

It can be difficult to edit a picture when the grid is turned on because the lines may get in the way. Using the quick keys to switch back and forth will make it easier to work.

Tip

● Select View→Snap to→Grid and the painting tools will follow the grid making it easy to paint in straight lines.

Guides

MENU	VIEW →
	SHOW →
	GUIDES
QUICK KEYS	Ctrl+;

These are horizontal or vertical lines that can be pulled out from the edge rulers to appear over the image. If the rulers aren't visible go to View→Rulers (Ctrl+R).

Guides can be used to align text or for laying out parts of the image in a symmetrical pattern. Go to Preferences→Guides & Grid to choose the guides' color and style (straight or dotted line). The guides will not print and can be removed or repositioned using the Pointer tool.

As with the Grid, Paint tools will snap to the guides if the Snap to Guides option is selected from the View menu.

Go to Preferences to change the number of lines per cm and the subdivisions. Choose a different color if the subject clashes with the current choice.

h

Hard light
(See Blending modes)

Healing brush

QUICK KEY J   This was one of the most exciting features to appear on Photoshop 7.0 and is located on the toolbar where the airbrush tool used to be. The healing brush is a glorified Clone tool and does a fantastic job on some things and makes a hash of others.

I would suggest that until you are familiar with this tool you can always try it first and if it doesn't work, undo the action and switch to the Clone tool.

The reason it's excellent when it works is that it takes the sample from the area you first select, just like the Clone tool, but when you paint over the area you are repairing the sampled pixels are not just laid down. The program looks at what you are cloning over and blends the two. In the photograph of a lime (right) there are a few blemishes.

I've sampled from a lighter area (highlighted in the red circle) knowing that if I tried cloning from here with the Clone tool it would produce a glaringly obvious patch (middle).

When the healing tool is used to sample from the same area it ensures the original pixel color and density are not lost.

If the area to be 'healed' had been a larger area of black then the original pixels would have influenced the result and it wouldn't have done much to cover the blemishes. Overall it's a stunning bit of technology that I'm sure will find its way into the competitors' products soon.

A close-up section of a scanned Polaroid Instant Black & White slide. As you can see it's a very dusty example. This would be very slow to sort out using the Clone tool, but this area took just over a minute using the Healing brush.

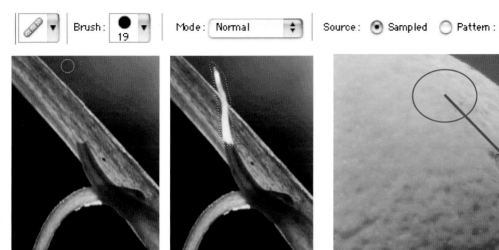

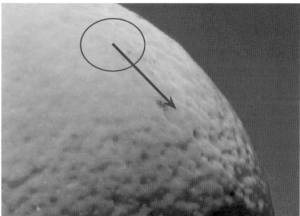

Sometimes it helps if you make a rough selection around the area that you want to heal. This prevents surrounding pixels affecting the blend. Top is the result of no selection and the bottom version is with the middle selection.

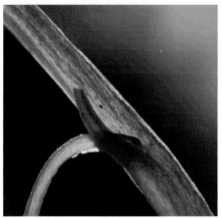

Make the source Pattern (activated from the options bar) to heal an area with a preset pattern. The pattern blends into the picture. Here I've turned the flower into a piece of Bridget Riley op art using the Darken blend mode.

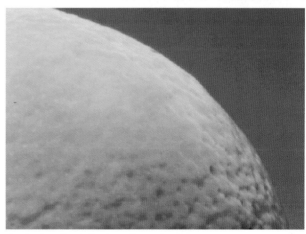

Here's where the Healing brush (bottom) is far more practical to use than the Clone tool. Try removing the couple of blemishes using the sample point indicated with the Clone stamp and you will create light blotches.

h

Help

QUICK KEYS F1 Photoshop CS's help menu has a bright interface with plenty of topics covered to ensure you understand the program and its functions. Each section is split up to make it easy to find. There is plenty of 'how to' material and a useful search. As well as linking to all the stuff provided on the CD that comes with the program, it goes direct to the Web as an extra resource. This ensures we can keep on top of the program and receive any updates that Adobe throw at us.

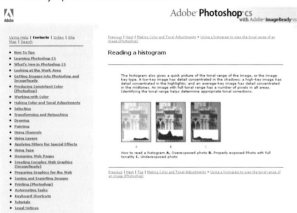

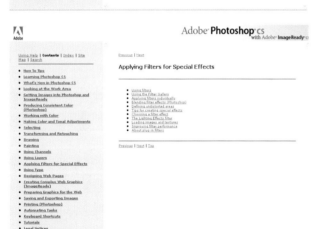

Highlights

The brightest parts of the image with detail that will still print. These can be adjusted using the clear triangle on the slider control that appears on the right-hand side of the Levels graph.

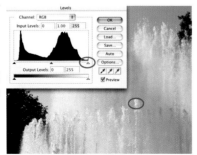

Histogram

MENU WINDOW → A graph that plots the image in a series of
HISTOGRAM pixel values from 0 (black) to 255 (white) and looks like a mountain range profile.

The horizontal scale represents shadow to highlight detail and the vertical axis is the number of pixels at a particular point. You can view the histogram of each of the RGB channels individually or as a group. It's used to check whether your image is suitable for printing and can be edited in the Levels palette by adjusting highlight, shadow and midtone sliders.

(Located in Image menu on earlier versions of Photoshop)

A low key image appears with most of the peaks concentrated in the shadow area at the left-hand side.

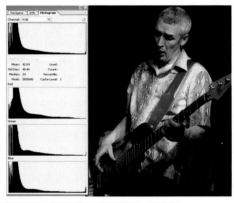

A high key image has the peaks in the highlight area to the right.

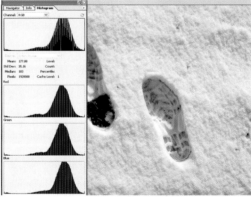

The average tone image should have a graph that rises from the far left, peaks across the middle section and falls to the far right.

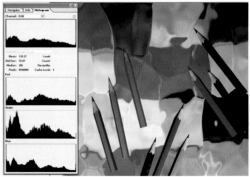

History brush

QUICK KEY **Y** Use this to paint in details from a previous stage of editing. Click on the box that appears in the History palette at the stage in the image editing process that you'd like to apply and paint onto the new level.

This is a great option if you're considering hand-coloring a black & white image. Cheat by starting off with a color image and convert it first to grayscale to discard all color information and then back to color. The black & white image can then be colored using the History brush. Click on the left of the opening image to turn on the History brush icon. Then click on the latest stage and begin to paint.

Also good for removing dust and scratches. Apply the dust & scratches filter and make the history brush active on that new layer. Then go back to a previous history level and paint with the History brush over dust & scratches to paint in the newer filtered layer.

Tip
● Set the brush opacity to around 50%, turn the Impressionist feature on and brush erratically over the image for a surrealistic watercolor wash.

History palette

Every task you perform in Photoshop 5.0 upwards is recorded as a step, or state, in the History palette. This allows you to go back up to 100 previous stages when an image you're working on starts to go wrong. A slider on the left-hand side can be dragged slowly through the stages to help you find when things start to go wrong. Simply click on the last stage that you were happy with and start again to change history – if it was just that simple in life!

Hue

MENU   **IMAGE →**
     ADJUSTMENTS →
     HUE/SATURATION
QUICK KEYS **CTRL+U**

Hue is the image color and varying the Hue slider changes the overall color. The scale runs through the colors of the rainbow starting at the left with blue.

    This cross polarized picture of a CD case shows the effect the Hue slider has over the color when adjusted in 30 unit increments. **(See Blending modes)**

Hue: 0 (original)

Hue: +180

Hue: +150

Hue: +120

Hue: -30

Hue: -60

Hue: -90

Hue: +90

Hue: +60

Hue: +30

Hue: -120

Hue: -150

Hue: -180

Image Assistant

A new feature that appeared in version 6.0 under the Help menu offering two assistants (wizards) – Export transparent image and Resize image.

These guide you through tasks that you may be struggling to understand. We expected

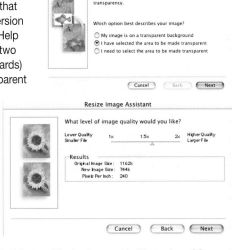

more to be added, but nothing's changed in Photoshop CS apart from a set of How to's that also appear under the help menu to give you a written guide to many Photoshop features.

ImageReady

ImageReady is a Web image editing program that's bundled with Photoshop. It has the same interface and allows seamless connection from within the program. We saw

a jump from version 3.0 with Photoshop 6.0 to version 7.0 with Photoshop 7.0. Now it follows suit with ImageReady CS. The program allows you to slice a picture up so that it can be used more effectively on a Web page. You can also optimize pictures, create rollovers and edit animation.

Image resolution

The measure of digital image quality, stated in pixels per inch (ppi). The more pixels per inch the higher the resolution. Not to be confused with sharpness, which is affected by a number of things, including lens quality.

The resolution needs to be high enough to suit the viewing media and should not be confused with dpi (dots per inch). If, for example, you only ever look at the images on a computer monitor for Web use you only need a resolution of 72ppi for Macs and 96ppi for a PC and each pixel will be displayed as a dot. If, on the other hand, you're wanting to send the images to a magazine or book publisher you'll need a resolution of at least 300ppi, while most desktop inkjet printers require files with 150 to 240ppi and lay down several dots per pixel to ensure accurate colors. **(See dpi)**

Image size

MENU   IMAGE →
        IMAGE SIZE

Is the physical size of the file, measured in kilobytes (K) or megabytes (Mb), that appears at the bottom left of your image. The larger and more complex an image the bigger its file will be. As an example, a simple 4x6in grayscale image, saved at 175ppi, has a file size of around 700K. The same file saved as an RGB increases to just over 2Mb and as a CMYK image to nearly 3Mb. A 300ppi 10x8in image suitable for magazine repro is 27.5Mb. Start adding Layers, or a History palette, and the file could quadruple in size.

You can either resize or resample a picture in Photoshop. Resizing allows you to adjust the number of pixels per inch and keeps the same amount of data by adjusting the dimensions to suit the new pixel setting. Resampling keeps the same dimensions and removes or adds pixels to reach the new pixel setting you key in. Increasing the number of pixels is usually referred to as interpolation.

Shows the size of the image in pixels or percentages. A link appears at the side when Constrain Proportions is on.

Gives size of output file. Can be set to inches, centimetres, pixels or percentages. A link appears when Constrain Proportions is turned on.

Turn on Scale Styles (new on Photoshop CS) to ensure Layer style effects keep in scale with the image as it's resampled. (above photo) Notice how the shadow and neon glow are exaggerated when Scale Styles is not selected.

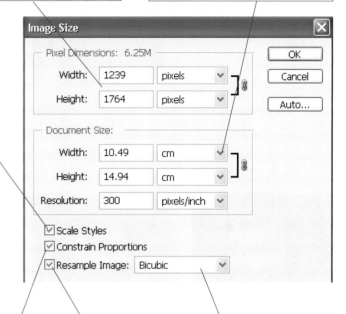

When turned on it ensures that the proportions of the width and height are maintained as one of the two values is changed.

When turned off, the file size is maintained. So, as you increase output resolution the file size dimensions are reduced.

If Resample Image is on the file size changes using interpolation. You then have a choice of five methods of resampling.

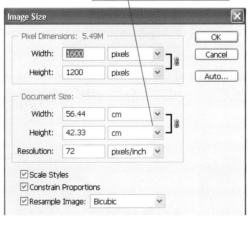

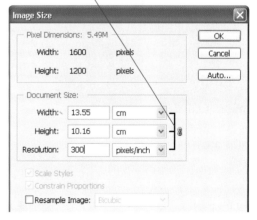

Tips

● Merge Layers to reduce the image's file size, but only when you're totally happy with the result as it can't be returned to a Layers state at a later date. **(See Flatten image)**

● Don't work with images larger than you need. Going to Image→Image size and resampling to a smaller size saves space.
● Images only need to be 72ppi for viewing on computer and TV monitors. They should be

between 150ppi and 240ppi for printing from most inkjet printers and 300ppi for magazine reproduction.
    Save at the maximum size you intend viewing/ printing out.

Indexed colors

MENU   **IMAGE →**
           MODE →
           INDEXED COLORS

Color mode used to reduce the image to 8-bit to suit viewing on older monitors or on the Web to keep the file size conveniently small.

Several color palettes can be selected from the menu including a Web palette with 256 colors that's widely used by Web browsers so your image will look the same whichever computer platform or Internet explorer the picture is viewed on.

Two pictures of the flower A and B. A is the original 16.7 million color image. B is index color with just 256 colors. At a glance they look similar. Enlarge just a small portion of the image and you'll see the lack of smooth gradation between colored pixels.

256 colors is fine for Web use, but when making prints stick with maximum color depth.

Info palette

MENU   **WINDOW →**
           INFO

Palette that displays a choice of RGB, LAB, Web, HSB and CMYK information for the image being worked on. Moving any tool across the image will change the value on screen as it passes over each pixel. The palette also shows X and Y co-ordinates and the width and height of any box or rectangular section that you create.

Input

Loading pictures into your computer can be done in a number of ways. The fully digital route is to use a digital camera, which can be connected to the serial or USB port; some have a docking station.

Alternatively the memory card can be taken out of the camera and slotted into a card reader that's like a small drive connected to the parallel, USB or Firewire port. Some newer cameras also have infrared, WiFi or Bluetooth remote transmission.

If you have a traditional camera and shoot negative film or transparencies you can buy a film scanner that converts the film image into a digital file and connects to the computer's SCSI, USB, parallel or Firewire port. A flatbed scanner is like a mini photocopier, designed to scan flat artwork such as prints. They're available to fit various computer ports.

Another option is to have the films scanned by a lab. Many shops now offer Kodak's Picture CD service where the films are processed as normal but you also get a CD with the images. **(See Picture CD)**

Finally you could have a shop scan your photos and place them on a Web server that looks after your images. You can then log on to the site and download the pictures you want to print.

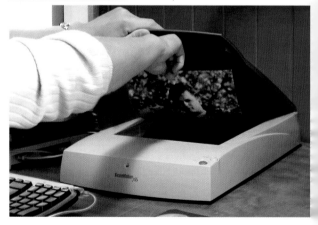

Interpolation

If you change the size of a digital file your software either adds pixels when increasing the size or removes them when making the image smaller. This is known as interpolation and relies on Photoshop knowing which pixels to add or dump.

There are now five methods of interpolation – Nearest Neighbour, Bilinear and Bicubic, with Bicubic Smoother and Bicubic Sharper added in Photoshop CS. One can be set as default by going to File→Preferences→General.

Nearest Neighbour offers the fastest method by copying the adjacent pixels, but results are often poor. Bilinear looks at pixels above and below plus left and right and averages out the result to give an intermediate pixel and a smooth blend. It's slower than Nearest Neighbour, but not as slow as Bicubic which looks at all the pixels surrounding each pixel and averages them all out to create the new ones. It then boosts contrast between each pixel to reduce softness. Bicubic Smoother is used when you enlarge the image and Bicubic Sharper when you reduce the image.

This star photo taken from the top of the building is 42x54 pixels. Increasing the image to create a 420x540 version requires a hefty interpolation job, and it's a good test for the various methods. A: Near Neighbour, B: Bilinear, C: Bicubic, D: Bicubic Smoother and E: Bicubic Sharper.

A

B

C

D

E

You don't have to use Photoshop's resampling tool. Several companies produce resizing plug-ins for Photoshop that work in different ways and usually offer more control. These include Genuine Fractals and Extensis pxl SmartScale that we used here. **(See plug-ins, App. F)**

Inverse

MENU   SELECT →   INVERSE

When the subject is difficult to draw round accurately, look at the background or surrounding pixels. Could Color Range be used, or the Magic Wand? If so, select the surrounding areas and then the Inverse to swap to the subject.

Inverting

MENU   IMAGE →   ADJUSTMENTS →   INVERT

QUICK KEYS CTRL+I

Changes a color negative image into a positive and vice versa.

As a negative you can still apply other filter effects – this example is Find Edges followed by Fade Find Edges at 100% with Difference blend selected.

j

abcdefghi**j**klmnopqrstuvwxyz

JPEG
Joiner

JPEG

Short for Joint Photographic Experts Group. The most popular method of image compression that's great for continuous tone photographs.

It supports CMYK, RGB and grayscale. It's a lossy compression method so information is discarded to save disk space, but when saved at a minimal compression level the image can be indistinguishable from the original.

The JPEG Options palette has a slider to adjust the compression level from 0 low quality/high compression to 10 high quality/low compression. Set 10+ for best printed results and around 6 for Web use, avoid lower settings where possible.

You also have three format options – Baseline Standard for normal use, Baseline Optimized, a higher compression method used for saving images for Web use, and Progressive, also for Web use. This option displays the image in stages so the viewer can skip by if the photo isn't interesting.

Warning

● Every time you close and reopen a JPEG file you compress and uncompress, and the effect can be cumulative so the image may gradually decrease in quality. Work in PSD format until you've done everything you want to the image then save to JPEG.

Joiner

A traditional photo technique is to take a series of pictures from the same position, each with a different viewpoint. Then the photographer mounts the images side by side to create a 'joiner', or panorama or a more random built up picture (below).

This can be done manually in Photoshop using gradient masks and the Clone stamp, but it's easier to use an auto stitching feature, such as Photomerge, which is now included with Photoshop CS. **(See Photomerge)**

A selection of photos was taken using a telephoto lens, some sharp, some out of focus (far left). These were then copied onto one canvas and arranged to build up this jagged picture.

This image shows the effect of JPEG compression. The original uncompressed file has a file size of 5.5Mb. Watch what happens to the file size and the quality as higher compression is chosen.

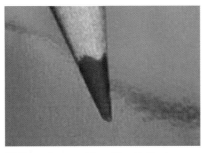

JPEG, maximum quality, setting 12, file size 1.5Mb. It's hard to spot any difference with this and the uncompressed file.

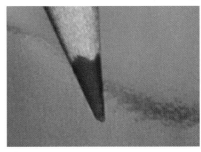

JPEG, maximum quality, setting 9, file size 736K. It's hard to spot any difference with this and the uncompressed file either.

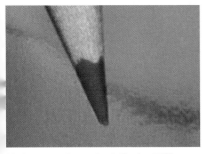

JPEG, high quality, setting 6, file size 448K. Very subtle changes in color of some pixels, but still very good.

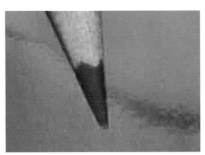

JPEG, medium quality, setting 3, file size 260K. It's now starting to clump groups of pixels in blocks noticeable in the outlined area.

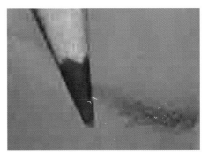

JPEG, low quality, setting 0, file size 172K. Low quality produces poor results and the recognizable problems of heavy compression.

You can use Photoshop to stitch pictures manually. Extend the canvas to the same length of the total length of the pictures you are joining. Paste them onto the canvas and position them. Reduce the opacity of the top one so you can see where it overlaps and adjust so they match. Use the gradient tool to get a good blend. Then use the Clone tool to help patch up bad bits. Repeat this on all the pictures.

Once you merge the layers you could add a gradient to the sky like I did in the second example of a joiner, taken at Rutland Water, UK. This one has an orange gradient to make the landscape look as though it's taken at sunset.

K

abcdefghij**k**lmnopqrstuvwxyz

Keyboard shortcuts
Keywords
Knockout
Kodak Photo CD
Kodak Picture CD

Keyboard shortcuts

MENU   EDIT ➜
           KEYBOARD
QUICK KEYS ALT+SHIFT+CTRL+K

Shortcuts to commands and options using individual or groups of keys. Learn ones you use regularly to speed up your work. When shortcuts are available they're listed in this book as Quick Keys for the PC. Mac users have similar shortcuts. Photoshop CS now lets you assign your favourite shortcuts. **(See Appendix C)**

Keywords

Photoshop CS lets you assign keywords to pictures.
(See Exif data)

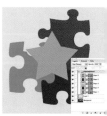

Knockout

A mode from Blend Options palette selected from the Layer Style menu that allows you to be more creative with the ways layers react with other layers. It can be used with text and vector shapes to great effect. To illustrate how it works I've created a blue star layer

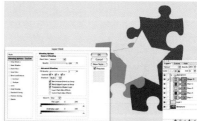

on top that will be used as the Knockout layer. It's above four jigsaw piece layers and all five are placed in a layer set. The background is a photo of bananas and there's a yellow layer above that. **(See Layers and Layer Sets)**

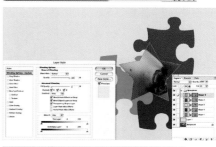

If the star is set to Shallow Knockout with opacity at 0% it would cut through the layer underneath and reveal the next layer. As the jigsaw pieces are in a set it cuts through them too and reveals the yellow layer below.

If the star is set to Deep Knockout with opacity at 0% it cuts through all the layers and reveals the background layer.

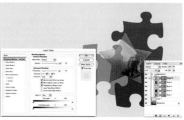

By turning off channels and adjusting opacity you can gain infinite control of how a layer blends with any layer below. It's the most complex area of Photoshop and much experimentation is necessary to understand this fully.

Kodak Photo CD

Kodak were way ahead of their time launching Photo CD in 1992 as a product designed to view photos on a television. Unfortunately it didn't take off until around four years later.

The service is offered by photo finishers and pro bureaux. Your images are scanned at high resolution using drum scan quality and recorded onto disc as Pict files. When you open the disc you have a choice of five file sizes from 192x128ppi to 3072x2048ppi. The smaller sizes are for using as positionals or for TV and Web use and the larger files are for making prints allowing up to around 7x10in enlargements.

Kodak Picture CD

Similar principle to Photo CD, but with a magazine style interface and free software, produced in association with Adobe and Intel. The CD opens up with a contents page and a range of options. Various menus let you edit and enhance your pictures, send them as e-mail postcards, catalogue them and print them. The service is available when you have a film processed and just requires a tick on the film processing envelope to ensure the lab produces a Picture CD of your film as well as a set of photos.

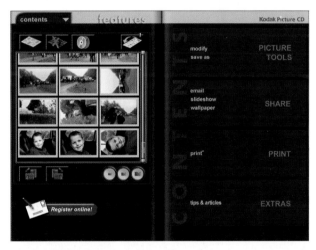

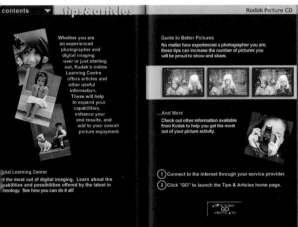

The interface is extremely friendly and easy to navigate. The first page that appears on screen is the contents page (above right). This has a menu of the items on the CD which can then be navigated using the linked buttons. You see your photos on the left and these can be edited using the basic software under the Picture Fixes heading (right). There are also tips and articles which change each time a new version of the CD is produced. Printing photos and sending them attached as e-mails is also made easy.

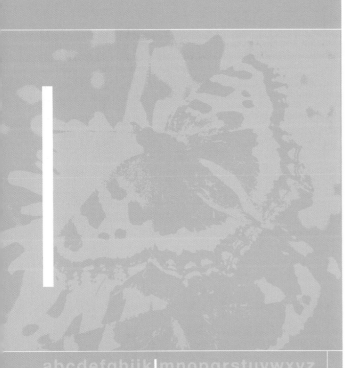

Lab Color

An international standard for color measurements developed by the Commission Internationale de L'Eclairage (CIE). It's capable of reproducing all the colors of RGB and CMYK and uses three channels – one for luminosity and the other two for RGB type color ranges.

Some users prefer to work in this mode as it's device independent and colors that fall into the CMYK gamut aren't changed when you convert to CMYK.

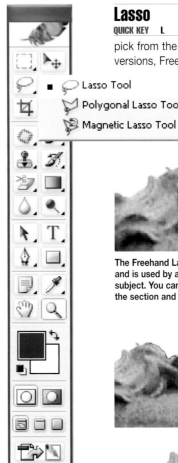

Lasso

QUICK KEY L There are three Lassos to pick from the toolbox. The two standard versions, Freehand and Polygon and a Magnetic version.

The Freehand Lasso is used in most programs and is used by accurately drawing round the subject. You can select a feather to be applied to the section and turn anti-aliasing on or off.

The Polygon Lasso is good for drawing round boxes and straight edged items as it creates a straight edge between the source and destination point

Magnetic Lasso is arguably the most useful Lasso. You draw roughly around the subject and the Lasso detects contrast changes and defines the edge. It then pulls the inaccurate drawing into line, often creating a very good selection.

Tip
● Don't worry too much about being spot on with your drawing. You can hold down the Shift key to add to the selection or the Alt key to take away from it.

Layers

MENU	LAYER →
	NEW →
	LAYER
QUICK KEYS	SHIFT+CTRL+N

One of the most useful features of Photoshop is Layers. Basically, using layers is like having several sheets of tracing paper, each holding part of the image. Laying the sheets on top of each other builds up the image and it's easy to remove any sheet to change the feel of the work. But, being digital, layers offer much more.

You can change how one layer reacts with another using the Blend modes (see individual entries). You can adjust the opacity so one layer is stronger than another, you can apply a filter effect to one layer and you can copy and paste from one layer to another.

Photoshop 6.0 introduced new Layer options on the palette. A selection of locks can be assigned to a layer to protect it from accidents later. The first is lock transparency. This used to be called Preserve Transparency and ensures that any areas that are transparent (indicated by the checked grid) will not be affected by paint or filter effects. Then we have lock paintbrush which, as the name implies, prevents you from using brushes. The third is a lock to stop you using the Move tool to move elements from this layer. All three can be individually selected or locked as a group.

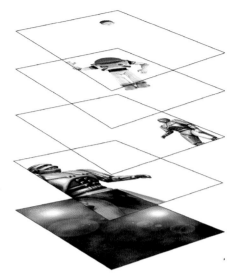

Layers are like sheets of glass or tracing paper, each one placed on top of the other to produce a combined multi-layer image.

Three images of a boy, flowers and colored pattern were combined for this shot, each with a blend mode selected that would allow the layers to mix and become diffused by each other.

The three bottom layers of this five layer image were merged using Overlay and Screen blend modes while the top two layers were set to normal so that they stand out.

Layer Based Slice

MENU	LAYER →
	NEW LAYER BASED SLICE

This feature, introduced with version 6.0, lets you cut up, or slice, your picture into several pieces. When the image is used in a Web page each slice is saved as an independent file with html code and becomes a fully functional part. The html code contains color palette info and links, rollover effects, and animations can be added in ImageReady.

Slices help you gain faster download speeds and increased image quality. Apply a layer based slice on a layer with a selection and the slice will be positioned around it. This can then be moved and scaled using the Move tool.

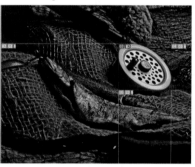

A selection was made around the fishing reel and this was copied and pasted onto a new layer. Now when you request a New Layer Slice it appears around the selection and can be set to be used as a hot link on a Web page.

Layer clipping path

MENU	LAYER →
	ADD LAYER CLIPPING PATH

Sharp edged shape around an object that can be edited using the Shape or Pen tools. The path can be converted into a layer mask: Layer→Rasterize→Layer Clipping Path.

Layer comps

MENU   WINDOW →
LAYER COMPS New Photoshop CS feature that lets you create a snapshot of a state of the Layers palette. Layer comps records a layer's position in the Layers palette and whether it's showing or hidden. It also records whether layer styles are applied. This is a useful feature if you want to try different effects to show a client. You can then turn each version on or off in the Layer Comps palette and view the differences with speed.

This Layer clipping path was a tick before I started to drag the points around.

I took this photo a few years ago for Sam, a drummer in a band, who wanted to create a promo card. It was shot on color negative film and scanned on, at the time, one of the better budget film scanners. This didn't have dust and scratch removal and grain was accentuated.

Sam was holding a potato (it seemed like a good idea at the time!) from which I originally had a lens flare spot appearing to make it look a little magical. This time I decided to replace it with a picture of a skull. And almost in the words of Shakespeare 'Alas, poor layer masks, I knew them well'.

With Layer masks you can edit each layer with ease, allowing areas of one layer to show through to the ones below. In this composite I have four layers: one with the skull, one with Sam the correct way round and the same image copied, flipped and enlarged to produce a ghost-like extra, plus a man-made background.

Layer Mask

MENU   LAYER →
ADD LAYER MASK A layer mask controls how much of that particular layer appears in the overall image. Black masked areas don't show through and white areas do. You can use the vignette and graduate filters to good effect using Layer Masks.

Masks can be turned off at any stage and any bits of the image that have been masked will show through on the overall image again.

Left: The skull has been very roughly cut from its background and pasted on the layer with Sam. It obviously looks like it has too! By adding a Layer Mask you can paint out areas of the skull layer using the Eraser. Above: Use a large Eraser brush to get rid of the surrounds and a small one for the detailed areas.

Above right: Now the second Sam layer was pasted, flipped and scaled up. Notice the rough selection around the shirt and hair. Eraser and Paint brush to the rescue.

Once complete I rearranged the pieces, added an adjustment layer and turned it sepia. I then flattened the layers and added grain and a green vignette on the background areas.

Layer properties

MENU   **LAYER →**
     LAYER PROPERTIES   Opens up a small box where you name the layer and select a color for it.

Layer set

A great feature introduced in version 6.0 that allows layers to be grouped and all the layer blend modes applied to the group. Alternatively the individual layers within the group can have their own set of blend modes that become active when you select Pass Through from the set's blend mode options.

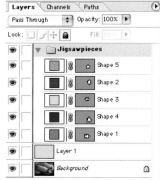

Layer style

MENU   **LAYER →**
     LAYER STYLE →   Control how a layer looks by adjusting its style from a new palette. This offers advanced blending options that lets you adjust the way each color channel blends with the layer below and each element can be adjusted from the palette. Global light lets all the layers have the same angle and altitude.

Lens Blur

(See Blur filters)

Lens Flare

MENU   **FILTER →**
     RENDER →
     LENS FLARE   Another one of those filters that will make lens manufacturers cringe. They spend millions on research to get a lens that you can point into the light without getting flare and then you go and stick some in using Photoshop! The truth is a touch of flare can sometimes add the extra bit that's needed to make the image work.

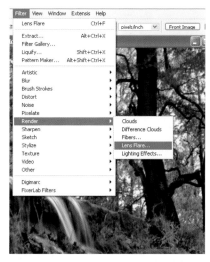

The palette offers a choice of four lens types (Movie Prime is new for Photoshop CS) and an adjustable brightness control, each can be seen in action in the series of pictures below. The preview window above allows you to check the result before you apply the effect to the main image.

35mm prime

50–300mm zoom

105mm prime

Movie prime

Levels

MENU   IMAGE →
        ADJUSTMENTS →
        LEVELS
QUICK KEYS   CTRL+L

Used to adjust the black and white points of an image to change contrast. Auto levels does this automatically, but it can affect the color of the image.

When you're in this palette there's a window with the histogram and sliders to control the darkest and lightest points. The left-hand triangle controls the shadow area, the right one looks after highlights and the middle triangle adjusts midtones.

If you drag the black triangle to the right you'll see the image becomes darker. This is because you are changing the value of the darker pixels to appear black. Dragging this too far over would make shadow areas with detail become black. Similarly dragging the white triangle left affects highlights and dragging it too far left will make highlight areas completely white without any detail. This is known as clipping because you are basically cutting off the black and white areas of your photograph.

As the right-hand slider is moved inwards the white point shifts. Here the white triangle indicates the new white point and everything that was beyond that also becomes white. The result is a compressed range of colors with washed-out highlights.

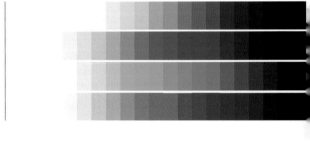

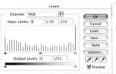

This test grid shows what happens when Levels are used. The original (left) displays a full range of gray tones in 5% increases from pure white to pure black. On the right are two versions showing what happens when levels are adjusted.

This time the left-hand black triangle was moved inward. Now the highlights stay the same but the shadows block up, so more black area exists and the color tonal range is reduced.

● To help you gauge the darkest and lightest points hold down the Alt key (Option on a Mac) while you click on the white or black triangle. This creates a posterized image showing the lightest point as white and the darkest point as black. As you drag the markers inwards you will see the white or black areas increase over the picture. This will give you an indication of how far to drag the sliders to make effective use of clipping the image. Use the values displayed as your highlight and shadow points.

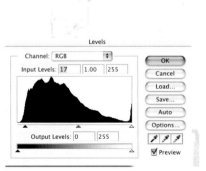

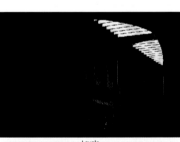

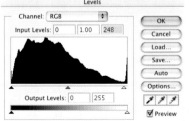

This is the original photograph with the Levels histogram showing a peak in the darker areas and a flat area where the highlights are.

If you drag the white highlight triangle to the left the image lightens in the highlight areas. Take it too far, as I have done here, and the lighter areas that should have detail become pure white.

The trick is to move the highlight slider so that the image lightens but you still maintain detail in the highlights. This is usually around the end of the black graph.

Now we drag the black triangle which takes care of the shadows. Again taking this just far enough to avoid the shadow area blocking up.

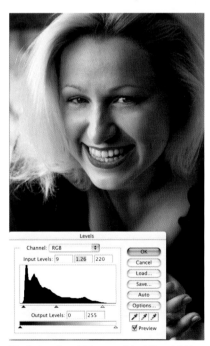

Finally drag the middle gray slider left or right to balance out the midtones. In this case slightly to the left towards the graph's peak.

Pull all three triangles into a similar point on the histogram and you create a posterized effect with only a few tones.

Lighten
(See Blending modes)

Lighting Effects

MENU **FILTER →**
RENDER →
LIGHTING EFFECTS

A superb range of filters that can be used to simulate various forms of light from spotlight to tungsten. There's plenty of choice so it's a case of picking a suitable image and sliding the controls to experiment. Remember to select undo (Ctrl+U) if you don't like the effect or click on a previous stage in the History palette.

Almost any lighting effect is possible using this filter. Here I've taken an icy cold winter scene and will add a sunrise lighting style while explaining the various sliders.

Several presets appear in the Style menu, but I'll stick with default and create my own. To do this select Omni, Spotlight or Directional from lighting type. Then pick a color – sunset orange in our case. Intensity controls the brightness of the light.

The properties section adjusts the lighting effect by emulating real life objects and how they react to light. **Gloss** makes the object's surface reflectivity low when you slide left towards Matte or high when you move towards Glossy.

Material controls whether the light or the object reflects more light. Plastic reflects the light's color and Metallic reflects the object's color. **Exposure** works like a camera – over exposure increases the intensity of light and under exposure decreases the light. There's no effect at 0. **Ambience** adjusts the balance of the light with a background lighting color that you've pre-selected. A 100 value puts full emphasis on the light source while a –100 value removes the light source. Go between to create an interesting balance of the two colors.

Omni light was selected with white light at a medium intensity. The point was positioned on the white flower to create a glowing effect. The ambient light was set to blue to contrast and give a wintery feel to the shot.

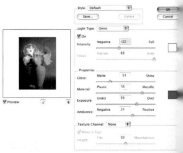

The two screengrabs below show the effect of adjusting the Exposure and Ambience sliders.

Tip

● If the Lighting filter is grayed out you are in 16-bit mode or CMYK color space. Convert to 8-bit, RGB.

99

Omni lighting was used with gray and black colors to create a moonlight effect which suits the mood of the powerful Stonehenge stone circle.

It's easy to turn lights on and create night time pictures using omni lighting and suitable colors. Here a warm yellow was selected for the light type and blue for the properties and the balance of both elements was adjusted using various sliders.

The original was lit using a snoot light for a low key effect. This placed emphasis on the rose petals. Digitally, using an omni light source, it's easy to bring back the underexposed areas and create a very different effect.

Line art

An image that's drawn using one color on a background color with no midtones. Line art is a popular giveaway on royalty-free CDs and web sites. This frog was found on <www.free-graphics.com>, a web site with over 130,000 free graphics for use when downloaded. I've picked a small size one to show you what happens to line art if the file size is too small. It looked sharp on screen, but here in print it looks smudged so choose with care.

Linear burn
(See Blending modes)

Linear dodge
(See Blending modes)

Linear light
(See Blending modes)

Line tool

QUICK KEY U Used to place lines in the image. When you draw with the Line tool it uses the foreground color and whatever width is set in the palette. You can change the color, width and style of line from the Options palette. You can also stick on an arrowhead making the tool useful for creating pointers.

A spotlight effect with dark tones can be used to place emphasis on one area of the photograph. In this case, blue was used making the shot look like a dark and moody Blair Witch style forest. Or you could try an orange hue for a misty morning sunrise.

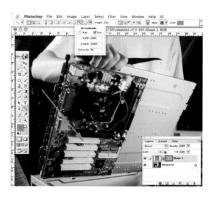

Liquify

MENU   **FILTER →**
             LIQUIFY

QUICK KEYS SHIFT+CTRL+X

This crazy filter first appeared in Photoshop 6.0's Image menu and is now in the Filter menu. It basically lets you smudge pixels to distort the image as if it was liquid and while it has many practical applications the most fun can be had by creating wacky portraits of people or pets.

Use the Pucker tool to shrink the nose, the Bloat tool to make the eyes and teeth bulge, the Twirl tool to add an artificial curl to the hair and the Warp tool to pull up the edges of the mouth.

The Liquid tool bar offers plenty of methods to smudge and distort a photo. From the top: **Warp** pushes the pixels wherever you drag the finger.

The **Reconstruct** tool undoes a Liquify effect at a local point without cancelling the whole work. **Twirl** rotates the picture (ideal to make hair curly). **Pucker** makes pixels smaller sucking in detail (the one to use to make a mouth or nose smaller). **Bloat** makes pixels bigger (the one I used for the eyes). **Shift pixels left** (as it says, Warp tool is better option). **Reflect** tool, mirrors pixels from start at other end of brush stroke. (Another pointless one). **Turbulence** creates a wave effect when you brush (this is ideal to make smoke look more wispy or fire look more raging). The two **Mask** tools are used to paint on and paint off the mask which protects areas from the Liquify tools. You will also see that the new palette in Photoshop CS has complete control of masks and ones from existing pictures can be used and modified with the Liquify masks. Finally we have the familiar **Move** tool and **Magnify** tool which need no introduction!

Hours of Dali style fun can be had with flowers.

Tips

● Use the mesh grid to help show you the extent of the effect you've added and change its color so it stands out from the picture you're working on.

Hours of Dali style fun can be had with just about any subject – laughing rocks, ultra slim lady things and wobbly bridges. Hmmm!

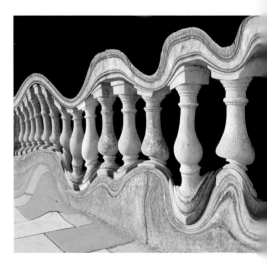

Liquify
(Cont.)

You can use the filter to stretch and warp the background too which, if done better than this, could be made to look like an oil painting.

Kids will love playing around with these pictures, but it's good fun for adults too!

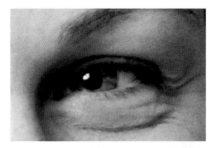

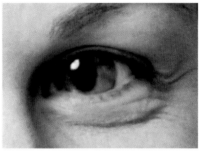

You don't have to go crazy – Liquify can be used to subtly change a photo. Here the Bloat tool was set to a low pressure and used to enlarge the eye slightly, making it appear a touch wider.

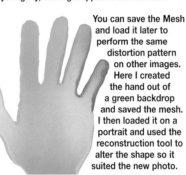

You can save the Mesh and load it later to perform the same distortion pattern on other images. Here I created the hand out of a green backdrop and saved the mesh. I then loaded it on a portrait and used the reconstruction tool to alter the shape so it suited the new photo.

Luminosity blend
(See Blend modes)

LZW compression

A lossless method of compression used with TIFF and GIF file formats to save space without affecting image quality. The disadvantage is it takes longer to open a compressed image than an uncompressed version.

Oh dear, this tool also gives you a licence to create all sorts of what's the point pictures.

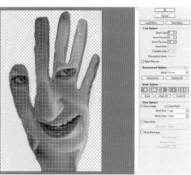

TIFF Options

m

Magic Eraser tool

QUICK KEY   E   Introduced on Photoshop 5.5, this tool, found in the Eraser compartment of the toolbox, is used to make pixels transparent. Click on the area you want to lose and the pixels disappear.

The palette has a number of options including the Opacity and Tolerance levels along with on/off options for anti-aliasing, Use all Layers and Contiguous modes.

Anti-aliasing makes some of the edge pixels semi-transparent to ensure edges of unremoved details are smooth for natural cutouts. Using All Layers mode makes pixels in every layer to be considered by the Eraser. Contiguous mode ensures just the pixels connected to the sampled color are selected. When turned off, any pixels with a similar value within the image are selected.

All this image needed was six clicks in various parts of the sky to completely remove it. When pasted onto another background it will show through in all the areas of transparency.

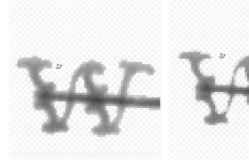

Turning Anti-aliasing on (right) ensures that edge pixels appear softer which, in turn, makes the cutout look more natural.

Magic Wand tool

QUICK KEY **W**   Click on the image using this tool to select an area that has the same brightness. If for instance your subject has a blue background that you want to change to green, click anywhere on the blue and you'll see the Magic Wand create a selection around all the pixels that have a similar color and brightness level. Adjust the Tolerance setting to increase or decrease the range in the selection. You can also select from an individual channel which is sometimes easier.

Make sure you enlarge to check what the Magic wand tool has selected. This close up shows it's not always that accurate.

Magnification box

Appears at the bottom left of a picture and lets you enter a value manually to change the size of the image on screen.

Enlarging the image on screen helps when you need to edit small areas of detail, but this may appear as blocks of pixels so you should use the Zoom tool to nip backwards and forwards.
(See Zoom tool)

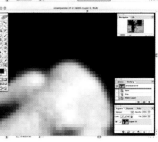

Top right: Image viewed on screen at 25%.
Middle right: Image viewed at maximum 100%. Bottom right: image viewed at maximum screen enlargement of 1600%

Magnetic Pen
(See Pen tools)

Magnetic Lasso tool
(See Lasso tool)

Marquee tool
QUICK KEY **M**

The marquee tool is used to make a rectangular, circular or single row selection from the subject. Then copy and paste can be used to pick up and drop the selection elsewhere.

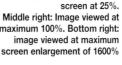

Masks

Used to protect parts of the image when you apply filter effects or change color. They can be added to channels or layers and converted into selections.
(See Alpha Channels and Quick Mask mode)

Match Color

MENU IMAGE →
ADJUSTMENTS →
MATCH COLOR

Another new feature introduced in Photoshop CS. This lets you apply the color from one photograph or layer to another. It's ideal when you are combining selected elements into one photo and ensures the elements look naturally placed in the montage. It can also be used when you want to match a series of photos that have slightly different coloring. One example of this would be a panorama that you'd stitch together, where the blue sky varies from print to print.

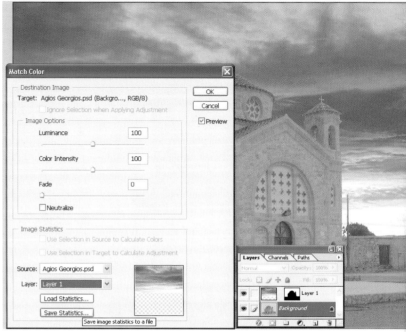

Another example would be when combining one element with another, such as adding this colorful pink sunset as a background to a dull church shot. Notice that the church goes pink too when the Match Color filter is applied. This is because in auto it's doing the job correctly and matching the brickwork with the pinks of the sky.

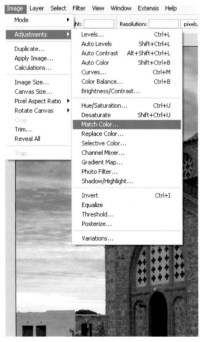

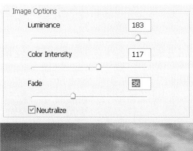

To get round the incorrect color we have full control of the sliders and can adjust the luminance, color intensity and also Fade which allows you to revert back to the original hue by adjusting the slider. A point mid way is a balance between the before and after Match color versions. I've also turned on Neutralize which detects and reduces any color cast.

In this example I've combined two indoor shots that have been taken under different lighting. In both cases the subject has a color cast. Yellow/green in the room and a warm magenta hue from the model servant. I made a selection around the model and cut it out pasting it into the interior. The colors are way off the mark. Match Color to the rescue!

First remove the color cast. Match color can be used to tweak color of a single image by selecting None as the Source. Then adjust the Image options sliders until you have a satisfactory color.

The model was pasted onto a new layer. Click on this layer in the layer palette and activate Match Color. The layer you clicked on appears as the target layer. Select the file as source and the Layer 0 (interior) as the source layer. The model will now take on the color of the source layer. In our example this is too hard and unnatural so we used the Fade slider to create a more natural coloring. You may have noticed I added a drop shadow too and used liquify to change the shape of the model slightly.

Match color makes montage creation really easy and accurate. It's a great feature!

Measure

QUICK KEY I The measure tool, found with the eyedropper, is an underused item designed to give precise details about subject distance and angle. It can also be the perfect assistant when you need to straighten up a wonky horizon or leaning wall. Click on it and draw a line along the sloping object. Then go to Image→Rotate Canvas→Arbitrary and the image will magically straighten up.

Memory

Photoshop is a hungry program, especially when you have a large History palette and several unmerged layers. The performance may drop if your computer doesn't have loads of RAM spare and you could find filters take much longer to apply.

Click on the arrow at the bottom of the window by the file size figures and select Scratch Sizes from the drop down menu. You'll see the figures change. The new left-hand figure represents the room required for the currently open images and the right-hand one is the space available in RAM. If the first figure is bigger than the second you're treading on thin ground and could find your computer crashes more often. The computer will borrow memory from the hard drive and will slow down as it accesses the info. Either work with one image at a time or upgrade your PC and buy more RAM.

Merging Layers

QUICK KEYS CTRL+E When you've finished editing an image and are sure you don't need to keep it in layers you can flatten the layers to make the image's file size much smaller. There are several ways to do this – all found at the bottom of the Layers menu.

Merge Layers and Merge Down combine the selected layer and the one below it in the Layers palette. Merge Visible combines all layers with an eye icon in front of the layer's name in the Layers palette.

Merge Linked brings together all the layers that you've selected using the linking box (including the one you were last working on). Merge Group combines all the layers that you've previously grouped using the Layer→Group Linked command. Flatten Image merges all layers that are visible and discards all the others. It's the option to choose when all your image editing is complete.

Masks are lost when layers are merged so if you intend revisiting an image to make further adjustments save a copy with all the necessary layers.

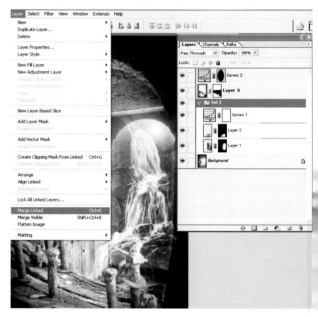

Mezzotint filter
(See Pixelating filters)

Minimum

MENU FILTER →
OTHER →
MINIMUM

Quite an unusual filter, placed in the 'Other' area which suggests that Adobe didn't really know where to fit it. In most cases the filter doesn't do much good, but when there are quite marked changes in tone from one area to another, it can be effective in a creative way. In this example set to 33 pixels, I applied fade with a Difference blend and it's created some funky glowing edges. Use with care, though!

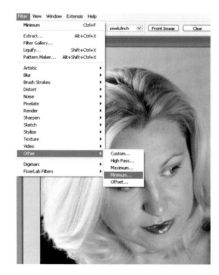

Moiré patterns

A mottled pattern caused when printed material is converted to digital using a scanner. Some scan software has a descreening feature that eliminates the pattern but this can soften the image.

You can also rotate the material to be scanned slightly in the scanner and straighten it up once scanned, which sometimes helps. **(See Noise filters)**

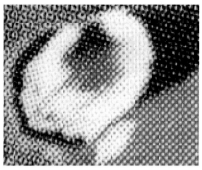

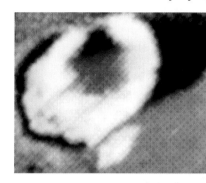

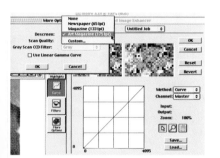

This scan of a peacock butterfly came from a 2x1in picture in a magazine. The Moiré pattern isn't obvious when the picture is small, but as soon as you enlarge it the criss-cross pattern becomes harsh. Use Photoshop's Median filter at a setting of around two to reduce the pattern.

Move tool

QUICK KEY   V   Hardly the most exciting item in the Photoshop toolbox, yet still useful. It's used to drag the image around on screen and can also be used to move Selections and Layers across to other Photoshop images.

Double click on the tool to call up the Options palette and just two options, Pixel doubling and Auto Select Layer. Turn Pixel doubling on to increase the speed the tool moves the selected image in the preview. Auto Select Layer makes the tool automatically select your image's top layer.

If you have opened another command, say Levels, and you want to scroll an open image that's larger than the screen area, click on the space bar and the mouse which then allows you to drag the relevant part of the image into a suitable view.

Just to prove two heads are better than one! The better expression was borrowed and blended into the other image.

Montage

A collection of images and text brought together on one canvas using features such as Layers, Blending modes and the Rubber Stamp tool to make seamless joins.

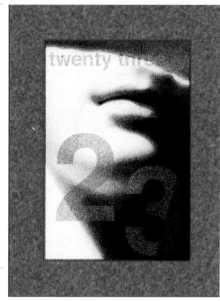

Motion Blur
(See Blur filter)

Multi-page PDF to PSD

MENU   FILE →
         AUTOMATE →
         MULTI-PAGE
         PDF TO PSD

New feature in Photoshop 5.5 that automatically converts Acrobat PDF files into Photoshop PSD. White backgrounds become transparent and images can be edited in Photoshop. Options are available to save at various resolutions in color or black & white.

Multiply
(See Blending modes)

Navigator palette

MENU **WINDOW→**
　　　　NAVIGATOR

This palette shows a small preview of the image you're working on. The palette preview can be made smaller or larger by dragging the bottom right edge of the box. At the base of the preview window is a zoom scale that you adjust to make the main image magnify or reduce in size.

The area that shows on screen

appears as a frame in the navigator's preview window which gets smaller as you increase magnification. The frame can be

moved around the preview to select the area of the main image you want to work on. It's a really useful feature to help you fly around a photo, especially when you're working on a vastly enlarged version.

New

MENU　　　　**FILE →**
　　　　　　　NEW
QUICK KEYS　**CTRL+N**

When opening a fresh file in Photoshop you follow the usual path that most programs offer, File>New. In Photoshop's past you then keyed in the measurements required and a blank canvas would appear.

Photoshop 7.0 added default options with a drop down list of popular preset sizes to save you keying in values. You can, of course, still set any size you want in the custom fields and Photoshop CS adds a save preset feature so favourites can be added to the drop down list. I've added the 10x4in panoramic format.

Noise filter

MENU   **FILTER →**   Four filters used to add grain or remove
            NOISE...   dust in an image to make it look natural.
Noise can also be used to reduce banding effects that are often
introduced by gradients.

To illustrate this I have created a color gradient which clearly
shows the lines between tones of the color gradient. Adding
a small amount of noise removes these, making the gradient
smoother and a little more natural. Adjust the slider and watch
the image. You can always undo (Ctrl+Z) if you are not happy
with the effect. I used a setting of 0.6%. Any more and the grain
became too noticeable.

ADD NOISE

When used in small amounts this filter can make a digital picture
with smoothed edges or an Illustrator file look more natural. Use
in larger amounts to recreate an effect you'd obtain using fast
film. Controls include an amount slider to vary from a very subtle
1 to an unbelievably gritty 999. Then you can choose between
Uniform or Gaussian distribution. Gaussian produces a stronger
effect. Finally turn Monochromatic on or off. When on, the Noise
filter works the same on all color channels, unlike off where the
effect is random on each channel.

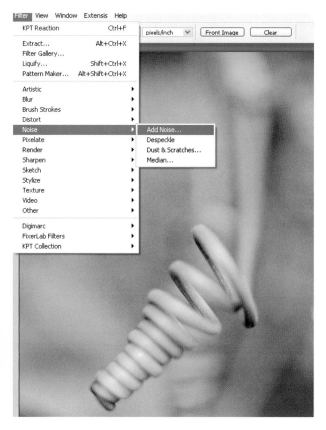

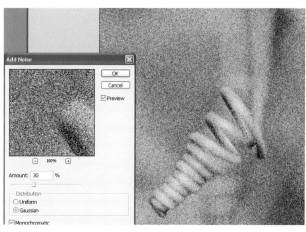

Adding 30% of Gaussian distribution with Monochromatic selected
produces an image that's far too grainy for most images.

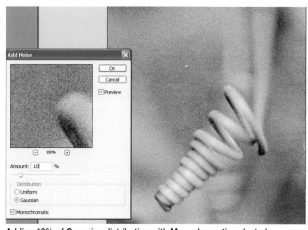

Adding 10% of Gaussian distribution with Monochromatic selected
produces a far more natural result.

Reducing to about 6% gives the best and more subtle effect.

Noise filter
(Cont.)

DESPECKLE
A subtle softening filter that helps reduce noise caused by poor scanning. When applied increase sharpness using the Unsharp Mask filter.

This close-up of a girl's eye was cropped from a 46Mb scan. The Despeckle filter helps reduce some of the problems of the scan, but does tend to soften the image slightly.

MEDIAN
Used to reduce noise, so it's quite effective with the Moiré patterns that are caused when scanning printed material. The downside is it tends to soften the image. Apply the Unsharp Mask filter to increase sharpness after this filter has been used.

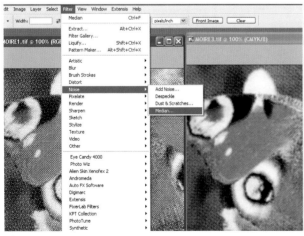

Median has a dialogue box with a sliding adjuster giving more control over the effect. The Moiré pattern is easily removed but the result is softer and needs the Unsharp Mask applying.

DUST & SCRATCHES
The most useful of the Noise filter range is Dust & Scratches, especially when used on scanned films. No matter how well you try to keep the surface clean it will attract dust and result in scans with marks. This is a noise filter that detects dramatic changes in adjacent pixels and blurs the surrounding colors to smooth out the tones.

It's not always clever enough to know what is and what isn't dust so don't think this is the answer to your prayers. You're more likely to end up with a soft result than a rescued one!

Try various combinations of the two Radius and Threshold sliders and adjust the settings until the best result shows in the preview window. Dragging the Radius slider to the right increases the effect, unlike the Threshold slider which reduces it.

Be careful how far across you set the Radius. Even just a small setting of 5 pixels has destroyed all the detail in the example on the right, but the dust has gone! Below is a more sensible 1 pixel setting, but here the image is softened and the dust is still present. 3 pixels was best.

Here's a handy tip to help you use Dust & Scratches over a whole image without affecting quality.

1 First apply the filter to the whole image. Then click in the box to the left of the Dust & Scratches level in the History palette. This puts the History Brush icon in the box.

The quickest way to get rid of big chunks, especially if there are only a few around your picture, is to use the Patch tool seen here doing a marvellous job with ease.

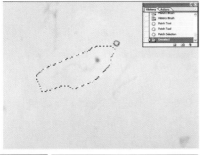

The Add Noise filter can be used to reduce banding when a gradient is produced.

Nonsquare pixel support
(See Pixel Aspect ratio)

2 Now click on the previous history state, in our case the crop stage. The dust and scratches will return but you can now use the History brush to paint over all the bad areas with the Dust & Scratches filter applied to the size of the History brush.

3 Keep working around using the History brush and when you get to a big chunk try the tip below or use the Patch tool.
(See Patch tool)

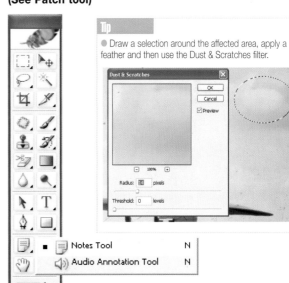

Tip

● Draw a selection around the affected area, apply a feather and then use the Dust & Scratches filter.

Note
A feature introduced on version 6.0 that allows you to leave messages around the picture. These appear as little notes on the image which, when clicked open, reveal the message you've left. Useful if you're working with a designer who needs to do something with the picture before it goes to print.

112

Opacity

The opacity slider appears in many of the palettes and is adjusted by either dragging the arrow left or right or typing in a new percentage value. Use this mode to adjust the layer's appearance in the overall image or adjust strengths of paints and editing tools.

Here's one of the ways you can use opacity in a more complex layer structure. I created a background and cut out three seagulls which were then pasted onto the background creating four layers. I wanted two of the seagulls to appear to be in mist, but just changing the opacity would make the background show through so I created a neutral gray layer with a gradient mask and reduced the opacity of this to partly reveal the birds.

Text displayed at various opacities.

Opacity set to 20%.

Opacity set to 40%.

Opacity set to 60%.

Opacity set to 80%.

Open

MENU	FILE ➜
	OPEN
QUICK KEY	O

Use this to open pictures from within Photoshop. It will point you to a folder or directory and you then go through the system to search for the picture. When you find the image double click it to open.

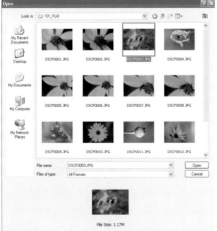

Open as

MENU	FILE ➜
	OPEN AS
QUICK KEY	ALT+CTRL+O

You may find that a file will not open with a message appearing that says incorrect format. This can happen when you accidentally add a wrong file extension when renaming a file or try to open a file that has no extension details. In such cases you can use the Open as option and select the file extension that you think the file actually is and it will open. On a Mac you need to go to File➜Open➜Select All Documents.

Open recent

| MENU | FILE ➜ |
| | OPEN RECENT |

First introduced on version 6.0, this feature shows a list of 10 recent images that you have had open in Photoshop and offers a shortcut path to find them. This saves you having to trawl through your entire system if you want to reopen an image you have previously worked on and forgot where you saved it.

Options palette

| MENU | WINDOW ➜ |
| | OPTIONS |

Double clicking on anything in the toolbox brings up the Options palette that usually has a range of settings, check boxes and sometimes grayed out items that can only be accessed when you're in certain modes. Ones at the bottom with a stylus next to them need a graphics tablet attached to be functional. The top right arrow reset tools.

Output levels

A slider at the base of the Levels palette is used to control the highlight and shadow detail of the image for printing. Dragging the left-hand marker right decreases shadows while dragging the right-hand marker left decreases highlights.

Tip

● If you get a bronzing effect on the blacks of your inkjet prints it's because too much black ink is being used. It occurs on some types of paper when they're not fully compatible with printers. Adjusting the shadow triangle from 0 to 5 or 10 reduces shadow density and helps avoid overinking the black.

Overlay mode (See Blending modes)

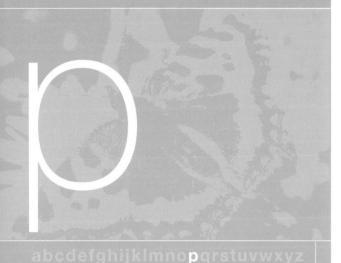

p

abcdefghijklmno**p**qrstuvwxyz

Page Setup

MENU   FILE →   PAGE SETUP

QUICK KEYS   SHIFT+CTRL+P

This takes you to your printer's settings where you select the paper size and orientation.

The depth of settings you see depends on the Operating System and print driver software. Clicking on the printer button takes you to the printer's driver and from here you can access properties and set paper type, size, resolution and a whole many more options.

Paint bucket

QUICK KEY   G   Use this to flood the selected area with the foreground color.

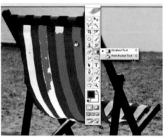

The Tolerance setting determines how many pixels are affected by the flood. A small amount results in a patchy paint effect, while a higher tolerance may color areas you don't want covered. The deckchair stripes, above, show the Tolerance at four settings. The left-hand one was set to 10, the second 20, the third 30 and the fourth 40. Click on Anti-aliased to soften the edge of the paint fill.

Paintbrush tool

QUICK KEY   B   One of three tools used to apply selected color to the image. The paintbrush can be used on full strength or less using the opacity setting to reduce the amount of color affecting the image.

With lower opacity the original pixel color can still be seen. This effect is like adding a wash to the image and is really useful for hand-coloring black & white images like the example below.

Palettes

The menu boxes that let you adjust settings of various tools.

Arrange them carefully on the desktop to avoid clutter. Many of them have shortcut keys to open and close the window, making it visible or invisible on the desktop.

Palettes can also be grouped to make the desktop even tidier.
(See Appendix C)

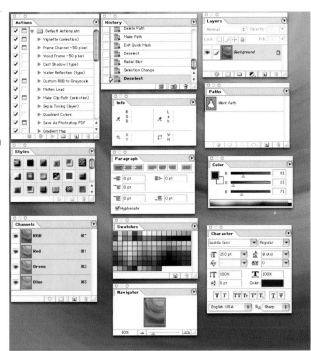

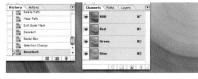

You can drag one palette onto another to combine them and save space on the desktop.

Palette Well

When several palettes are open your screen may become cluttered. Photoshop CS makes it easy to arrange things by having a Dock to Palette Well mode that moves the palette to a position at the top of the page. The palette can then either be used as a drop down from the well or dragged back onto the screen.

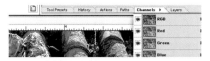

Paste into

MENU	EDIT →
	PASTE INTO
QUICK KEYS	**SHIFT+CTRL+V**

Used to paste an image into part of another that's been previously selected. The new pasted image appears within the selection. The area around the selection becomes a Layer Mask and the icon appears by the pasted image by the layer thumbnail. You can use the mask to hide or reveal sections of the pasted in image.

The background was selected and the cloudy sky was pasted into this selection. The pasted image's position and size was then adjusted using the Move and Transform tools followed by Match color to make it similar in hue and Motion blur to give the clouds movement.

Patch tool

One of the star features of Photoshop 7.0, this astounding tool has been made even better in Photoshop CS. It does a

🖌 Healing Brush Tool	J
■ 🩹 Patch Tool	J
🖌 Color Replacement Tool	J

similar job to the familiar Clone tool but makes a much better and faster job of repairs. You select an area that you want to repair. This could be wrinkles on portraits, blemishes on skin or fruit, dusts on scans, or even unwanted birds in a sky. You select either source or destination and draw a lasso around the area you want to use as the source (pixels that will be the sample) or Destination (area you want to repair). Then you drag the selection to the new spot and the job's done.

A few laughter lines, catchlights from the flash on the nose and chin and an odd crease here and there – put away the Nivea, we have a much better option! Photoshop CS shows the pixels that you are sampling in the Patch tool sample area making it easier to sample the best area.

Moving around the face and neck with the Patch tool took no longer than five minutes and you can't see where the repairs are. All you do is select nearby areas and drag to match up the photo. Alan's 10 years' younger now.

Here's an old photo that was scanned on a flatbed scanner. I selected the area I want to repair, dragged it to the new sample point and let go. The Patch tool selection automatically returns to base and the sampled pixels are blended.

Photoshop CS has a transparent option in the menu bar. This allows new sampled pixels to be patched over existing pixels without the existing ones being removed. So the new ones merge with the old rather than replace them.

Path component selection tool

QUICK KEY   A   This tool is used to select a whole path shape and move it on screen. Unlike the direct selection tool which lets you click on an anchor point and drag to distort the path's shape.

Paths

Paths are outlines created by drawing with one of the Pen tools. They are vector-based so don't contain pixels and appear separate from a normal bitmap image.

A thumbnail of the path can be viewed in the Paths palette, and from here you can select a number of options to apply to the active layer from a row of icons along the base or from the arrow's drop down menu. These options include: Filling the path

with the foreground color; producing a Stroke to add the foreground color along the selected path and making a Selection from the path.

A path can be moved to a new image by dragging the original path icon from the palette and pulling it over a new image. You can also copy paths from one location and paste them into another using the normal copy & paste option.

Paths can be converted quickly into selections and selections can be turned into paths.

Paths are also used by designers who turn the selection into a clipping path and import it into a page layout. The clipping path ensures everything outside the frame appears as transparent on the layout. This ensures text wraps around the subject and the subject blends well with the layout.

(See Pen tools)

Use the Quick Mask mode to paint a mask around the subject. Magnify an area and use the Eraser and Airbrush to remove or add to the mask, then convert the masked selection into a path.

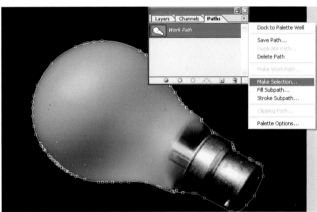

When a path is drawn you can turn it into a selection, fill it or produce a colored outline using the Stroke Path option.

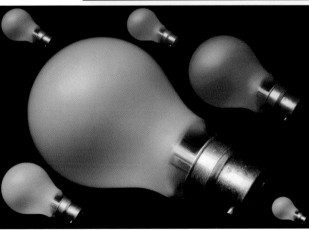

Paths can be turned into selections and then cut and paste the selected object. In this case the lightbulb was copied and colored using the Hue/Saturation command.

Pattern Stamp tool

QUICK KEY S Like the Clone Stamp, but it takes the sample from a preselected area that you've defined. To use this select an area you want to clone using the Rectangular

| | Clone Stamp Tool | S |
| | Pattern Stamp Tool | S |

Marquee and use this to create the pattern. Then select Edit→Define Pattern.

Now when you use the Pattern Stamp tool the defined area will be repeated as you draw across the canvas. If the Align box is checked the pattern will be repeated in uniform tiles in the shape of the selection. If you uncheck the Align box a tile appears wherever you draw. Blend tools are also available in this mode.

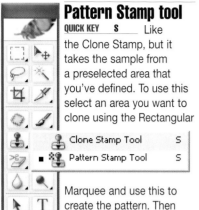

First make a selection of an area that you think will suit the Pattern Stamp tool. Then go to the Edit→Define Pattern and the new pattern will appear in the Patterns Presets box. Then you can paint a pattern using the pattern stamp and it will repeat whatever pattern you select.

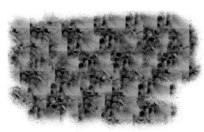

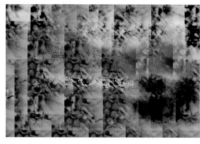

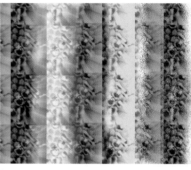

As illustrated here you can also use Blend modes to change the way the pattern appears on the page. Above left is the pattern painted with Diffuse blend mode and align turned off. Left is various blend modes painted on top of each other and above is a strip of five blend modes from left; Normal, Difference, Luminosity, Hardlight and Dissolve.

A selection from a mushroom, painted in using the aligned turned off for the top version and turned on for the bottom version.

Right is the same brush with the Impressionist option turned on and changed to purple.

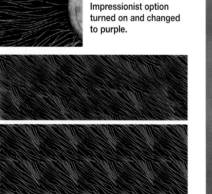

Tip

● Make your own mini gift wrapping paper by selecting a part of a subject that would look good repeated and use the Pattern Stamp tool in aligned mode to cover an A4 or A3 sheet.

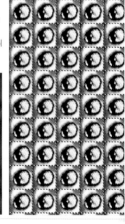

PDF

Short for Portable Document Format, this file format is used to convert Quark documents that contain words and pictures into a format that any one can view using the free Adobe Acrobat reader. Pictures that have been edited in Photoshop can also be saved in this format. Photoshop 7.0 introduced an option to password protect the PDFs too.

PDF presentation

MENU **IMAGE →**
AUTOMATE →
PDF PRESENTATION

At last! Photoshop has a slide show mode. This mode is new to Photoshop CS and lets you create PDF presentations (slide shows) that you view using Adobe Acrobat. The images can be set to change at selected intervals with one of many transitions. You can also choose to save as a multi page document. You can access this mode from the File Browser menu.

Pencil tool

QUICK KEY **B** Produces a hard-edged line and is more useful for drawing than retouching images. The Options palette has a fade feature that gradually reduces the pencil color opacity to zero giving a gradual fading effect. There's also an Auto erase that replaces the image with the background color as you draw.

Pen tool

QUICK KEY **P**

Creates a path that can be turned into a selection. It's unusual to use at first, but spend some time getting familiar with it and your drawing and selection skills will improve tenfold.

The Pen tool icon on the toolbar has several options. The first is Pen tool which you use to add points, known as anchor points, around the subject. Points are automatically linked to make a path. This is ideal when you want to draw straight lines and smooth curves. You can have as many anchor points as you like and they can be removed by clicking on them.

To draw a straight line, click at a start point then move to the finish point and click again. To complete a straight path click the Pen tool icon in the toolbox when you reach the end. To complete a round path click on the original start point to complete the shape.

The Freeform Pen tool is like the normal Lasso and creates a path wherever you draw. It's like using a normal pen and is very accurate, providing you are! Anchor points are added along the path, and their positions can be changed when the path is complete. The Magnetic Pen tool works like the Magnetic Lasso and automatically locates high contrast differences between pixels and lays the path along the edge.

Tips

● When using the Magnetic Pen tool go slowly so the Pen locates the edge you're drawing along to ensure it picks up what you expect it to.
● Hold down the Shift key to create a straight line running at a 45° angle.
● Click the Rubber Band box in the Options palette to see the curve of the path you're about to create as you move the Pen tool.

Perspective

MENU EDIT →

TRANSFORM →

PERSPECTIVE

Use this to either reduce converging verticals or exaggerate them. Drag the handles at the edges of the selection to pull in or pull out the canvas. A tall building that's been taken from a low angle with a wide-angle lens will appear narrower at the top. Stretch the canvas outward to make the walls upright.

Alternatively a road going off into the distance can be made to reach a pinpoint at the horizon by pulling the canvas in at the top.

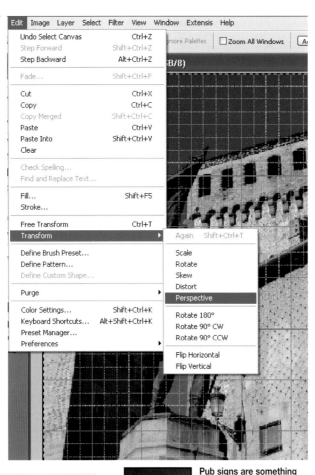

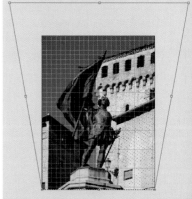

Whoops!

● If the Transform option is grayed out go back to the picture and select the area you want to transform. Select All if it's the whole picture you're changing.

Pub signs are something that rarely appear square, and that's not because of the few you've just had indoors! The distort tool is a better option to use.

Photo Filter

MENU   IMAGE ➜
        ADJUSTMENTS ➜
        PHOTO FILTER

Those traditional photographers who have been wondering how to emulate an optical photographic filter can now do so with ease. Photoshop CS adds this option that places a color over the photo without you having to worry about variations, hue/saturation or adjustment layers.

This new adjustments feature has a range of preset options including the 81 warm, 80 cool and sepia, plus a color option where you can select any color from the color picker and apply that. The only other control is an opacity slider which reduces the amount of color as you reduce the opacity and a preserve luminosity box that keeps the tonal values the same just allowing the color to adjust. If this is not checked the image will go darker if you choose a dark color.

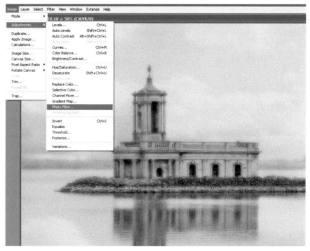

Warm up filters are no longer required and you can even add warmth to a toned photo. You can adjust the density while watching the preview.

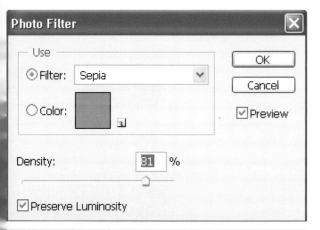

Click on the color box to manual select a color from Photoshop's standard color picker.

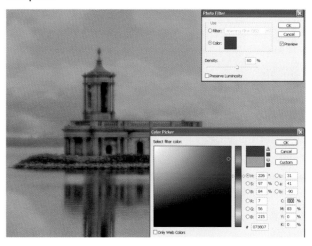

Photomerge

MENU	IMAGE →
	AUTOMATE →
	PHOTOMERGE

This first appeared in Photoshop Elements and it's good to see that the same option is now included within Photoshop CS. This feature automatically joins photographs together that have been taken from the same position but pointing at different sections of a scene. It's a great feature when you see a landscape in front of you and find you are restricted by the angle of the lens you use. You simply shoot several photos to cover the width of the scene and then let the program automatically stitch them together. Each photo should be taken allowing around 20% overlap and ideally with manual exposure so that all the shots have the same tonal value. This makes it easier for the software to match and create an even join.

Settings gives you the choice of a straight stitch (Normal) or one that takes into account the view you see would be arced and perspective would be different at the edges. This is the option I've used. Notice the photos at each edge are stretched and made bigger, giving the illusion that you are looking around the scene rather than at a flat, two-dimensional view.

Click on Cylindrical Mapping Composition setting to remove the bow tie shape created when you use perspective setting. Use Advanced Blending to minimize color changes where blending images with exposure differences overlap.

You can save the composite as a .pmg file which can then be called up in future and reworked.

When you first activate this mode it asks you to select the photos you want to join. These then appear in the centre window in sequence, usually overlapped and ready for you to confirm acceptance. You do have several options to improve the results.

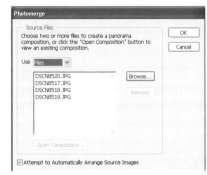

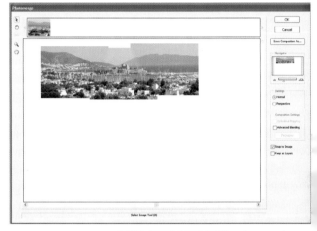

Left is a version created when Normal is selected from the Settings option. The version below is when Perspective is selected and this is the option I used for the main photo at the bottom.

You may find the merge leaves a line where two tones have been blended. Use the Patch tool to make a selection over the poor merge and sample from a spot outside the merge area.

PICT file

Is widely used by Mac operators for use in graphics and page layout programs, and is ideal for transferring between the two. It supports RGB and allows a single Alpha channel, Index colors and Grayscale.

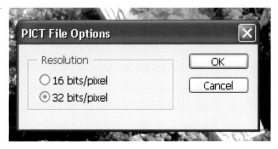

Picture Package

MENU   **FILE →**
         AUTOMATE →
         PICTURE PACKAGE

An auto mode that resizes a selected picture to a specified resolution and fits a variety of sizes on an A4 page, ranging from one to 16 pictures.

First you choose the source image which then opens into one of the templates. You can change the size of the page and the number of pictures displayed in the layout. The source image appears in each of the picture frame areas on the layout and then you either print that or click on individual boxes in the layout to change pictures into a multiple print page.

Photoshop CS adds a layout editor where you can choose the shape, size and position of pictures on the page and save the layout as a custom file for future use. Custom files can be deleted by going into Photoshop Folder and presets and layouts.

CHOOSE YOUR TEMPLATE
Picture Package has a range of layouts you can choose from. This is a great automated tool to help you print multiple photos from one or several images on a sheet of A4 paper.

Pin light
(See Blending modes)

Pixel Aspect ratio

MENU   **IMAGE →**
         PIXEL ASPECT RATIO

A new feature in Photoshop 8 that enables either DV or D1 video format files which are composed of rectangular (non-square) pixels to be viewed accurately on screen.

DV or IEEE 1394 is a digital video standard with a 4:3 frame aspect ratio and a screen resolution of either 720x480 (NTSC) or 720x576 (PAL). D1 is also known as CCIR-601 and has a screen resolution of either 720x486 (NTSC) or 720x576 (PAL).

If you were to view files created in either of these two formats the image would look squashed. By selecting the correct non-square format you can view the files as they will appear on a video display or in video editing software such as Adobe After Dark.

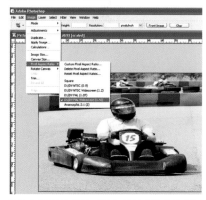

Pixel dimensions

Number of pixels measured along the width and height of an image, quoted as 640x480 pixels on a basic digital camera and 1280x960 pixels on a megapixel model. The latest six million pixel cameras have dimensions of around 3072x2048 pixels.

Pixelating filters

MENU   FILTER ➜
                PIXELATE ➜

A range of seemingly pointless filters that convert the selected area into varying patterns of clumped pixels.

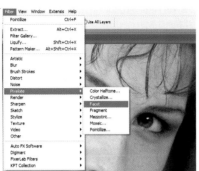

CRYSTALLIZE
Takes pixels into lumps and converts them into a polygon shape of solid color. The size of polygon can be varied between 3 and 300 pixels, although anything past 3 starts to look ridiculous.

FRAGMENT
Duplicates pixels and offsets them to create an effect that you'd normally only see after a few too many drinks!

MOSAIC
Clumps pixels into square blocks and makes them the same color. The effect is like a very low resolution image and another one we'll avoid.

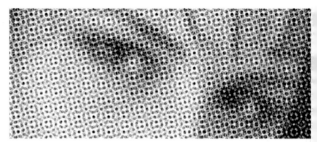

COLOR HALFTONE
Divides the image into rectangles and replaces them with circles to create an enlarged halftone effect. The menu lets you select the radius of the halftone dot, with pixel values from 4 to 127, and you can enter screen-angle values for each channel. It can take ages to apply and you'll wonder why you bothered!

FACET
One of the better pixelating filters, changes clumps of similar colored pixels into blocks of the same color pixels to make images look like they're paintings.

MEZZOTINT
Brings up a dialogue box that has nine options – each scrambling the picture to look as though it's a badly tuned television picture. One to avoid, unless, of course, you like looking at badly tuned images!

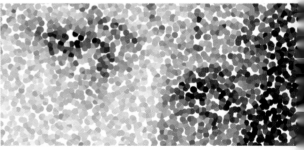

POINTILLIZE
Makes the image look like a pointillist painting. Yuk!

Plastic Wrap filter
(See Artistic filters)

Plug-in filters
A filter that offers additional features to the standard program. Photoshop supports third party filters that can be added to Photoshop's plug-ins folder to increase the program's flexibility. The files have .8bf as their description. Many of the current supplied range used to be third party options.
(See Appendix E)

Polygonal Lasso tool
(See Lasso tool)

Posterization

MENU	IMAGE →
	ADJUSTMENTS →
	POSTERIZE

Converts the image into a number of brightness levels between 2 and 255 to produce a graphic effect. 2 is too harsh, 255 too subtle. A good balance is between four and eight.

Preferences
(See Appendix D)

Preserve luminosity
(See Color balance)

Preserve Transparency
When this box is ticked in the Layers palette the areas of transparency are protected from brush strokes or other changes made to that layer.

The examples below show the result of varying levels of Posterization on color and black & white images

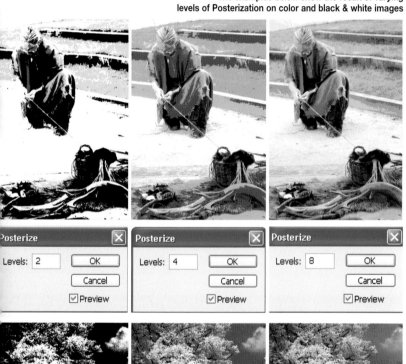

To show the effect I cut around the leaping bather and pasted him onto a new layer. Then I painted over him using Preserve Transparency turned on (above) and off (below).

Preset manager

MENU   EDIT ➔
PRESET MANAGER

Brings all the preset palettes into one box so you can create new ones, load and edit existing ones or delete unwanted ones. These categories include Brushes, Swatches, Gradients, Styles, Patterns, Contours, Custom Shapes and Tools, each with its own set of presets.

Tools, for instance, contains Crop & Marquee, Art History, Brushes, and Text presets that can be loaded or new ones saved.

Print Options

MENU   FILE ➔
PRINT WITH PREVIEW
QUICK KEY   ALT+CTRL+P

Adobe created this sensible printing system on version 6.0. When the message saying 'image too big, do you wish to proceed' appears come here and select Scale to fit Media which automatically adjusts the image to suit the paper you're using in your printer. You can also adjust the size and position of the image so it prints in a certain part of the paper. Show bounding box lets you adjust by dragging the corner boxes or you could manually adjust size and position by keying in known measurements. All done with minimal loss of brain cells! There are plenty of options for repro houses too including allowing bleeds and printing crop marks.

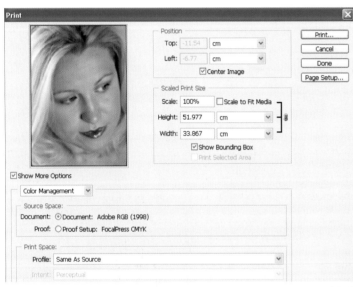

Left: The preview window shows the default setting and how the print will appear on an A4 sheet, in this case it's too big and will be heavily cropped and a message will appear when you try to print saying the image is too large.

Below left: Click Scale to fit media to get a full image inside the preview window and a useful print. The Color management section lets you set the source (image) and print space (output) profiles. This ensures that Photoshop works with the inkjet printer to deliver a good quality result.

Below right: Uncheck 'centre' and key in a size to print a custom size and position anywhere on the page. The Print options window has many more options to choose from that were introduced in version 7.0. To see these change the Color Management drop down to Output. To show you a few in this example I've changed the background color to blue, selected crop marks which help when you, or a repro house wants to trim the print. I've also selected registration marks.

Print resolution

The number of dots along the length and width of a print, measured in dots per inch. Generally the more dots per inch the higher the resolution. Most inkjet printers print out at between 600dpi and 1440dpi, but these are slightly misleading as the figures allow for between three and six ink color droplets which are used to make up each dot.

A 1440dpi printer that uses six individual ink colors actually means the print resolution is more like 240dpi. The highest true resolution is around 400dpi for dye-sub printers and most books and magazines print at around 300dpi.

Progressive JPEG

A file format used on the Web for quicker downloads. The image opens up progressively so you can get a rough idea what it looks like and either wait until it is at its highest resolution or click off and go elsewhere.

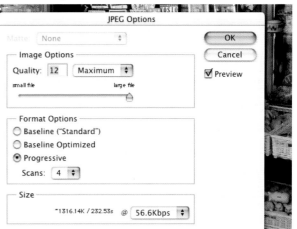

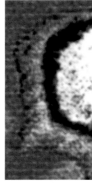

This close-up of the tip of a peacock butterfly's wing shows how the dots make up the image. This is the equivalent of a 1/4in area printed out at 300dpi, so it shows the formation of around 75 dots across the length.

Proof Setup

MENU   VIEW →
        PROOF SETUP →

Lets you view the image on the monitor as it will appear when reproduced on a specific output device. This is known as soft-proofing and saves you printing a hard copy of your document to preview how the colors will look. It is only any use when you have calibrated your monitor.

PSB

A new format for huge documents to get around the file size limits in the old formats. In the same way PSD stands for Photoshop Document, PSB is short for Photoshop Big! You have to enable large document format in the File handling Preference window first before it will show up. Then you can work on files with up to 300,000 pixels in any dimension.

PSD

Photoshop's native format. Use this to save photos when you want to keep individual layers, but files are large.

Purge command

MENU   EDIT →
        PURGE

This clears stuff out of the computer's memory such as the pattern held in the buffer ready for use by the Pattern Stamp tool.

You'd use the Purge command when the computer is starting to run slowly or can't finish an action due to a lack of memory. Several options are available from the Purge drop down menu including Undo, Clipboard, Patterns, History.

abcdefghijklmnop**q**rstuvwxyz

Quadtones
Quick Mask mode

Quadtones

MENU   IMAGE ➔
           MODE ➔
           DUOTONES

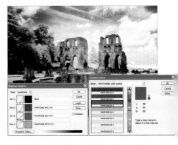

Quadtones, like Duotones and Tritones, are grayscale images that use process or Pantone colors to give a subtle color tone, almost like the sepia, blue and gold toning of the conventional darkroom but with much more control and repeatability. Photoshop has a selection of preset Quadtones in the Duotone folder found in the Preset folder.

(See Duotones and Tritones)

From the preset selection, this adjusts the grayscale without adding a colour hue and is used to ensure better printing in high quality books.

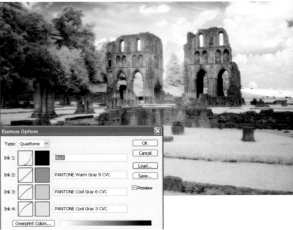

Another preset using Pantone colours to give a subtle green hue. This would be effective on still life shots but less so on a portrait.

One of the Pantone presets that gives a slight sepia style glow.

A process color preset that may work well with a vintage portrait.

Blue colors like this, created using the process color preset, can work well with glamour images.

Playing around with the Quadtones colors can be very rewarding when you stumble, by chance, on a pleasing tone as a result of mixing colors.

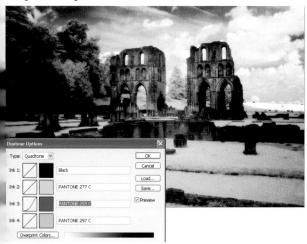

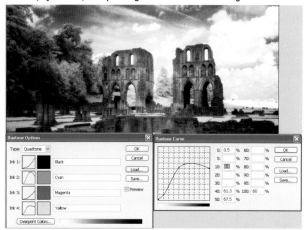

Quick Mask mode

QUICK KEY   Q   Enter this mode by clicking on the icon near the bottom of the toolbar. It's a quick way to create a mask around a section. The mask can be increased using one of the Painting tools or decreased using the Eraser.

When you've made all your adjustments to the mask, click the off icon at the base of the toolbar and a selection will appear on the edges where the mask meets the unmasked area. Use the Paint or Erase tool set to a small brush size to clean up rough areas.

RAM
Raster image
Rectangle tool
Replace Color
Resample Image
RGB
Rotate Canvas

Radial Blur
(See Blur filters)

Radial Fill
(See Gradient tool)

RAM

Short for Random Access Memory – the part of the computer that's used to run programs. Photoshop needs a minimum of 128Mb to run, 192Mb for anything more than basic manipulation and as much as you can stick in to do complex multi-layer picture editing of large files.

Most computers can be upgraded and RAM, while fragile, is easy to install. You just take off the computer's side, back or lid, locate the memory slots and clip a stick of RAM into the hole. RAM used to be very expensive – a 128Mb chip cost around £900 a few years ago – now it's around 20p per megabyte.

 Could not open "Page 1.eps" because there is not enough memory (RAM).

OK

Raster image

Another name for a bitmap – an image made up of a grid of pixels.

Rectangle tool

QUICK KEY **U** One of the vector-based shapes that you draw on the page. The shape fills with the foreground color and can be resized to suit the job you're doing. It appears on a new layer and has an adjustment icon where you can change its color. These can also be used to mask individual image layers. The

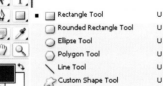

Rectangle Tool	U
Rounded Rectangle Tool	U
Ellipse Tool	U
Polygon Tool	U
Line Tool	U
Custom Shape Tool	U

list also includes Rounded rectangle, Ellipse, Polygon, Line and Custom shape. Here a layer effect has been applied which then affects any shape that's added to the canvas.

Rectangular Marquee tool
(See Marquee tools)

Replace Color

MENU IMAGE →
ADJUSTMENTS →
REPLACE COLOR

Use this to select and change the color of your subject. The palette that appears has a fuzziness scale that works like the tolerance setting – the higher it's set the more pixels are selected around the original color. This mode is useful when the subject you want to change has a strong color dominance as it's easier to select the area you want. Set the preview window to Selection and click on either the preview image or the main image using the Eyedropper tool to select the color you want to change.

The preview image shows the color selected as

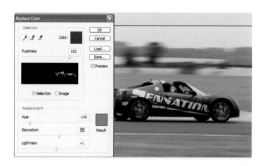

white and the surrounding areas as black. You can then adjust the Hue, Saturation and Lightness. Use the +/- Eyedroppers to add to, or remove from, the color selected.

Resample Image

MENU IMAGE →
IMAGE SIZE

If you want to make a picture smaller for use on a Web page, or bigger to enlarge for the wall, you have to take away or add pixels – known as resampling. The Image Size palette lets you change the image using the pixel dimension or measurements. Make sure Resample Image is checked.
(See Image size and Interpolation)

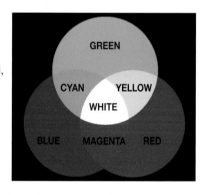

Resolution
(See Image Resolution)

RGB

Mode used to display colors on a computer monitor – R being Red, G green and B blue. The colors are mixed together in various proportions and intensities to create most of the visible spectrum with over 16.7 million colors.

Photoshop assigns an intensity value to each pixel ranging from 0 (black) to 255 (white) for each of the RGB colors. Cyan, Magenta and Yellow are produced when different proportions of color overlap, for example R and G values of 255 mixed with a B value of 0 result in 100% Cyan.

Gray is created when there's an equal amount of R, G and B. When all the values are 255, the result is pure white and when the values are 0, pure black. This is known as additive color.

Ripple filter
(See Distort filters)

Rotate Canvas

MENU IMAGE →
ROTATE CANVAS →

Scanned images can often appear the wrong way up or back to front. This option lets you rotate the canvas by 90° clockwise or anti-clockwise, 180° or flip horizontally or vertically.

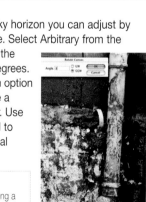

If you take a photo with a wonky horizon you can adjust by slightly rotating the whole picture. Select Arbitrary from the Rotate Canvas menu and key in the amount of rotation required in degrees.

You can also use the Transform option Edit→Transform→Rotate to rotate a selection or whole selected layer. Use the Grid option View→Show Grid to help align the horizontal or vertical elements.

Tip

● Draw a line, using the measure tool, along a sloping object that you want straight, then go to Image→Rotate Canvas Arbitrary and the image will magically straighten.

S

Saturation

MENU   **IMAGE →**
        ADJUST →
        HUE/SATURATION
QUICK KEYS **CTRL+U**

A slider control to adjust the colors in the image from –100 to +100.

Dragging the slider to the left decreases the color in the image which is useful if you

want a pastel effect or black & white.

Dragging to the right is the recipe for vivid colors – go too far and the image will look unnatural.

The Sponge tool can also be used to apply the effect on smaller areas. **(See Sponge tool)**

Saturation reduced to –100 knocks out all the color.

Increase to +100 and the colors become unreal.

Save

MENU	FILE →
	SAVE
QUICK KEYS	CTRL+S

When you click on the close box to close a photograph a message box will appear asking you if you want to Save, Cancel or Don't Save which may seem like a silly message if you've clicked on the picture to close it. This is your chance to save changes before closing. If you click Save, the latest version will be saved. If you click cancel you can go back and make a final adjustment that you may have forgot as you clicked on close. If you click on Don't Save it will save the file as the last saved version so any corrections or editing you have done will be lost. This is a useful option if you've opened a picture to try out an effect that you don't want to apply. **(See Save As)**

Save As

MENU	FILE →
	SAVE AS
QUICK KEYS	SHIFT+CTRL+S

If you prefer to keep the original and have a different file for the new edited image, select this option and change the name. To make things easy just add 2 at the end of the current name so you know it's version two. It also lets you change file format.
(See individual file format entries)

Save for Web

MENU	FILE →
	SAVE FOR WEB
QUICK KEYS	CTRL+SHIFT+ALT+S

One for Web designers which was introduced in version 5.5. Open a picture you want to convert for the Web and when you've done all your retouching or enhancing go to Save for Web. This brings up a palette to the side of your picture with a range of options to reduce the file size by resampling, file change and color reduction.

If you're not sure what effect various options will have on your image you can split the screen into two or four versions and apply a different setting to each.

Save a version

MENU	FILE →
	SAVE A VERSION

New to Photoshop CS, this feature works within an Adobe Version Cue Workspace, which is only available if you are using Photoshop CS as part of the new Adobe Creative Suite. It allows you to save a version of an image that you are working on to ensure that no one overwrites the file of someone else working in a Version Cue project. **(See Version Cue)**

Scale command
(See Transform)

Scratch disk

When your computer lacks the RAM needed to perform a complicated Photoshop task, the program uses its own virtual memory system known as a Scratch disk. The Scratch disk is best assigned to the hard drive – removable drives are not recommended for this type of use. If you have partitioned your hard drive use a separate partition to hold the Scratch disk to the one that's running Photoshop for the best performance.

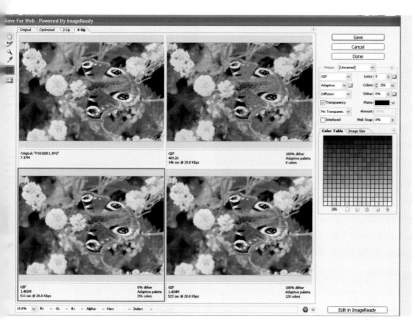

S

Screen mode

MENU	VIEW→SCREEN MODE
QUICK KEYS	F SELECTS IT
	FROM TOOLBOX

If, like me, you have loads of desktop icons floating around untidily and, often, several applications open at once you may find it becomes difficult to work with Photoshop and its many palettes. The full screen mode, selected from the toolbar, removes all the clutter to make it much easier to see the image. Choose full screen with menu items when you need to access modes or full screen when working on a picture. The F key runs through each option in a cycle.

Selecting

When you want to edit part of an image it has to be selected. A selection can be made using several Photoshop tools such as the Lasso and Pen tools, Pens, Marquees, Magic Wand and Color Range. These are all explained in their relevant sections. The selection appears with a moving dotted line border that's often described as marching ants. Select→All puts the marching ants around the whole image.

Selective color

MENU	IMAGE →
	ADJUSTMENTS →
	SELECTIVE COLOR

Use this color correction mode to remove a color cast or add creative color. The palette has a drop down menu of the six additive and subtractive primary colors along with blacks, neutrals and whites. Select which you want to modify and then adjust the Cyan, Magenta, Yellow or Black content.

Adjusting the cyan slider in the red does not affect the cyan in any of the other areas. For color casts it's often just a case of nipping into the Neutral colors and adjusting the four sliders until the image looks balanced on screen.

You also need to choose between Relative and Absolute adjustment methods. With Relative selected you adjust the cyan, magenta, yellow and black sliders by a percentage of the total. A 25% magenta pixel becomes 30% when you add 20% (20% of 25% = 5%). Add 20% using the Absolute method and a 25% magenta becomes 45% magenta.

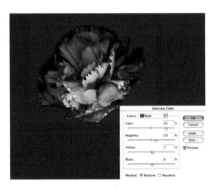

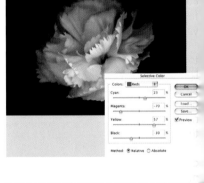

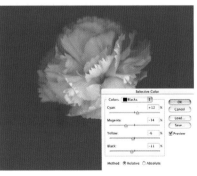

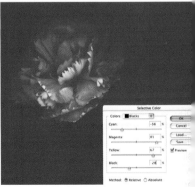

Playing around with the color sliders can produce some creative color effects.

Shadow/Highlight

MENU   **IMAGE →**
        ADJUSTMENTS →
        SHADOW/HIGHLIGHT

A clever new feature introduced in Photoshop CS that allows you to adjust the shadow and highlight areas of an image by correcting each pixel based on the luminance values of neighboring areas. Image contrast can be increased in the shadows or highlights or both without significantly sacrificing contrast in other regions.

As with many Photoshop adjustments you have several sliders to fine tune your corrections. The Shadows and Highlights sections each have an Amount, Tonal Width and Radius slider.

The Amount slider controls the steepness of a brightening or darkening curve. Larger values lighten shadows and darken highlights. A value of zero for both Shadows and Highlights produces a straight line and no modification of the pixel, while a value of 100 produces a very steep curve with maximum modification. The default is a setting of 50 which is fine for most backlit subjects, but for severe backlighting with very dark subjects, you will need to increase this towards 100%, while images needing moderate correction can be set to smaller values of around 20%.

The Tonal Width slider adjusts how much modification you make to the shadows, midtones and highlights. When correcting shadows select a small value in the Tonal Width to place emphasis on the darker regions of the image. Larger values place emphasis on midtones and highlights as well.

The default is set to 50%. If you are trying to lighten a dark subject but the midtones or lighter regions are changing too much, move the Shadow Tone Width slider to the left so only the darkest regions are lightened. If you need to brighten up the midtones as well as the shadows, move the slider to the right.

The Radius averages out the luminance of neighbouring pixels so that each pixel is modified according to its surrounding data. A larger radius increases the extent that the neighborhood luminance is averaged out.

As you adjust the slider you can obtain a good balance between subject contrast and differential brightening or darkening of the subject compared with the background.

The bottom sliders let you adjust color brightness and midtone contrast. The clip values entered here determine how much of the extremes are clipped when you adjust the slider. Set this too high and the adjustments will appear dramatic, with detail in highlights and shadows being lost or clipped.

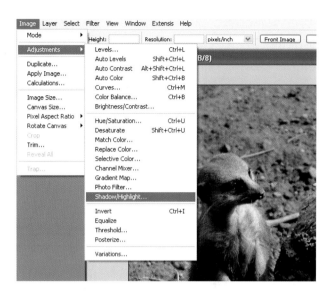

When you first choose Shadow/Highlight a basic two slider control opens (right) which is usually fine for basic control. Click on Show More Options to gain access to the full range of sliders (below) that we use on the next page.

S

Shadow/Highlight
(Cont.)

Here's a good example of a photo that can benefit from the Shadow/Highlight adjustment. It was taken on a Minolta Dimage 7Hi digital camera and was one of those

scenes where the camera couldn't win. The exposure was a compromise between the dark foreground and bright sky. The result is it lacks detail in the sky and shadow areas. So the first job is to sort out the shadow areas using the top three sliders (right). Secondly let's make the highlights darker using the middle three sliders (below). Notice how the gray in the sky is now really dramatic. Finally we can brighten up the colors using the bottom two sliders (below right). Look how vivid the red roofs are now.

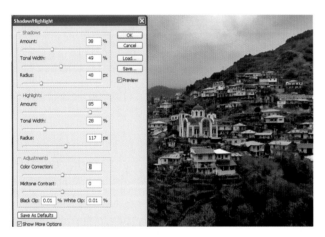

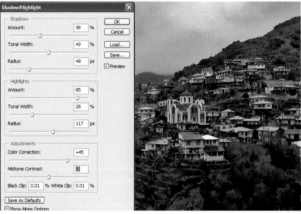

Tip

● Set the radius to a value that roughly represents the size of the subject, it then takes the data from the surround and averages the intensity over the face, ignoring the background. If you select a radius that's much larger than the subject it will average out the subject values too and make the whole thing too bright. If the radius is too small you lose contrast in your subject. If the radius is too large, you will brighten or darken the whole image rather than affecting just the subject.

137

Sharpen

Filters used to give an apparent sharpening effect by increased contrast between light and dark pixels. Three of the Sharpening filters perform automatic operation. You have much more control using the last option, Unsharp Mask. **(See Unsharp Mask)**

Sharpen

Sharpen Edges

Original

Sharpen More

Single Column Marquee tool
(See Marquee tools)

Single Row Marquee tool
(See Marquee tools)

Sketch filters

MENU   **FILTER →**
      SKETCH →

A selection of filters that add hand-drawn texture to your images using the foreground and background colors. The image becomes two tone but you could always use the History Brush to bring some more color back.

BAS RELIEF

Changes dark areas to the foreground color and light areas to the background color. Two sliders control the detail and smoothness of the effect. Here the foreground color was set to blue.

CHALK & CHARCOAL

Recreates the image with solid mid-gray highlights and midtones. The background becomes coarse chalk using the foreground color, and shadow areas are replaced with diagonal charcoal lines using the background color. Sliders control the balance of Chalk and Charcoal and the Stroke length.

Tip

● Set Detail at maximum and Smoothness at minimum for the kind of bas relief you'd create in a darkroom, especially when foreground and background colors are set to black & white.

S

Sketch filters
(Cont.)

CHARCOAL
Similar effect to Chalk & Charcoal. The foreground color, in this case blue, is sketched on top of the background color.

CONTÉ CRAYON
Uses the foreground color for dark areas and the background color for light areas to supposedly recreate the effect of a Conté Crayon drawing – it's more like a tapestry effect. Sliding controls let you adjust the strength of the foreground and background colors along with the Texture, Scaling, Relief and Light direction of the effect. Here yellow was selected as the foreground color and purple as the background color.

HALFTONE PATTERN
Produces a circle, dot or line pattern using the foreground and background colors. In this example I have used green as the foreground color and selected the line pattern.

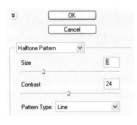

CHROME
Produces an image with smooth edges and a variety of gray tones, making it look like highly reflective chrome.

Tips

● Images can look dull when this filter has been used. Adjust Levels to add contrast to the image.
● Doesn't work well with all subjects – go for bigger subjects with less detail.

GRAPHIC PEN
Changes the image to a series of fine ink strokes which ensures detail of the original is still present. The foreground color is used for the pen's ink and the canvas becomes the background color. Controls allow stroke length and direction to be adjusted along with the pen and paper color balance.

NOTE PAPER
I can't see the point of this one! Controls let you adjust the proportions of the foreground and background colors, add grain and adjust the relief of the texture. Try a few settings then give up!

PHOTOCOPY

Another pointless effect that is supposed to turn the image into a photocopied effect. One of the filter's creators is obviously using a vintage photocopier!

PLASTER

Creates a slight 3D effect that looks like spilt fluid on a glass sheet. Dark areas are raised and light areas sink, unless you select Invert to reverse the effect.

RETICULATION

Use the Density, Foreground and Background sliders to control the reticulation effect that you'd normally only achieve by accident in the darkroom.

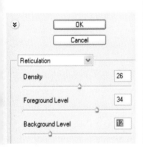

STAMP

Lightness/darkness and smoothness controls are all that are available for use with this potato-printing filter. Another one to avoid!

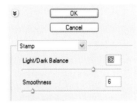

WATER PAPER

Makes the foreground and background colors flow into the image just as watercolor paint or ink would when applied to blotting paper.

TORN EDGES

Normally one of the more interesting Sketch filters that simulates a ragged paper effect. You need to spend time adjusting settings to get the best effect.

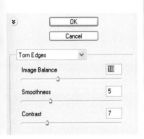

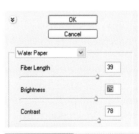

Tip

● Use the Edit→Fade … and experiment with the Blend modes and different opacities. Here the Water Paper fade has been blended using Overlay mode to create an effect that looks like a cheap color photocopier print.

S

Slice tool

QUICK KEY K The Slice tool lets you cut a picture up ready for use on the Web. The overall picture will still appear seamless but each slice has its own Web code and can be adjusted so that it appears to change color, dim down, glow or whatever other effect you apply when the cursor goes over it. Each area is designated with a number.

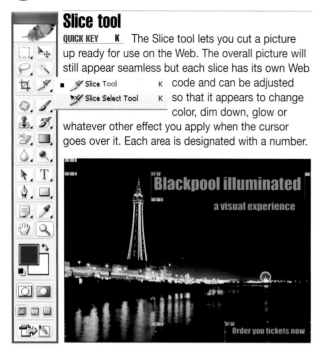

Smart Blur (See Blur filters)

Smudge tool

QUICK KEY R Click on the finger icon that's shared by the Sharpen & Blur tools in the toolbox and use it to push or smudge color from pixels into neighbouring pixels. It creates an effect like rubbing your finger through wet paint and, as with all paint tools, you can select the size of your fingertip.

The Smudge tool can also be used to remove blemishes and spots by rubbing around the area to blend the dust spot with its surroundings.

The tool's Options palette allows the Blending mode and pressure to be adjusted and it picks up the color under the pointer to paint, unless you select the Finger Painting option which uses the foreground color. Change to Finger Painting by pressing Alt (Windows) or Option (Mac OS) as you drag with the Smudge tool.

Selecting All Layers makes the Smudge tool use color from all the visible layers. When deselected it uses colors from just the active layer. You can also choose Size or Pressure when a pressure-sensitive drawing tablet is connected. These are grayed out when not available.

Snapshot

Lets you make a Snapshot (temporary copy) at any stage in the editing process. The snapshot appears in a list at the top of the History palette and can be recalled by clicking on the Snapshot you want to return to.

You can make as many snapshots as you need to compare editing stages, return to certain states or compare two or more final techniques.

Tips
● Select the Allow Non-linear History option from the triangle drop down menu in the Options palette. Then you won't lose the current History state when you return to an earlier History palette.
● Snapshots are not saved with the image so when you quit snapshots are lost.

The Smudge tool can also be used to blur objects by rubbing over the surface in all directions. The effect can look like water's dripped onto a watercolor painting.

Soft light mode
(See Blending modes)

Solarizing
(See Stylize filter)

Spherize filter
(See Distort filters)

Sponge tool

QUICK KEY **0** Shares a place with the Dodge & Burn tools in the toolbox. The icon looks like a sponge and when dragged over the image surface either increases localized saturation or decreases saturation depending on which you selected from the Options palette.

The Sponge tool does locally what the Saturation option does for a whole selection.

Tip

● Use the view Gamut Warning option with a bright color to see where the sponge could be used and the effect it has.

Stroke

MENU **EDIT →** **STROKE** Used to place a border around a selection using either foreground or background color pixels. You can choose the width of the border, the position from the selection, Blend mode and opacity. Version 6.0 brought the color selector within the palette rather than you having to go to the toolbar foreground color to choose it. In this example I sampled a green from the statue to use as the Stroke border.

Tips

● As with all border creating methods, avoid colors that clash and distract from the subject.
● Use the Stroke command when you want to highlight part of a picture. Draw a circle round it using the Circular Marquee and apply a two or three pixel stroke in an eye-catching color.

Spot Color channels

Allows you to add and print a color that would normally not be possible from the normal CMYK gamut. You select the color using Pantone reference in a special Spot Color channel.

Select New Spot Channel from the Channels drop down menu and click on the color square to call up the color picker. Ignore the Out of Gamut warning and pick that lush fluro green or pink for the vivid heading or background. Selecting 100% solidity simulates a metallic color while 0% is more like a clear varnish effect.

Tip

● The Spot Color option works best when you have the image printed with a fifth color ink. Desktop printers use CMYK so you need to add the color to the normal channel's Merge Spot Channel. The printer will then simulate the color using CMYK, but it may not be as vivid.

S

Stylize filter

MENU   **FILTER →**   Use these
       STYLIZE →   filters to create
impressionist effects. They often work
better when the Fade command is
applied afterwards, especially if you
choose the right blend mode.

DIFFUSE
Shuffles pixels around randomly to create a soft,
ragged looking image. Darken Only replaces light
pixels with darker pixels. Lighten Only replaces

dark
pixels
with
lighter
pixels.

EMBOSS
Locates high contrast
edges and adds light
and dark pixels to
emphasize these
edges. The strength
of relief is increased
using the Amount
slider and the Height
slider increases the
3D effect by making
the image appear
raised from its
background. You can also adjust the angle
that the embossing takes effect through 360°.

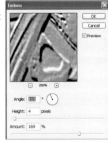

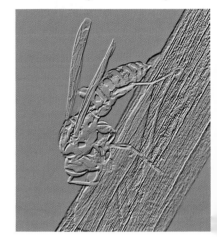

EXTRUDE
Produces a 3D building block or pyramid effect.
The height and size of blocks can be adjusted.

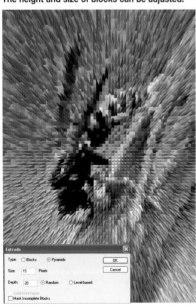

Tip

● Try applying the
Pyramid Extrude after
the block. Use small
pixel values for the
most detailed effect.

● Select Solid Front
Faces to fill the front
of each block with the
average color. Keep it
deselected to fill the
front with the image.

FIND EDGES
Emphasizes edges of a subject by detecting areas with high contrast edges
and turning them black, while areas with low contrast appear white and
medium contrast go gray.

Tip

● Try using the Fade
command and a
blend option after
applying Find Edges.
Here the Hard Light
blend mode was
selected with an
opacity of 59% to
create a pencil style
sketch around the
original photo.

143

GLOWING EDGES

Opposite effect of Find Edges which makes the white edges that replace high contrast areas appear with a neon glow.

Tip

● Selecting Image→Adjust→Invert makes Glowing Edges look like Find Edges and vice versa.

SOLARIZE

Produces an image like the photographic technique popularized by the likes of surrealist Man Ray where a print was exposed briefly to light during development to fog and turn highlights to black. Yuk!

TILES

Makes the image break up into a series of tiles. You can select tile size, gaps between the tiles and the color of gaps between the tiles.

Tip

● Reapply the tile filter on an already tiled photo and select a larger maximum offset, then go to Edit>Fade and select Overlay blend mode set to about 50% for a crazy effect.

TRACE CONTOUR

Creates thin outlines that vary in color around high contrast edges.

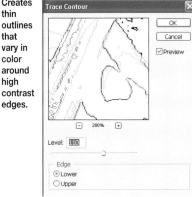

WIND

Imitates an unrealistic wind effect by producing streaks from the pixels. Three options include Wind, Blast and Stagger which can be applied coming either from the left or right.

t

Texture filters

MENU   **FILTER →**   A series
       TEXTURE →   of filters
that gives the image a textured appearance as though it has been ironed onto a textured surface.

CRAQUELURE
Produces a fine patch of cracks that looks a little like flaking paint. Choose your image carefully!

GRAIN
Adds grain to an image making it look more like a traditional photograph. This is a useful mode to apply to make a digital camera image blend with a traditional shot and look more natural when combined. There's a choice of grain types and the intensity and contrast can be controlled.

MOSAIC TILES
Breaks the image up into tiles separated by grout. The size of tiles can be adjusted along with the width and contrast of the grout.

OK
Cancel

Mosaic Tiles

Tile Size	60
Grout Width	8
Lighten Grout	9

PATCHWORK
Changes the image into a grid of colored squares. The colors produced are an average of all the enclosed pixels of each particular square. The size of grid can be changed and appears in varying depths to simulate a very realistic looking patchwork.

OK
Cancel

Patchwork

Square Size	8
Relief	14

STAINED GLASS
Draws a series of irregular shaped cells over the image, outlined by the foreground color, and fills them with an average of the contained pixels.
The cell and border size can be changed.

OK
Cancel

Stained Glass

Cell Size	10
Border Thickness	5
Light Intensity	3

TEXTURIZER
Adds a texture to the image making it look like it's printed on canvas or, like this example, a jigsaw puzzle.

OK
Cancel

Texturizer

Texture: Puzzle	
Scaling	167 %
Relief	37
Light: Top Right	

☐ Invert

TIFF format (Tagged-Image File Format)

A versatile format that can easily be read by Macs and PCs using a variety of software programs. It supports CMYK, RGB, and grayscale files with Alpha channels plus Lab, indexed-color and Bitmaps without Alpha channels. TIFF files can be compressed, without any loss in quality, using the LZW method to gain storage space, but they'll be slower to open and save.

Tiles filter
(See Stylize filters)

Tolerance settings
(See Magic Wand)

t

Threshold mode

MENU   IMAGE ➜
         ADJUSTMENTS ➜
         THRESHOLD

Makes a normal
grayscale or color
image appear like
a high contrast lith
image by discarding
all tones including
grays and leaving just
black and white.

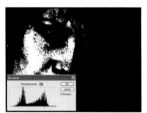

You can control where the black and
white crossover points are using a
slider on the Histogram. Go too far to
the right and the image will look mostly
black, too far to the left and it will look
mostly white. A point mid way is usually
best, but it does depend on the subject.

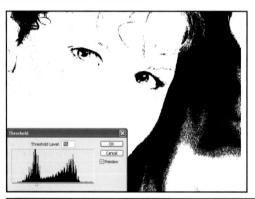

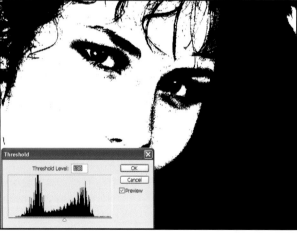

Tip

● Create a silhouette using
the Threshold mode then go
to Hue/Saturation and with
Colorize selected make a
color. This gives effects similar
to those using graphic art
papers in the darkroom such
as Kentmere Kentona papers
or bleach etch effects.

Tolerance setting

Found in the Magic Wand options. It's used to adjust the
number of pixel color variations selected from the one the magic
wand touches. If the tolerance setting is high more pixel colors
will be selected. If it's low fewer will be selected. Trial and error
will help you determine what to set this to.

Tip

● Start small and work up or start big and work down until the wand is selecting
more or less the area you want it to. Then adjust the tolerance to minimal setting
and pick up wanted areas using the wand with the Alt key held down or remove
parts of the selection with the wand and the Command key held down.

Toolbox

The area on the desktop where all the tools are
located. Ones with arrows have pull-out sections
with a choice of alternative tools.

Most of the toolbox icons can be double clicked
to bring up the palette options box.

The bottom two icons allow easy transfer from
Photoshop CS to ImageReady CS.

Tool shortcut keys are given throughout this book
on the separate entries for toolbar contents.
(See Appendix C)

Tip

● The tab key hides all the desktop palettes, including the toolbar.
Hold down the Shift key while clicking on the Tab key to keep the
toolbar on view, while you hide palettes.

Tool presets

Store your favourite
settings for Brushes, Crops
and text styles to access
them with ease from the
preset menu.
(See Brushes)

Transform

MENU   EDIT →
           TRANSFORM → A series of options that lets you change the size, shape, and perspective of a selection as well as rotate and flip it either manually or numerically.

The selection appears with squares, or handles, in the corners that you drag to change the dimensions. It's ideal for resizing an object when it's copied and pasted into another image. You can also use it to stretch landscapes and give them a panoramic feel.

The area you want to change must be selected before you can use these modes.

Studio photographers can't always shoot from an angle that will ensure uprights are parallel. For this reason many commercial photographers use large format that allows perspective control. You can of course sort it out in Photoshop like this, using Transform→Distort.

Transform→Distort was used here to create a slightly more dramatic looking perspective.

Whenever you shoot a subject from below it will appear to be leaning back and look like the top is thinner than the bottom. Use Transform→ Perspective to pull the top outwards equally from both sides.

Copy and resize your subject using Transform→ Scale to create a more realistic looking perspective.

t

Transform
(Cont.)

Take any ordinary landscape and stretch it using Transform→Scale to create a panoramic print.

Tip
● When making the image grow out of the canvas area increase the canvas beforehand to allow the new 'stretched' area to appear.

Transform Again
Remembers that last Transform that you applied and repeats the action. This is a useful option if you're creating a composite picture and are pasting in and adjusting several elements.

Transparent layer
A layer with areas that contain no pixels, such as a new Layer, appears with a chequered pattern. Any subsequent layers that are merged will only be affected by the non-transparent areas. These are available in Photoshop's PSD format and the TIFF format, but need to be merged if saved as JPEGs. Transparent areas are then replaced by white. Cutouts can be saved by converting to clipping paths which prevent the white background appearing on the document.

Transparency masks
Use the Gradient Editor with the Transparency option selected to create a transparency mask. This can be used to help blend two layers or add a graduated filter effect to an image.

The original on the left was shot on an overcast day and could quite easily do with a lift. I copied the statue and pasted her on a new layer and then added a transparency mask as a new middle layer. A blue fill was added and the blue only shows through where the mask is clear.

Trapping
MENU   IMAGE →
          TRAP

Produces an overlap on colors by the amount of pixels you key in. The overlap prevents gaps appearing between CMYK colors if there's a slight misalignment or movement of the printing plates. This technique is known as trapping and your printer will tell you if it's needed and what values to enter in the Trap dialogue box.

Tritones

MENU   **IMAGE →**
MODE →
DUOTONE

Part of the Duotones series using various color schemes from the presets folder in the Photoshop folder. The image first needs to be in grayscale before it can be converted to a Duotone.

Here are a few examples of an image that started life as a color photo taken on a Coolpix 995 digital camera. The image was layered with a diffuse glow version, flattened and converted to grayscale before it became a duotone/tritone.
(See Duotones and Quadtones)

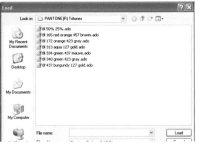

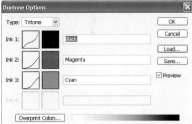

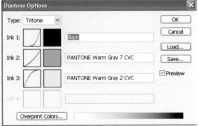

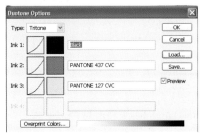

t

TWAIN

TWAIN, or Technology Without An Interesting Name, is a file that comes with scanners that you place in the Mac's Preferences folder or the TWAIN folder of the PC's Windows Directory. To scan with in Photoshop go to File→Import→ TWAIN Acquire. If more than one scanner is installed

select the one you want first, File→Import→Select TWAIN Source. You can keep within Photoshop while scanning pictures. Once scanned the image appears in a new Photoshop document named Untitled. It's wise to save this Untitled file straightaway, because if the computer crashes you'll lose the file and will have to scan the photograph again.

Type tool

Photoshop CS's Type tool continues to improve making it even easier for designers to create stunning text treatments. As well as being able to call from the system's usual font size, color and styles you can create type with selection borders using the Type Mask tool and fill with images or textures. Version 6.0 introduced vector-based type that you can increase in size without any jaggedness. This also offers more control so you can distort and bend the text alone or around objects. Photoshop CS adds the ability to add Text along a Path or Shape.

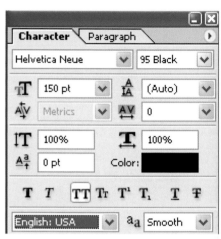

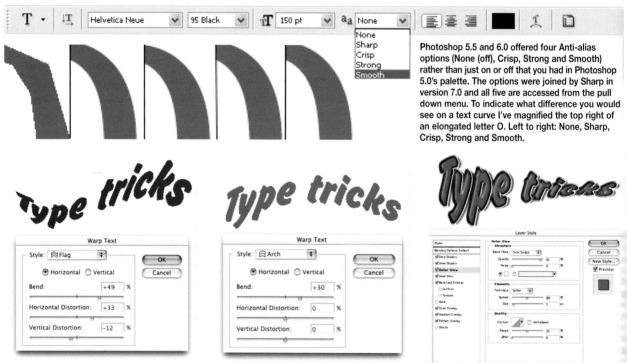

Photoshop 5.5 and 6.0 offered four Anti-alias options (None (off), Crisp, Strong and Smooth) rather than just on or off that you had in Photoshop 5.0's palette. The options were joined by Sharp in version 7.0 and all five are accessed from the pull down menu. To indicate what difference you would see on a text curve I've magnified the top right of an elongated letter O. Left to right: None, Sharp, Crisp, Strong and Smooth.

Type can be bent and shaped in any direction. First select a style and then drag the sliders to warp the text. Here I've illustrated Flag (left) and Arch (middle). You can then add a style using the Layer Style drop down options (right).

Once you're familiar with using the type warp tool you'll be able to warp it to suit a shape that you place the type on. Here the type has been warped so it looks like it's following the shape of the 3D sphere.

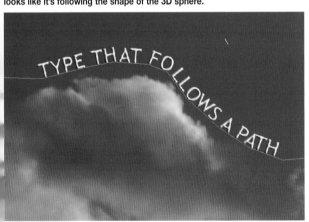

Photoshop CS has introduced a type to path option. First create a Path where you want the type to go then position the type tool over the path where you want the type to start. The Type tool cursor icon will show a path through the middle and when it does click to begin typing along the path. This works for shapes too.

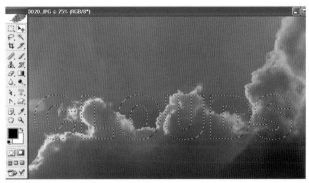

Use the Horizontal type mask tool if you want to create an instant selection around the letters you type. Then you can copy and paste so that the image appears in the letters and add a Layer effect such as a drop shadow or bevel as seen in the two examples below.

If you are using the Type tool to add a paragraph of text use the Bounding box option. With the Type tool selected click on the point where you want the text to start, hold the mouse down and drag. This creates a box that can be formatted to ensure the text appears as you prefer. You can change Character and Paragraph formatting.

u

abcdefghijklmnopqrst**u**vwxyz

Undo
Use all Layers
Unsharp Mask

Undo

MENU	EDIT →
	UNDO
QUICK KEYS	CTRL+Z

If you don't like the effect of a filter you've just applied, or you've gone wrong with a brushstroke you can use Undo to take you back one step. Edit→Step Forward/Step Backwards makes life even easier. It's like the History palette but uses shortcut keys to speed things up. Whatever you do can be simply undone. **(For multiple undos see History palette)**

> **Tip**
> ● Use Undo to revert to a previous setting when making adjustments to palette settings that have several options.

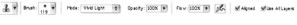

Use all Layers

Select this mode in the Rubber Stamp, Paint bucket or Sharpness/Blur/Smudge palettes to ensure the colors of all layers are considered when an effect is applied to the active layer. When Use all Layers is not selected only the colors in the active layer are sampled, cloned or smudged.

Here's what happens when we clone from a source image (Untitled 1) to a destination document (Untitled 2). The image has text on each of three layers. The first example (top) doesn't have Use All Layers selected. When you clone from source to destination only the active layer is picked up and cloned onto the new document. When Use All Layers is selected (right) all three layers are cloned.

Unsharp Mask

MENU   **FILTER →**
       SHARPEN →
       UNSHARP MASK

A filter used to sharpen edges in an image and reduce blurring caused at the photographic, scanning, resampling, or printing stage. Unsharp Mask locates pixels that differ from neighbouring pixels and increases their contrast. It's perfect for sharpening pictures that are taken with digital cameras and scanned images that often have a slightly soft edge sharpness.

The dialogue box has Amount, Radius and Threshold settings that are adjusted by dragging sliders or manually entering values.

Amount changes the pixel contrast by the amount you set. When producing images for on-screen viewing you can judge the effect quite accurately and a setting of 50–100% is fine, but for printed output it's not as easy. Try a setting of 150% to 200%.

Radius controls the number of pixels surrounding the edge pixels that will be affected by sharpening. A lower value sharpens just edge pixels while a higher value sharpens a wider band of pixels. The amount you set also depends on the size of the image – use a smaller number for a lower resolution image and increase the number for a higher resolution image. Go too high and the edges become too contrasty.

Threshold, set at a default of 0, sharpens all the pixels. Moving the slider upwards prevents the filter from affecting pixels that are similar to neighbouring pixels. A value of between 2 and 20 is a good starting point. The higher you go the less effect Unsharp Mask will have on the image.

Above: Amount set at 500% with low radius and threshold values is acceptable.

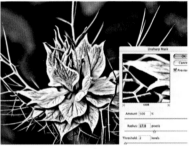

Above: Increase the radius and the result is too harsh with extreme contrast on all edges.

Above: Reducing the Amount and Radius and increasing threshold produces a better result.
Below: Applying Unsharp mask to the lightness layer of the image in Lab color mode is best.

Tips

 Bright colors can become overly saturated when Unsharp Mask has been applied and dust marks are easily enhanced. Try converting the image to Lab mode and apply the filter to the Lightness channel only to sharpen the image without affecting the color.
 Run Unsharp Mask twice at half the single settings for a more subtle effect.
 Hold down the Shift key and click within the preview window to show the original unfiltered version.

Above left: Magnified section of original shot on a Nikon Coolpix 995. Above right: Same shot with Unsharp Mask applied in Lab color's lightness channel.

V–Z

Variations

MENU   **IMAGE →**
       ADJUSTMENTS →
       VARIATIONS

This color balance control, which also lets you adjust image contrast and brightness, is the most colorful window of all the Photoshop dialogue boxes with its series of preview images.

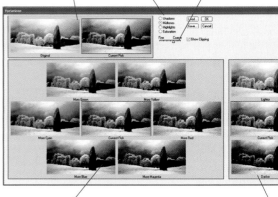

The original selection and the adjusted selection appear at the top.

The menu appears at their side and from here you select Shadows, Midtones, or Highlights to adjust dark, middle or light areas.

Set the Fine/Coarse slider to control the amount of adjustment.

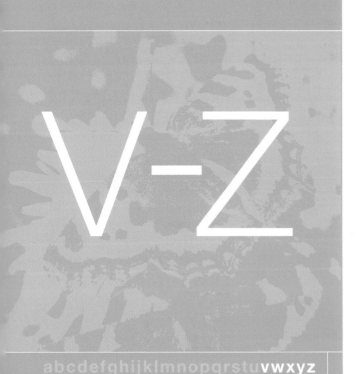

Seven pictures appear with the current example in the centre and the color options around the edges.
To add a color to the image, click the appropriate color image and to subtract a color, click the image on the opposite side.

These three preview images are used to adjust image brightness. The centre is the current version, the one above makes the centre lighter and the one below makes it darker.

Whoops!

● If the Variations command is missing from the Adjust sub-menu check that the Variations plug-in module has been installed.

Version Cue

If you buy Photoshop in Adobe's Creative Suite bundle you have access to this new feature which helps you be more productive when working with other team members on projects. With Version Cue, you create, manage and locate different versions of your project files and share them in a multi-user environment that protects them from being accidentally overwritten.

Vivid light
(See Blending modes)

Watercolor filter
(See Artistic filters)

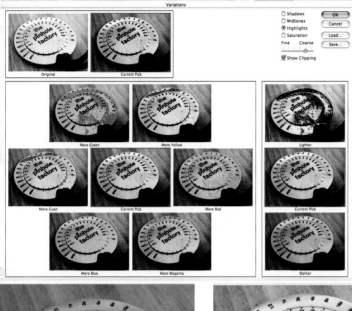

Turn Show Clipping on to display a preview of channels that have been clipped as a result of your adjustment. The neon color indicates the affected channel or channels. In this example if you clicked on darker the clipping would disappear.

Watermarks

MENU **FILTER →**
       DIGIMARC →
      EMBED WATERMARK

Adding a watermark to your image is a safe way of protecting the copyright. Digimarc embeds a digital watermark to the image. It's imperceptible to the human eye but is durable in digital and printed forms and will survive typical image edits and file format conversions. A © symbol appears by the title to warn viewers that copyright should be respected. To use this feature you have to register with Digimarc and receive a special ID number.

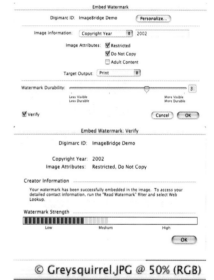

© Greysquirrel.JPG @ 50% (RGB)

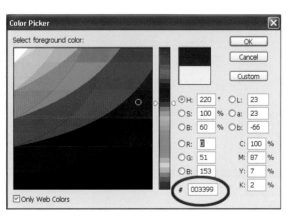

Left: The original photograph of a brass calculator dial was photographed using window light and lost the lovely yellow color. Variations enabled me to bring this back to something like the original item. It's easy to use and you can see instantly which way to go to ensure better results. By careful control of lighten and darken I could ensure that the highlights didn't get clipped while adjusting color.

Web colors

When using pictures on the Web there are a limited number of colors that can be selected when writing HTML code. Photoshop versions back to 5.5 let you select the Web palette from the Color Picker and when you pick a color, the HTML reference code appears for the selected color. The medium blue color I picked here has an HTML code of 003399.

Wet edges

An option in the Brush palette that produces a brushstroke with a build-up of color on the edges to simulate a watercolor paintbrush effect.

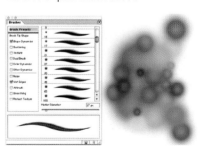

Web Photo Gallery

MENU FILE ➔
AUTOMATE ➔
WEB PHOTO GALLERY

It's never been easier to get your pictures on-line with this new feature, introduced first in Photoshop version 5.5. This auto mode converts your pictures into Web manageable sizes, then writes some HTML code so that they appear as thumbnails on an opening index page. Clicking on an individual picture brings up a full screen version. The code includes arrows to navigate backwards or forwards through the gallery. Pages can be edited if you have a web design program such as GoLive or DreamWeaver.

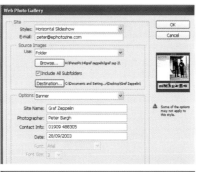

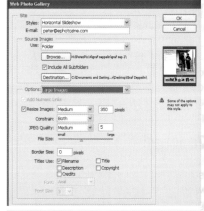

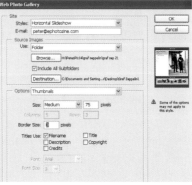

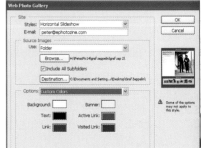

Opening up the main page in this basic design template gives a thumbnail index of all the pictures on the site. Click on the arrow at the top of the page to navigate backwards and forwards through the pages.

Various menu options let you set up this feature so that it creates the ideal Web page and style for you.

You can select the number of images shown per page, the layout, text color and size, along with image quality, destination folder and even add links. The palette has options to generate the pictures at various sizes. The site will work quicker when small files are selected, but image quality will be poorer. All the HTML pages, pictures and thumbnails are stored in the destination folder.

If you have a Web editing program you can customize the text and position.

In this version the thumbnails appear in a strip down the left-hand side. When you click on an image in this strip it appears in the main window. You can select the size up to 450 pixels for the main image.

Workspace

MENU WINDOW→
WORKSPACE →
SAVE WORKSPACE
Feature introduced in version 7.0 that lets you save the screen positions of the Toolbar and palettes for a personalized desktop. Ideal if you share the computer with another user or tend to often end up with palettes all over the place.

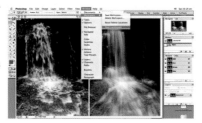

Zoom tool

QUICK KEYS   SHIFT+Z Used to magnify or reduce the image on screen. The zoom options palette has one choice – resize windows to fit. When selected the window grows or contracts with the image.

When PC users click on the right-hand mouse key with the Zoom tool selected you're greeted with a new menu to fit to screen, view at 100% or print size. You can also select zoom in and zoom out from here. If you hold the Alt key down and click on the mouse the image will zoom out.

(See Navigator palette)

Zoom set to 100%.

Zoom set to maximum 1600%.

ZigZag filter
(See Distort filters)

Image fits on screen, Zoom at 28%.

Tips

● You don't have to call up the Zoom tool to change magnification. Go to the image size box in the bottom left corner of your picture and manually key in a percentage to change size.
● Click and hold down the mouse at the top left of the area you want to magnify and drag to the bottom right. The image will magnify to the selected area.

ZoomView

MENU FILE →
EXPORT →
ZOOM VIEW
Introduced in Version 7.0 when Adobe teamed up with Viewpoint to offer direct connection to the ZoomView Portal to help you display high resolution images on the Web.

Zoom View is a technology that overcomes bandwidth constraints by dividing high resolution images into bite-size tiles. As a viewer zooms into the image, more and more detailed tiles are transmitted and displayed. This allows your viewer to zoom in on detail at high resolutions using the free Viewpoint Media Player.

To publish ZoomView on a Web site you need a Viewpoint Licence Agreement which removes a VIEWPOINT watermark that is displayed in front of all non-licensed images that are displayed with the Viewpoint Media Player.

Registered Photoshop users are entitled to a free Viewpoint licence for non-commercial hobbyist purposes, such as showcasing a portfolio.

Index

Appendix A: Photoshop versions compared

Every time Adobe update Photoshop, users ask whether it's worth upgrading. Often there are only a few changes, but they're usually 'must haves', making it hard not to want to upgrade. Throughout this book I've illustrated features that come with Photoshop 7.0, but many of these came with previous versions. If you have an earlier version or a light edition (LE), use this chart to see whether the feature is available on your copy.

I've also included the recent addition to Adobe's portfolio, Elements (Ele), which is like a light version of Photoshop, with some new, easier, automated modes, making it more accessible for beginners.

Photoshop feature changes	v3.0	v4.0	v5.0	LE	v5.5	v6.0	Ele	v7.0	v8.0
Tools									
Annotation tools						☺		☺	☺
Art History Brush					☺	☺		☺	☺
Background & Magic Eraser					☺	☺	☺	☺	☺
Crop tool with transform feature						☺		☺	☺
Healing brush								☺	☺
Measuring tool			☺		☺	☺		☺	☺
Magnetic Lasso			☺	☺	☺	☺	☺	☺	☺
Magnetic Pen			☺		☺	☺		☺	☺
Painting tools	☺	☺	☺	☺	☺	☺	☺	☺	☺
Patch tool								☺	☺
Photo Merge						☺			☺
Retouching tools	☺	☺	☺	☺	☺	☺	☺	☺	☺
Replace color brush									☺
Text tools	☺	☺	☺	☺	☺	☺	☺	☺	☺
Vector shape and text support						☺		☺	☺
Web support									
Export to ZoomView								☺	
Import/export GIF, JPEG and PNG files			☺		☺	☺	☺	☺	☺
ImageReady				v2.0		v3.0		v7.0	v8.0
Image slicing					☺	☺		☺	☺
Save for Web					☺	☺	☺	☺	☺
Version Cue									☺
Web palette	☺	☺	☺	☺	☺	☺	☺	☺	☺
Non-Square Pixel support									☺
Integrated Camera Raw support								opt	☺

Photoshop feature changes

	v3.0	v4.0	v5.0	LE	v5.5	v6.0	Ele	v7.0	v8.0
Creative features									
3D Transform plug-in			☺		☺	☺	☺	☺	☺
Adjustment Layers		☺	☺		☺	☺	☺	☺	☺
Auto Shadow, Bevel, Glow			☺		☺	☺	☺	☺	☺
Channel editing			☺		☺	☺		☺	☺
Color correction controls	☺	☺	☺	☺	☺	☺	ltd.	☺	☺
Color Range command	☺	☺	☺		☺	☺		☺	☺
Extract Image command			☺		☺	☺		☺	☺
Layers	☺	☺	☺	☺	☺	☺	☺	☺	☺
Layer alignment and layer effects			☺		☺	☺		☺	☺
Layer comps									☺
Layer sets						☺		☺	☺
Layer styles						☺	☺	☺	☺
Liquify						☺	☺	☺	☺
Match Color									☺
Number of special effects filters	42+	90+		95+	95+	95+	99+	95+	95+
Paths	☺	☺	☺		☺	☺		☺	☺
Pattern maker								☺	☺
Shadow/Highlight correction									☺
Functionality									
Auto editing using the Actions palette		☺	☺		☺	☺		☺	☺
Batch processing		☺	☺		☺	☺	ltd.	☺	☺
Contact sheet			☺		☺	☺	☺	☺	☺
Digital Watermark		☺	☺		☺	☺		☺	☺
File browser							☺	☺	☺
Guides & Grids for precise alignment		☺	☺		☺	☺	☺	☺	☺
History palette for multiple undo			☺		☺	☺	☺	☺	☺
Navigator		☺	☺	☺	☺	☺	☺	☺	☺
Open recent						☺	☺	☺	☺
Palette well							☺	☺	☺
Picture package						☺	☺	☺	☺
Preset manager						☺	☺	☺	☺
Spot color channels			☺		☺	☺		☺	☺
Color support									
CMYK, Lab, Duotone and Multichannel	☺	☺	☺		☺	☺		☺	☺
Color management and color sample			☺		☺	☺	☺	☺	☺
Color separations	☺	☺	☺		☺	☺		☺	☺
RGB, Indexed Color and Grayscale	☺	☺	☺	☺	☺	☺	☺	☺	☺
Compatibility									
Comprehensive 16-bit editing									☺
CMYK, Illustrator, PostScript and Acrobat Import	☺	☺	☺		☺	☺		☺	☺
Enhanced Tiff								☺	☺
Exports paths to Illustrator	☺	☺	☺		☺	☺		☺	☺
Print preview and soft proofing						☺		☺	☺

Appendix B: Typefaces

Your computer will, no doubt, come preloaded with a selection of typefaces, known as fonts. These can be accessed from Photoshop's Type tool and used in many ways with your images.

One option is to make postcards or greetings cards and use the type as the main message. You could also use the type to caption pictures, or as a supplement to a creative image, faded back as a layer.

The main thing to consider is the font you use. A modern face used on a sepia toned collage will look out of place. This book is created using Helvetica Neue and here's a selection of other fonts that you're likely to have access to. They are all set in 12 point. Select with care!

Two of the safest fonts to use on the Web are Arial and Verdana because all PC and Mac computers will have these two installed which means your viewers will see what you intended. If you use a font that your viewer doesn't have installed on their computer, it will select a substitute and your page may then look badly designed.

Before we look at the sets. Here's some you can use to add impact to your pages. Webdings and Zapf Dingbats create icons instead of letters. A to N are displayed here:

Photoshop A to Z in ARDS1

Photoshop A to Z in Academy Engraved LE

Photoshop A to Z in Arial

Photoshop A to Z in Baker Signet

Photoshop A to Z in Banjoman Open Bold

Photoshop A to Z in Banshee

PHOTOSHOP A TO Z IN BERMUDA

Photoshop A to Z in Blackletter686 BT

Photoshop A to Z in Book Antiqua

Photoshop A to Z in Bookman Old

Photoshop A to Z in Broadway

Photoshop A to Z in Bruno

Photoshop A to Z in Calligraph421

PHOTOSHOP A TO Z IN CASTELLAR

Photoshop A to Z in Cataneo

Photoshop A to Z in Chaparral

Photoshop A to Z in Comic Sans

PHOTOSHOP A TO Z IN COPPERPLATE

PHOTOSHOP A TO Z IN CREEPY

Photoshop A to Z in Curlz MT

PHOTOSHOP A TO Z IN CUTOUT

Photoshop A to Z in EraserDust

Photoshop A to Z in Eurostile bold

Photoshop A to Z in Figaro

Photoshop A to Z in Flyer

Photoshop A to Z in Folio

Photoshop A to Z in Footlight MT Light

Photoshop A to Z in Franklin Gothic

Photoshop A to Z in Frutiger

Photoshop A to Z in Futura Bold

Photoshop A to Z in Futura Light

Photoshop A to Z in Garamond

Photoshop A to Z in Georgia

Photoshop A to Z in Giddyup

Photoshop A to Z in Gill Sans bold

Photoshop A to Z in Goudy OldStyle

Photoshop A to Z in Greymantle MVB

Photoshop A to Z in Haettenschweiler

Photoshop A to Z in Helvetica

Photoshop A to Z in Helvetica Neue 65

Photoshop A to Z in Helvetica Rounded

Photoshop A to Z in Humanist 521

Photoshop A to Z in Impact

Photoshop A to Z in Jokerman

Photoshop A to Z in Khaki

Photoshop A to Z in KidTYPE

Photoshop A to Z in Kids

Photoshop A to Z in Lucida Console

Photoshop A to Z in Lucida Sans Unicode

Photoshop A to Z in Maiandra GD Reg

Photoshop A to Z in Microsoft Sans Serif

Photoshop A to Z in Milano LET

Photoshop A to Z in Minion

Photoshop A to Z in MisterEarl BT

Photoshop A to Z in Mistral AV

PHOTOSHOP A TO Z IN MONO

Photoshop A to Z in Mono Corsiva

Photoshop A to Z in Myriad

PHOTOSHOP A TO Z IN NYX

Photoshop A to Z in OCRA

Photoshop A to Z in OldDreadful

Photoshop A to Z in One Stroke Script

Photoshop A to Z in Orbus Mul iserif

PHOTOSHOP A TO Z IN OUCH!

Photoshop A to Z in Sand Palatino Linotype

Photoshop A to Z in ParkAvenue BT

PHOTOSHOP A TO Z IN PLUMP MT

Photoshop A to Z in Pompeia

Photoshop A to Z in Postino

Photoshop A to Z in Pristina

Photoshop A to Z in Rockwell

Photoshop A to Z in Russell Square

Photoshop A to Z in Script MT Bold

Photoshop A to Z in Shuriken Boy

Photoshop A to Z in Silentium Pro

Photoshop A to Z in Spumoni

Photoshop A to Z in Space Toaster

Photoshop A to Z in Swiss 721 Bold

Photoshop A to Z in Tahoma

Photoshop A to Z in Tekton Pro Bold

Photoshop A to Z in Trebuchet MS

PHOTOSHOP A TO Z IN TWENTIETH CENTURY

Photoshop A to Z in Univers 67 Bold Condensed

Photoshop A to Z in Univers 85

Photoshop A to Z in Verdana

Appendix C: Useful shortcuts

TOOLBAR

All of the tools in Photoshop's toolbar can be accessed using shortcut keys. Hold down the Alt + shortcut key to scroll through multiple options.

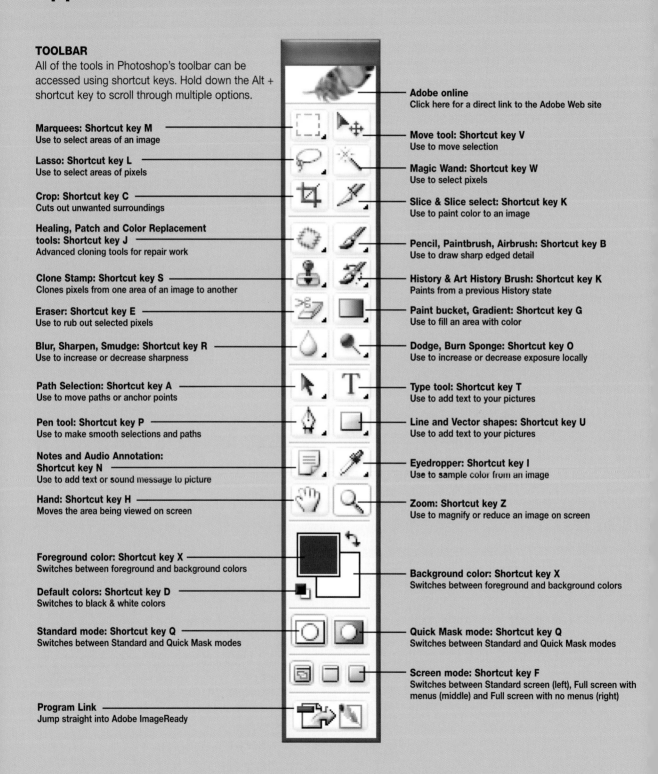

Adobe online
Click here for a direct link to the Adobe Web site

Marquees: Shortcut key M
Use to select areas of an image

Move tool: Shortcut key V
Use to move selection

Lasso: Shortcut key L
Use to select areas of pixels

Magic Wand: Shortcut key W
Use to select pixels

Crop: Shortcut key C
Cuts out unwanted surroundings

Slice & Slice select: Shortcut key K
Use to paint color to an image

Healing, Patch and Color Replacement tools: Shortcut key J
Advanced cloning tools for repair work

Pencil, Paintbrush, Airbrush: Shortcut key B
Use to draw sharp edged detail

Clone Stamp: Shortcut key S
Clones pixels from one area of an image to another

History & Art History Brush: Shortcut key K
Paints from a previous History state

Eraser: Shortcut key E
Use to rub out selected pixels

Paint bucket, Gradient: Shortcut key G
Use to fill an area with color

Blur, Sharpen, Smudge: Shortcut key R
Use to increase or decrease sharpness

Dodge, Burn Sponge: Shortcut key O
Use to increase or decrease exposure locally

Path Selection: Shortcut key A
Use to move paths or anchor points

Type tool: Shortcut key T
Use to add text to your pictures

Pen tool: Shortcut key P
Use to make smooth selections and paths

Line and Vector shapes: Shortcut key U
Use to add text to your pictures

Notes and Audio Annotation: Shortcut key N
Use to add text or sound message to picture

Eyedropper: Shortcut key I
Use to sample color from an image

Hand: Shortcut key H
Moves the area being viewed on screen

Zoom: Shortcut key Z
Use to magnify or reduce an image on screen

Foreground color: Shortcut key X
Switches between foreground and background colors

Background color: Shortcut key X
Switches between foreground and background colors

Default colors: Shortcut key D
Switches to black & white colors

Standard mode: Shortcut key Q
Switches between Standard and Quick Mask modes

Quick Mask mode: Shortcut key Q
Switches between Standard and Quick Mask modes

Screen mode: Shortcut key F
Switches between Standard screen (left), Full screen with menus (middle) and Full screen with no menus (right)

Program Link
Jump straight into Adobe ImageReady

EDITING KEYBOARD SHORTCUTS

Press Shift+Ctrl+Alt+K to create your preferred Keyboard Shortcuts on Photoshop CS.

BLEND MODES

All the Blend modes have shortcuts. Hold down the Shift key + Alt with the corresponding letters below. Items in yellow were new to Photoshop 7.0 and the item in red is new to Photoshop CS.

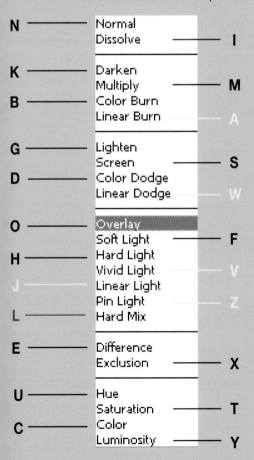

N	Normal
	Dissolve — I
K	Darken
	Multiply — M
B	Color Burn
	Linear Burn — A
G	Lighten
	Screen — S
D	Color Dodge
	Linear Dodge — W
O	Overlay
	Soft Light — F
H	Hard Light
	Vivid Light — V
J	Linear Light
	Pin Light — Z
L	Hard Mix
E	Difference
	Exclusion — X
U	Hue
	Saturation — T
C	Color
	Luminosity — Y

COMMON KEYBOARD SYMBOLS

Several keys are mentioned regularly in this book to use as shortcuts and as most readers will be PC owners I've mentioned the PC versions. Below are Mac equivalents with symbols to help you identify these on the keyboard.

⇧ Shift key is same on both systems

PC Enter key is Return key on a Mac

PC Ctrl key is Command key on Mac or ⌥

PC Alt key is Option key on Mac or ⌘

PALETTES

Keeping your desktop clear of junk is essential for clean working, especially if you have a smaller monitor. Palettes are one of the biggest culprits for clogging up space. Fortunately F keys will open and close palettes with ease.

F5 shows or hides **Brush palette** on version 5.5 and before. Shows brush presets on version CS.

Color palette
F6 shows or hides it.

Layers palette
F7 shows or hides it.

Info palette
F8 shows or hides it.

Actions palette
F9 shows or hides it.

PALETTE VIEWS

The Tab key shows or hides all palettes. Shift + Tab keys show or hide all but the toolbox.

IMAGE HANDLING

Open Image: Command(Mac)/Ctrl(PC)+O
Browse: Command(Mac)/Ctrl(PC)+Shift+O
New Canvas: Command(Mac)/Ctrl(PC)+N
Save Image: Command(Mac)/Ctrl(PC)+S
Save As: Command(Mac)/Ctrl(PC)+Shift+S
Close Image: Command(Mac)/Ctrl(PC)+W

Print with preview: Command(Mac)/Ctrl(PC)+P

Undo: Command(Mac)/Ctrl(PC)+Z
Cut: Command(Mac)/Ctrl(PC)+X
Copy: Command(Mac)/Ctrl(PC)+C
Paste: Command(Mac)/Ctrl(PC)+V

MOVING SELECTIONS

Use the Move tool and the up, down, left and right arrows to move the selection one pixel at a time.

Hold down the Shift key when using the arrows to move the selection 10 pixels at a time.

EXTRACT MODE

The Extract toolbox of Photoshop CS has the following quick keys.

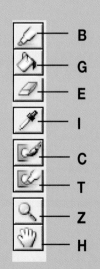

	B
	G
	E
	I
	C
	T
	Z
	H

Appendix D: Preferences

Use these for setting up Photoshop to run just as you want it. The palette has several submenus that can be scrolled down by using the up and down arrows. Before you first use Photoshop it's worth becoming familiar with the options and setting up the program to run smoother by turning off options you won't need. Go to the Edit menu and then Preferences and choose General to see the palette below. Mac OSX users will find the item under the Photoshop menu, not the Edit menu.

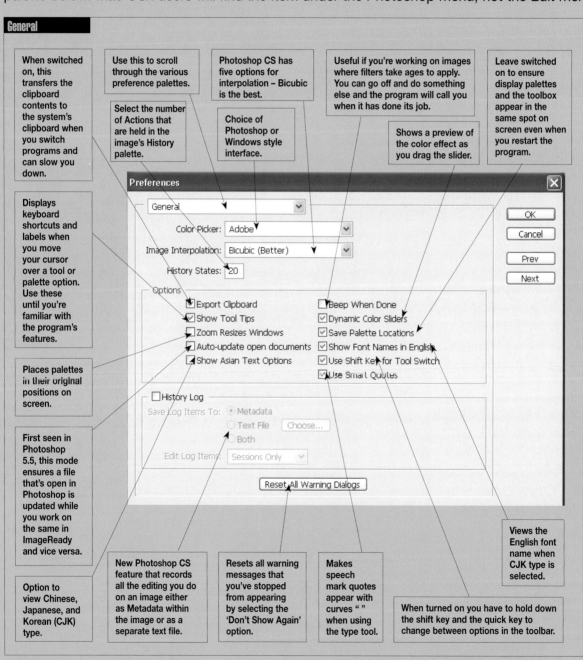

General

When switched on, this transfers the clipboard contents to the system's clipboard when you switch programs and can slow you down.

Use this to scroll through the various preference palettes.

Select the number of Actions that are held in the image's History palette.

Photoshop CS has five options for interpolation – Bicubic is the best.

Choice of Photoshop or Windows style interface.

Useful if you're working on images where filters take ages to apply. You can go off and do something else and the program will call you when it has done its job.

Shows a preview of the color effect as you drag the slider.

Leave switched on to ensure display palettes and the toolbox appear in the same spot on screen even when you restart the program.

Displays keyboard shortcuts and labels when you move your cursor over a tool or palette option. Use these until you're familiar with the program's features.

Places palettes in their original positions on screen.

First seen in Photoshop 5.5, this mode ensures a file that's open in Photoshop is updated while you work on the same in ImageReady and vice versa.

Option to view Chinese, Japanese, and Korean (CJK) type.

New Photoshop CS feature that records all the editing you do on an image either as Metadata within the image or as a separate text file.

Resets all warning messages that you've stopped from appearing by selecting the 'Don't Show Again' option.

Makes speech mark quotes appear with curves " " when using the type tool.

Views the English font name when CJK type is selected.

When turned on you have to hold down the shift key and the quick key to change between options in the toolbar.

Never save: Saves files without previews. Always save: Saves files with previews. Ask when saving: Saves previews on individual file basis.

New in Photoshop CS. Ignores color space info stored in exif data when ticked.

Ensures the file is fully compatible with earlier versions of Photoshop but it makes the file size larger.

Lists specified number of images previously worked on for quick recall from File→Open recent.

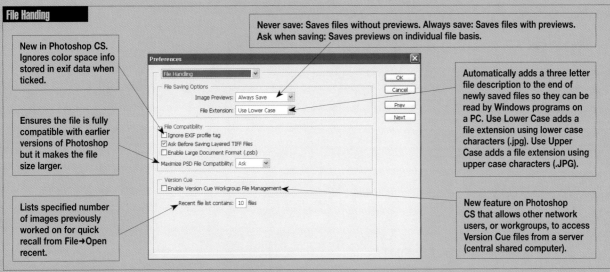

Automatically adds a three letter file description to the end of newly saved files so they can be read by Windows programs on a PC. Use Lower Case adds a file extension using lower case characters (.jpg). Use Upper Case adds a file extension using upper case characters (.JPG).

New feature on Photoshop CS that allows other network users, or workgroups, to access Version Cue files from a server (central shared computer).

Memory & Image Cache

Increases the speed that a histogram appears by producing it from the cached sample. The preview won't be as good, though.

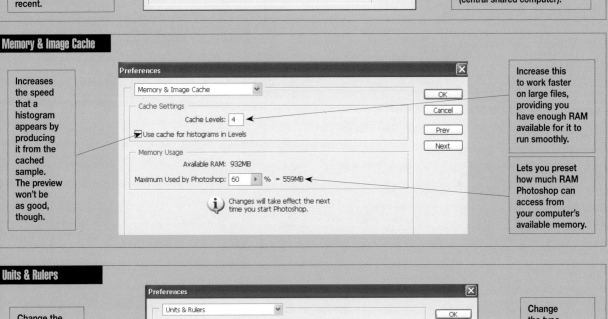

Increase this to work faster on large files, providing you have enough RAM available for it to run smoothly.

Lets you preset how much RAM Photoshop can access from your computer's available memory.

Units & Rulers

Change the measurement scale used on the ruler from this box.

Size images up to fit in the columns of a newspaper or magazine.

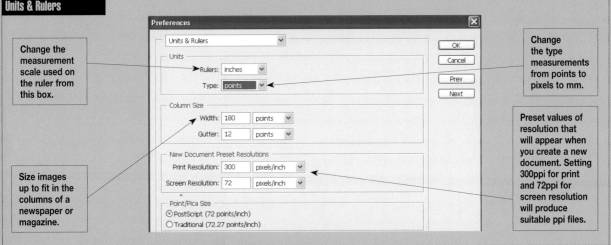

Change the type measurements from points to pixels to mm.

Preset values of resolution that will appear when you create a new document. Setting 300ppi for print and 72ppi for screen resolution will produce suitable ppi files.

Appendix D: Preferences Continued.

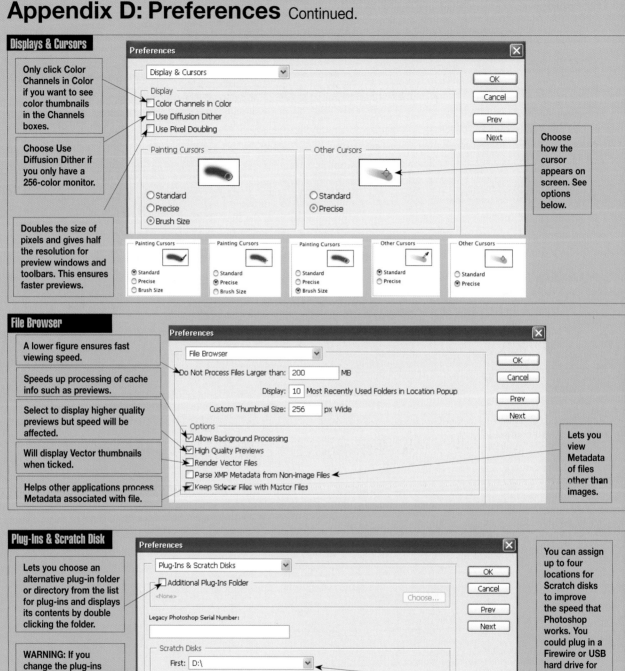

Displays & Cursors

Only click Color Channels in Color if you want to see color thumbnails in the Channels boxes.

Choose Use Diffusion Dither if you only have a 256-color monitor.

Doubles the size of pixels and gives half the resolution for preview windows and toolbars. This ensures faster previews.

Choose how the cursor appears on screen. See options below.

File Browser

A lower figure ensures fast viewing speed.

Speeds up processing of cache info such as previews.

Select to display higher quality previews but speed will be affected.

Will display Vector thumbnails when ticked.

Helps other applications process Metadata associated with file.

Lets you view Metadata of files other than images.

Plug-Ins & Scratch Disk

Lets you choose an alternative plug-in folder or directory from the list for plug-ins and displays its contents by double clicking the folder.

WARNING: If you change the plug-ins location, the usual Photoshop plug-ins, filters and scanners will be unavailable until you change back to the Plug-Ins location inside the application folder.

You can assign up to four locations for Scratch disks to improve the speed that Photoshop works. You could plug in a Firewire or USB hard drive for extra space, but don't use removable storage, such as a Zip drive, as a location.

Transparency & Gamut

The transparent areas of a document appear as a checker board pattern that can be varied in size. Choose None and the transparent areas in the layer will appear white.

The color and size of grid you select are displayed in the preview window.

Grid Colors lets you pick a gray pattern or a color.

Use Video Alpha should only be checked if you have hardware with a chroma key facility.

Shows when colors in an RGB image won't print out correctly. Select a color by clicking on the square in this palette and any colors in your image that are out of the printer's gamut will appear covered with this warning color.

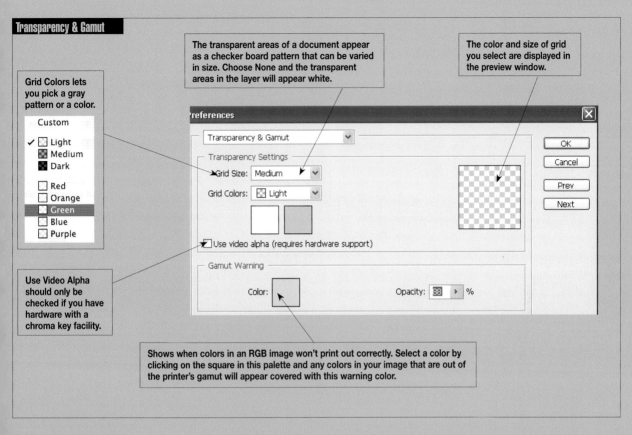

Guides and Grids & Slices

Pick a color for guides or the grid from the pre-selected range or from the Color palette. Choose one that will be seen above your images, such as bright yellow.

Choose straight lines or dashes for guides and grids.

Adjust the grid spacing by entering an amount in this box.

Enter an amount to subdivide the grid.

Introduced with version 7.0 to allow slice line color and number of slices to appear.

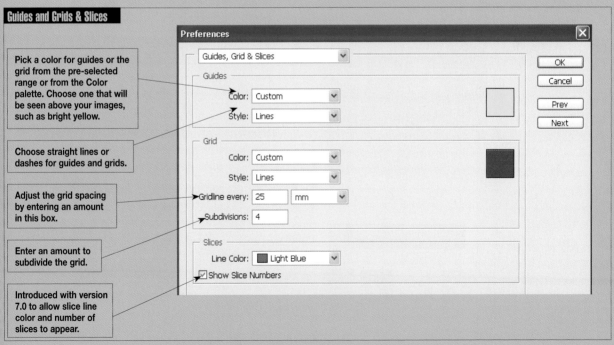

Appendix E: Useful Web sites

Adobe

www.adobe.com/products/
photoshop/main.html

Slick design, as you'd expect from the masters of imaging software. The home page guides you to several areas including support and products. It's the Expert Centre where the action is. Register to gain access to a stunning collection of material with lots of tips and tutorial pages, plus downloads and a training resource.

Apple

www.apple.com/creative/resources/ttphotoshop

One of the most useful sites for Photoshop movie tutorials with the work of Deke McLelland. Learn useful time saving shortcuts, how to use levels and much more in a very good series of tutorials. Being part of the Apple site you first have to bypass the sales blurb and Deke also mentions Apple products a few times. This doesn't spoil the enjoyment though.

Alien Skin

www.alienskin.com

From the makers of Photoshop plug-ins, Xenofex and Eye Candy, along with the recently introduced Splat. You can download trials, read about features, see the effects the programs create or buy full versions.

AutoFX

www.autofx.com

The company who make the fantastic Photo/Graphic Edges plug-in that comes with a CD of over 10,000 editable edges for ragged treatments and Polaroid style film effects. Also newer Dreamsuite range of effects. **(See Appendix F)**

Barry Beckham

www.bbdigital.co.uk

Barry is one of the most enthusiastic digital photographers in the UK and although he's an amateur his work puts shame to many professionals. This site has 47 galleries of pictures with great examples of digital photography and manipulation. There are also loads of Photoshop tutorials and reviews.

CoolType

webdeveloper.com/design/

If text is something you want to add to your pictures, go here for some, as the name suggests, cool effects. There are plenty of step-by-step techniques to help you improve the way text looks, including fire, bevels, charcoal and chalk.

Creative Mac

www.creativemac.com

Heavily commercial magazine with lots of flashing ads and with the title clearly aimed at Mac users but PC users can still follow the tutorials. Some really good Photoshop ones that are hard to find due to the news headline style layout. There is a search which can find some goodies. Work hard and you'll be rewarded.

The Digital Dog

digitaldog.imagingrevue.com/tips/

The Digital Dog is Andrew Rodney, an authorized Photoshop trainer from the US who shares lots of information with us providing we don't mind downloading PDF files. The page illustrated has various PDF files that look at color management and various articles on scanners and digital cameras.

ePHOTOzine

www.ephotozine.com

I couldn't go without dropping a plug for my own Web site. This will suit photographers of all types. Digital photographers can pick up reviews of equipment, download Photoshop tutorials and check out the work of other digital image makers. It's crammed to the brim with useful stuff.

Human Software

www.humansoftware.net

Human Software is a site that makes and distributes software plug-ins with interesting options that allow you to correct colour, sharpness and, as seen here, lens distortion. The site has lots of interesting products, but no helpful tutorials or free downloads.

Eyeball fx zone

www.eyeball-design.com/
fxzone/index.htm

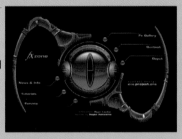

Fantastically well designed site which doesn't appear to have been updated since 2001, but there are some useful tutorials to help you make graphics like this menu page.

Intangible

members.madasafish.com/~cmci/

The portfolio site of one of my favourite digital artists with some beautiful images. Naked bodies are combined with found objects on multiple Photoshop layers. Catherine has since gone on to produce a book and more superb work using old photographs, animal skeletons and such like. A great introduction to her work. Go here for inspiration.

Graphicxtras.com

www.graphicxtras.com/

Graphicxtras.com is the website of Andrew Buckle, developer of Andrew's Filters, 1000+ plug-ins set. The site contains a huge selection of commercial (Andrew's plug-ins) as well as freebie plug-ins and extras for Photoshop, such as shapes, styles, gradients, and brushes.

Luminous Landscape

www.luminous-landscape.com

A resource site created by photographer Michael Reichmann that looks at pro digital equipment and delivers a series of in-depth advanced level tutorials as well as an Understanding series of articles on things such as depth of field and lens contrast.

Gurus Network

www.gurusnetwork.com/tutorials/
photoshop

A gathering of experts on different software programs, including Photoshop. Not that easy to navigate from the home page or when you're in deep, but the link above gets you to the Photoshop section where there are very good in-depth step by step tutorials.

Mccannas.com

www.mccannas.com

An odd site that offers loads of great tutorials, yet it looks like the designer of the site could do with reading a few of the tips. You are presented with a mishmash of styles, typefaces and layouts but it's worth putting up with for the large supply of great material within.

172

Appendix E: Useful Web sites Continued.

Mike's SketchPad

www.sketchpad.net

Easy to navigate and many Photoshop Tutorials within a huge collection of tips on using various graphic software. The tutorials are split into pages which you'll either love or hate. Well worth a visit for some nugget of useful info – at the time of writing there were 43 Photoshop Tutorials. Also includes a helpful links page.

Photoshop for Photographers

www.photoshopforphotographers.com/

Martin is a pro-photographer, Photoshop user and author of the Photoshop 7.0 for Photographers. The site offers free PDF downloads of several Photoshop tutorials and examples of sections of the book. Visit **www.martinevening.com** for great inspirational photography of beautiful models.

MyJanee

www.myjanee.com/PSRL/ tutfind.htm#photoart

Site includes a vast list of links that may be useful for Photoshop users and there are several step-by-step techniques, a gallery of pictures and a regular competition.

The Photoshop Guru's Handbook

photoshopgurus.info

Split into beginner, intermediate and experienced sections with lots of tutorials in the first two categories but little, if anything in the third. Also includes a good forum with over 1000 registered users and a links page, gallery and download section.

NAPP

http://www.photoshopuser.com

The website for the National Association of Photoshop Professionals – the largest graphics-related association in the world. It's a membership based site with an annual fee but plenty of stuff can be found on the outside for free, including a whole Photoshop CS guide with tutorials explaining many of the new features.

Photoshop techniques.com

photoshoptechniques.com

Another animated site that takes ages to load, even on an ADSL connection. Once there you have some fantastic Photoshop tutorials with a very active forum section. Worth a look for the fire and rain drop tutorials.

Phong

phong.com/tutorials/

Fancy design treatments with animated graphics. Even the tutorials have real marching ant selections! Superb tutorials if you want to create fancy text, buttons and graphics with reflections, natural curves and such like. Also well worth a look just to see that web sites don't have to look dull.

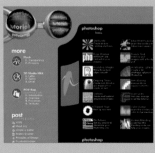

Photoshop Today

photoshoptoday.com

Not the prettiest sites going with dull color design schemes and the top half is taken up with large banner ads, but there's plenty to find of use. The sections are split into tutorials, reviews and links. More focused on the graphic design than photography, but very useful if you want to learn more.

Planet Photoshop

www.planetphotoshop.com

A fast site to move around in, which is important when your time is precious. The menu items call up loads of great tutorials with lots of links and a mass of extremely useful tips, techniques and advice on all things Photoshop.

Steve's Desktop Photography

showcase.netins.net/web/wolf359/

Stunning, that's the only word needed to describe this site – a veritable bonanza of interesting goodies for Photoshop owners. Nicely designed and crammed with useful stuff, including dozens of collections of filter effects by Andrew Buckle.

The Plug Page

www.boxtopsoft.com/plugpage/

Go here to find interesting plug-ins to download and expand the flexibility of Photoshop. It's a dull looking site but you'll find some useful stuff. Back at the home page there are some useful programs available including a GIF animation application and a high quality JPEG compression utility.

Tutorial Hunt

www.tutorialhunt.com

This site doesn't look that busy in terms of visitors, but with links to over 1000 Photoshop Tutorials in alphabetical order it's well worth you visiting. It links to tutorials in other software programs too and has over 6000 links in total.

The Plugin Site

www.thepluginsite.com/

Full of useful links to sites that offer plug-ins. There's also a great selection of reviews or plug-ins for Photoshop with ratings of each product to help you narrow down the options.

Trevor Morris

user.fundy.net/morris

Visit this site just to look at the superb design. Unlike most fancy designs that grind your PC to a halt, this one loads quickly. Trevor Morris is a graphic designer by trade so most of the material leans towards graphical effects with Photoshop, and there are some extremely interesting effects too.

PSWorkshop

rainworld.com/ psworkshop/

Over 730 Photoshop tutorials covering everything from text to graphical effects. The tutorials are borrowed from other sites so it acts like a central resource. Nice idea and useful material.

WZ2K

www.psmeg.co.uk

Excellent site by someone who obviously knows a thing or two about design. There is a good range of Photoshop tutorials and Navigation is first class with tutorials grouped into Quick Tips, How-tos, Primers, Regular Tutorials and videos.

Appendix F: Plug-in filters

Plug-ins offer additional features to the standard program. Photoshop supports third party filters that can be added to the plug-ins folder to increase the program's flexibility.

You can buy plug-ins such as Corel KTP Collection, AutoFX Photo/Graphic Edges and Alien Skin's Eye Candy 4000 off the shelf. Many can be downloaded from the Web. I've included a tiny selection of interesting ones over the next few pages.

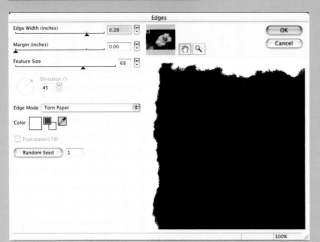

AutoFX Photo/Graphic Edges (PGE) is a useful plug-in that adds an edge to your image. The edges range from rough, ragged effects to elaborate designs. Some emulate the edges that you'd get using Polaroid – a technique that's often used by fashion photographers. AutoFX have recently revamped the interface (above right) to include a Layers palette where earlier effects can be deleted. The four examples here are from PGE 6.0 and include the new transfer style Polaroid (above) a typical soft edge (below left) a modern artistic style (left) and the new stamp frame (below right). The program comes with over 10,000 effects including patterns, frames and vignettes.

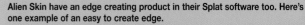

Alien Skin have an edge creating product in their Splat software too. Here's one example of an easy to create edge.

175

Corel took over Kai's Power Tools which is a great box of tricks and have added new effects over the last two versions renaming it the KPT Collection. Above is a superb cloud maker that puts Photoshop's Render Clouds to shame. Below is Pyramid Paint which makes photos look like art.

The interface is one of the most lively looking of all programs and offers excellent control over styles and effects. Above is a far more advanced lens flare option than Photoshop. Below is a texture creator.

KTP's projector filter lets you produce tiled effects with amazing perspective. One for fans of horror or sci-fi maybe!

20/20 Color MD is a new program that works like an eye exam. Two options are displayed – you pick the best. Another two options appear and you pick the best again. This is repeated several times and you usually end up with an image with natural good colour and brightness.

Appendix F: Plug-in filters

Continued.

The Flaming Pear Web site has a range of downloads including these filters.
Top: The interface for Glitterato (a galaxy and space generator), middle: a
typical result created by Glitterato and bottom LunarCell (a planet creator).
The interface is based on a series of sliders that control the effects precisely.

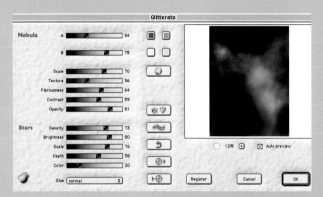

A cloudy galaxy was created using
Glitterato and this was blended
with the Windmill image to create
a misty, cloudscape.

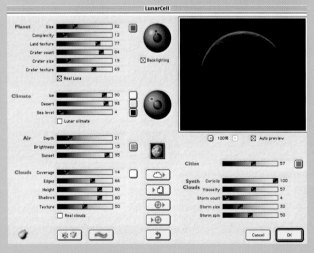

Andromeda make a
good range of plug-ins
for Photoshop. This
is one of the best and
offers perspective
control using arrows
to adjust the angle
of view and direction
of the image. You
can also zoom in
or out and rotate.
Download a trial from
<www.andromeda.com>

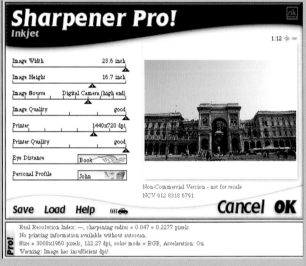

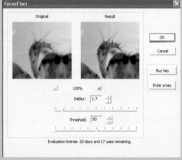

Programs such as Nik
Sharpener Pro! (above) and
Focus Fixer (left) are useful if
you need to sharpen pictures
but don't want to mess them
up through oversharpening.
In Sharpener Pro! there are
several sliding controls to
help you match sharpness
to the output device and
size you intend to print to
and view. Focus Fixer is a
simplified adjustment and
is more natural than some
sharpening applications.

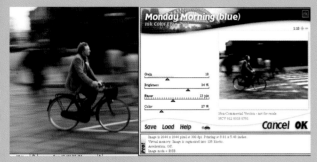

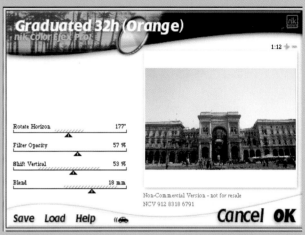

Nik Color Efex Pro is a superb set of color effects filters that adds color and/or dreamy softness to pictures. It takes the Photoshop editing to a new level by adding some easy to apply graduated filters and color temperature filters, plus some crazy special effects.

AutoFX
DreamSuite is one of my favourite products. It's sometimes a bit slow to process, but the interface is really cool and the effects you can create are even cooler. Here are a few that will make your photos stand out when used in newsletters and design projects. Left: create four types of sticky tape. The tape can be aged, made more ragged, curled, stretched, thickened and much more.

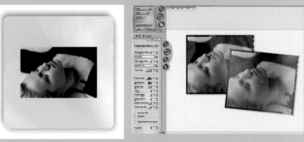

DreamSuite comes in two series. Series 1 has 18 special effects and series 2 has 12. Below is the film strip option from series 2 and right a 35mm slide frame from Series 1. Your photo is automatically placed in the frame when this is selected. Far right: There's also an option to create medium and large format transparencies in Series 2. Above right: The soft focus filter lets you control the depth of focus in Series 1.

178

Appendix F: Plug-in filters
Continued.

Xenofex, from Alien Skin, is a useful addition to the vast filter range provided with Photoshop. It has a collection of 16 additional filter effects that can be put to good use include Baked Earth which gives a dry mud cracked appearance. Lightning (top right) that adds forks of lightning. Crumple (below) gives a screwed up and reopened paper feel. This photo also has burnt edges applied. Flag creates the wavy shape you'd see when a flag is blowing and Mosaic (right) gives a tile mosaic style effect. The shot above is using the obvious Jigsaw puzzle filter. The pieces were then selected, cut and paste around the edge and a drop shadow was added.

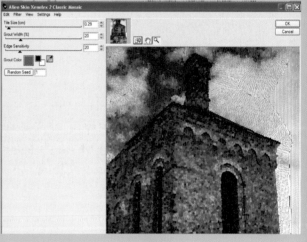

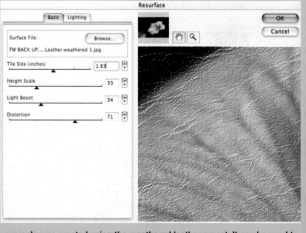

Alien Skin's Splat program was used here. Left: light pegs have replaced all color values in Patchwork mode. Right: In Resurface mode you can choose a texture or pattern and edit it to suit your photograph. This example was created using the weathered leather preset. It can be used to create tapestry style photos from your color originals.

Above: FocalBlade has been used here to create a glow around the subject. The program is more tempting for its detailed blur and sharpening modes.

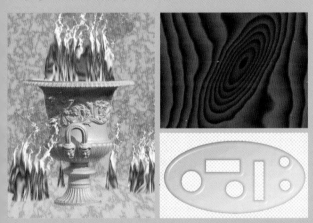

Eye Candy 4000 offers 23 effects including Plastic, Marble, Fire, Smoke, Wood and Weave effects all created above. Its an ideal program for designers and Web Masters.

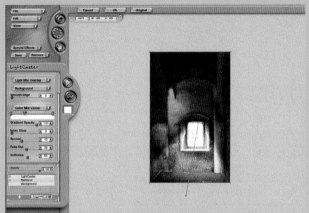

AutoFX Mystical plug-in is sold in two packages Mystical Tint, Tone and Colour and Mystical Lighting. LightCaster and Rainbow have been used here.

Extensis' pxl SmartScale is a new program designed to help you enlarge your digital images up to 1600% of the original size with, Extensis claim, no discernible loss in print quality. In this example I've increased the print from 2066x2500 to 6000x7260pixels.

Appendix G: Recording sheets

Use these to make notes of all your favourite filter settings.
Photocopy the sheets if you prefer not to mark this book

UNSHARP MASK

Photograph	Size	Amount	Radius	Threshold
Blue racing car	1280x960	123%	1.4	103

GAUSSIAN BLUR

Photograph	Size	Radius	Fade	Mode
Portrait of Joseph & William	1760x1200	7.3 pixels	70%	Soft Light

INNER & OUTER GLOW

Photograph	Mode	Color	Opacity	Noise	Technique	Spread	Size	Range	Jitter
Neon Test	Hard Light	Green	75%	8%	Softer	4%	6px	50%	4%

BEVEL & EMBOSS

Structure						Shading		Highlight			Shadow		
Photo	Style	Tech	Depth	Size	Soft	Angle	Altitude	Mode	Color	Opac	Mode	Color	Opac
Pencils	Inn.B	Sm	100%	5px	1px	30°	25°	Screen	Black	23%	Inner	Blue	23%

DUOTONES, TRITONES & QUADTONES

Photograph	Ink 1	Ink 2	Ink 3	Ink 4
Market Deeping village	Black	Pantone 431 CVC	Pantone 492 CVC	Pantone 556 CVC

DROP SHADOW

Photograph	Mode	Color	Opacity	Angle	Global	Distance	Spread	Size	Noise
Web button	Multiply	Blue	75%	120°	On	5px	7%	8px	4%

FILTER MENUS

Photograph	Filter	Value 1	Value 2	Value 3	Value 4	Value 5
Green pepper still-life	Colored Pencil	4	8	25	n/a	n/a
Garden of delight	Underpaint	6	16	95%	4	top

LIGHTING EFFECTS

Photograph	Style	Light type	Intensity	Focus	Gloss	Material	Exposure
Stonehenge	Crossing D	Omni	35	-23	39	-32	-23

HUE & SATURATION

Ambiance	Texture Channel	Height
-23	Red	88

Photograph	HUE	SATURATION	LIGHTNESS
Robin	+27	-13	-8